ONE
SINGULAR
SENSATION

The Michael Bennett Story

DOUBLEDAY

New York London Toronto Sydney Auckland

ONE SINGULAR SENSATION

The

Michael

Bennett

Story

BY KEVIN KELLY

Lines from "The Sea and the Mirror" by W. H. Auden reprinted
by permission of Random House, Inc.

PUBLISHED BY DOUBLEDAY
a division of
Bantam Doubleday Dell Publishing Group, Inc.
666 Fifth Avenue, New York, New York 10103

DOUBLEDAY and the portrayal of an anchor
with a dolphin are trademarks of Doubleday,
a division of Bantam Doubleday Dell
Publishing Group, Inc.

Library of Congress Cataloging-in-Publication Data
Kelly, Kevin, 1934–
One Singular Sensation
The Michael Bennett story / by Kevin Kelly.—1st ed.
p. cm.
Includes index.
ISBN 0-385-26125-X
1. Bennett, Michael, 1943 Apr.8– 2. Choreographers—United
States—Biography. I. Title.
GV1785.B38K45 1990
792.8′2′092—dc20
[B]   89-35025   CIP

BG

FOR C.M., FOR GAY,
AND FOR AIDAN

*O what authority gives
Existence its surprise?*

—W. H. Auden
The Sea and the Mirror
*(Preface: "The Stage Manager
to the Critics")*

CONTENTS

PREFACE

———

In August 1966, on the bucolic grounds of the Eastern States Exposition close to Springfield, Massachusetts, where the Storrowton Music Fair once offered summer musicals, the name Michael Bennett appeared on the program's shiny pages as the choreographer of *A Joyful Noise*. Like the show itself, Michael Bennett was an unknown quantity. Supposedly both were headed to Broadway. As drama critic for the *Boston Globe*, I'd driven up the Mass Pike to Storrowton without much hope, hope being a religious belief daily drama criticism quickly drains to accidie. My experience was that summer circuit pre-Broadway tryouts usually were acts of fantasized ego. The most I could hope for would be music loud enough to soften the buzz (if not the bite) of mosquitoes.

A Joyful Noise immediately set up a promise that it would be different. It had talent and energy. It was interesting. If it lacked focus, it had potential. And, within its musical means, there was something new and exciting and full of zip: the dance patterns devised by Michael Bennett.

Reviewing the production for a *Globe* Sunday piece a week later, I expressed delight, stating that the young Mr. Bennett would be "a major Broadway discovery." While critics are more rightly known for pans rather than prophecy, I had no idea how major he would be. But I sensed—from my iron seat on the edge of the Storrowton ramp—the presence of someone sharp, original and restive. Although his dances had a vitality that enlivened the entire show, *A Joyful Noise* finally would be unable to fuse all of its elements and would flop four months later on Broadway.

It was two years after the Storrowton tryout when Bennett and I met. In Boston with the pre-Broadway break-in of *Promises, Promises*, which he had choreographed, he called me at the *Globe*. During drinks at the Ritz Carlton, we talked about the theater as though it were the only thing in life that truly mattered. He was hardly my image of a Major Discovery, who, had I thought about it, would have been august, remote, autocratic, leonine. Here was this kid (I knew he was young; I didn't expect him to be an adolescent). He was small and pallid and pocked, and his eyes had the burn of bulbs about to brown out. I don't remember that he hummed, although, later, his humming became the equivalent of a tic douloureux. As adolescent as he seemed, when he talked, his words—with their syntactical leaps, solecisms and italics—displayed a mind quick as wind. He was unlettered, but he was smart.

Michael Bennett and I became professional acquaintances, then friends—not close friends, but steady enough so that I'd occasionally get one of his late-at-night (or *very*-early-in-the-morning) phone calls. We went to the theater together; had dinners at Sardi's, Jilly's, Wally's, Joe Allen's, Claire's and Backstage; shared a number of parties, four or more at his Central Park South penthouse, three at my house in the country. In the course of this friendship, I interviewed him for the *Globe* on several occasions and, once, for *New York* magazine.

The basis for this book was ten tape-recorded conversations between Michael Bennett and me, some with his best friend, Robert Avian, and with Susan MacNair and various colleagues during the *Ballroom* tryout in Stratford, Connecticut, where I spent the better part of two weeks in October 1978. The course of the book has

developed through an additional seventy-seven hours of taped interviews and innumerable telephone conversations with his widowed
mother, his brother and his half brother, his ex-wife, his lovers (male
and female), his friends and enemies (sometimes one and the same),
his colleagues, his associates, all of whose voices speak and echo
through these pages.

When I began to question my way through Michael Bennett's
life, I thought I knew him. In the Pirandellian shadow play of perhaps
all our conflicting identities, I came to realize I knew only aspects of
his personality. The real person seemed as changeable as the light. At
various times, he had told me intimate details of his life, the early
struggles in Buffalo, the beginning of his career, the career taking off
and crowding him so there was barely breathing space and certainly
less than elbow room for a wife or lover. He wanted, he once said,
to find someone permanent, but permanency in his personal life—
until near the end—was impossible. He achieved what most people
simply dream: unqualified success in his work, considerable artistic
freedom, extravagant praise, fame and money. But he yearned for
what he could not have: deep emotional commitment, sincerity, sharing, stability. He came to think that this deprivation was the price of
his talent and, though painfully high, accepted it. If, as Emerson has
it, "Art is a jealous mistress," the theater may be the most demanding
of all her sisters, and certainly the meanest.

As I listened to the people who had been close to Michael Bennett
talk, I wondered how all these memories, anecdotes, dialogues and
variously slanted perceptions could explain the person he was, as well
as the person he would become as death neared. He was warped in
complexity. Hand-me-down psychology wouldn't help. Psychoanalyt-
ically structured motivations might have given insight, but Bennett's
analyst chose not to talk. So did some others, including his last gay
lover. My decision was to present the memories exactly as they were
given, the Bennett story filtered through the sometimes paradoxical
sides of "truth." If there's synthesis between his life and his work, so
are there links between his maniacal will and his spiritual plight.

Michael Bennett directed his own story as though it was a musical he might fully control but never did. He found relief and consolation only in work, "another show." To me, the fulcrum of his forty-four years is a line from Francis Bacon: "But men must know that in this theatre of man's life it is reserved only for God and angels to be lookers on."

Four memories: Late on the night of February 24, 1979, in the long-gone Fan Club in Boston, Michael Bennett, in the company of three friends, hummed his way across a sea of vodka. Although he pretended to be happy when he was anonymous in a bar or a disco, this attitude was, at best, a havering pose. As closing time approached, the Fan Club, which was then Boston's equivalent of Sardi's and Backstage (the walls were hung with Broadway posters), learned that Bennett was present. After last call, the waiters, intending a tribute, lined up across the small oak stage as the sound system blared out the *Chorus Line* finale. The performance was impetuous and, of course, ragged.

Beaming when it began, Bennett waited for it to get better. When it didn't (there is no way it could have), he became impatient, frantic as an ant after sugar. Twitching and muttering, he rapped the beat on the table, then suddenly stood up. Teetering drunkenly, he made his uncertain way through the closely angled tables. Almost falling up the three steps to the stage, he cut to the center of the shuffling line, grabbed the wrists of a waiter on his right and a waiter on his left, saying, "No no no no! *No!* Here's the way it goes. And, by the way, it's my dance, so I know."

The finale was played again, then again. By the third repetition the waiters—though still sloppy—had a semblance of rhythmic shape. Acknowledging the whistling, stamping, hollering ovation that greeted this subtle but noticeable change in the number, Bennett stumbled off the stage in triumph.

In early spring 1980, when *A Chorus Line* had been running in New York five years and its reputation had spread through touring companies, Bennett flew to Boston to accept an award from Emerson College and have dinner—with Ron Field—at my house on the South Shore. The Emerson honor made him ebullient, yet he was emotionally and physically depleted. *A Chorus Line* had become "like a nagging child," and he was sick of restaging it for the road. When he had turned his attention to other work, to *Ballroom*, for example, in 1978, *A Chorus Line* had suffered, especially on the road, and he—with Bob Avian's assistance—really was the only one who could help. In New York it was fairly easy to check on the company and insist on a standard of performance; frequently he did.

But the strain of directing what seemed an endless repetition, a performance going on forever like the dancer in *The Red Shoes* destined to spin through time, was a paralyzing responsibility. He had sat in balconies in Toronto, London, San Francisco, and Baltimore looking down on his work and, more often than not, he "couldn't see it anymore, couldn't identify, couldn't understand." Plot and characters, music and lyrics had become so familiar they could only be half remembered. Despairing, he had begun to think the capstone of his career was going to drown him. Yet all those eager, promising *Chorus Line* kids were depending on him. Recently he had had a squabble with them in San Francisco.

Explaining all of this when he arrived, Bennett then said he'd like to be by himself for a while before dinner. Accompanied by Stolichnaya and Marlboros, he went out to the pool, paced the deck, then sat staring into the woods as twilight came down like a curtain. As the dark deepened, all I could see from the house was the occasional firefly glow of his cigarette. Finally, after about two hours, I interrupted his revery.

"I've figured it out," he said. "I've listened to all those kids in San Francisco, planned their steps, heard their problems, been a good father. But it's time to leave. Know why? Because it's not art anymore. Now it's business, strictly business, big business, cut and dried. They all have to grow up. And I know that. And I have to do it. So why do I feel like a father abandoning his children? Because, by the way, I know all about that . . ."

During the run of Peter Shaffer's *Amadeus* in New York, I took Michael Bennett to see it. Given that I would later review the production for the *Globe*, there was an unspoken agreement that the evening would not be discussed. As Shaffer's play tracked the rivalry Salieri felt with Mozart, the rivalry between a nonentity and a genius, Bennett said not a word; sitting next to me, he somehow seemed either disinterested or distracted.

Midway through the intermission, he remarked in the lobby that the scenic design—specifically, the glossy blue floor—was remarkable. He thought a play could be written "around the floor." He offered no further opinion or explanation. When the curtain came down, he said nothing and applauded politely. Ambling up the aisle of the Broadhurst, we walked outside in silence.

Upstairs at Sardi's, talking of other things (the possibility of doing *1984* as a musical), he abruptly interrupted himself, like someone fearful of misinterpretation and desperate to clarify a point. Clearly identifying with Mozart, possibly unaware either of immodesty or of self-aggrandizement, Michael Bennett said, "*Amadeus?* I just don't understand the dramatic problem."

Except for a telephone call from him in Providence, where a revised version of his most recent production, *Dreamgirls*, was playing late in 1986, the last time Bennett and I talked was April 26, 1983. It was an impromptu and devastating meeting.

In the company of Angela Lansbury, I had stopped by Eight Ninety Broadway, the sprawling complex he owned, where Lansbury was due for a costume fitting by Barbara Matera, a tenant in the building. (A revival of Lansbury's 1966 hit, *Mame*, was shortly to open on Broadway.) Rather than wait through the fitting, I went upstairs to visit Bennett. Harry Kalkanis, a member of his staff, knew me and palmed me into the well-guarded inner office, a vast rehearsal-size space seven floors above lower Broadway.

Unannounced, I found the room empty except for a sleek dog curled near a black-and-silver tub holding a tall, spindly tree. Calling out "Michael," I stood at the far end facing the dais-like desk maybe fifty feet away. The atmosphere was intimidating, more so in its silence. I called again, then knelt and talked to the dog.

In the dead quiet, I thought about leaving.

Then, in the passageway separating the office from a long, gleaming, narrow kitchen and a gymnasium and apartment beyond, Michael Bennett appeared, wispish, forlorn, agitated. His greeting was forced, his smile faked. I'd blundered into something, had interrupted him. He wasn't pleased. He sat behind his enormous desk, lit a Marlboro, and the smoke and the desk became an effective wall between us. Our conversation was perfunctory, with awkward pauses, no real connection. Sniffling, he shoved up the sleeve of his sweatshirt and tapped his watch without looking at it.

About to leave, I looked in his eyes, as he came out from behind the desk, and saw dilated pupils. There were no other telltale traces, but the slicked-over stare and the surliness behind it were telltale enough. His hands shook when we said goodbye. He walked me partway down the length of the vast office to where his dog was still curled on the floor.

I knelt again and stroked the dog.

"What's her name?"

"Kila."

"What breed?"

"Hungarian Vizsla," Michael Bennett said, pinching his nose with thumb and forefinger. "She's the first thing in my life, by the way, that's all mine."

Thornton Gore, New Hampshire
March 11, 1989

ACKNOWLEDGMENTS

I wish to thank some close friends who helped with the manuscript in specific ways as well as with unflagging support: Charles and Harriet Ball, John Malcolm Brinnin, Gay Jacobson, Reverend Ida Marie Miller, Father Aidan Shea, Frank Taylor and Charles Martin Wirth. In addition, through the two years it took to research, document, write, and complete the text, I was given specific support from professional colleagues, among them my editor Nan A. Talese, Gail Buchicchio, and Kathy Trager. While not directly involved in the project, there were others who provided pathways and were willing to listen, among them *Boston Globe* colleagues: John Driscoll, Richard Dyer, John Koch, Lincoln Millstein, Christine Temin, and Ande Zellman.

I wish to thank the people who contributed to the book through extended interviews, answers to specific questions or written material: Victoria Allen, Robert Avian, Gerald Bordman, Patricia Botsworth, John Breglio, Ralph Brown, Mary Bryant, Sabine Cassel, Mary Coniglio, Salvatore Coniglio, Nicholas Dante, Ron Field, Helen DiFiglia, Frank DiFilia, Joanne DiGuilio, Merle Debuskey, Tom Eyen, Bob Fosse, Larry Fuller, George Furth, Vincent Gardenia, Larry Gelbart, Norma Ferrara Gelose, James Georgedes, Alyce Gilbert, Marvin Ham-

lisch, Katharine Hepburn, Robert Herr, Jennifer Holliday, Betty Ja-
cobs, Bernard Jacobs, Diane Judge, Jerome Kass, Lainie Kazan, Larry
Kert, James Kirkwood, Elaine Krauss, Marvin Krauss, Henry Krieger,
Daniel Kublitz, Baayork Lee, Jack Lenny, Kenneth Lipper, Dorothy
Loudon, Bob MacDonald, Susan MacNair, Donna McKechnie,
Tharon Musser, Edward Padula, Joseph Papp, Michon Peacock, Scott
Pearson, Michael Peters, David Powers, Harold Prince, Tom Porter,
Joseph Raposo, Frank Rich, Dr. Grant Rodkey, Dennis Rosa, Matty
Serino, William Schelbe, Dr. Robert Schooley, Randy Shilts, Marvin
Schulman, Treva Silverman, Neil Simon, Liz Smith, Elaine Stritch,
Dr. William Strole, Sada Thompson, Tommy Tune, Robin Wagner,
Thommie Walsh, Jimmy Webb, and Dr. David Yocum.

CHAPTER ONE

Buffalo Shuffle

(1943–1960)

No matter where he was—slouched in the back of his homeroom waiting for the bell to clang, sliding across the floor in his tap class, showing off on television on *TV Saturday Dance Party*—all Mickey DiFiglia thought about was *Ice*. He couldn't sleep. He almost couldn't sit still. When he did sleep, body images slipped through his dreams, bending, arching, spinning, the bodies moving like water, water caught in sunlight, polished water, the whole thing like ice skating and, magically, without blades.

Had anyone ever thought of this before, dance as ice skating?

His mind flipped through the Astaire and Kelly movies his mother had taken him to at Shea's Buffalo. He thought about the Broadway show he had seen four years ago when he was eleven, *The Pajama Game*. His memory raced through *Damn Yankees*, *Guys and Dolls* and *Ankles Aweigh*, which he had seen the summer after *The Pajama Game*, when his mother had allowed him to take dance lessons on West Forty-fourth Street. He watched all the shows from the balcony, high up, distant from the dancing and the lights, but he could remember the dance patterns, not in their specifics, but in blurred overall shape.

Running through these memories, he couldn't find anything that even approximated his idea for *Ice*. Of course, there was the ballet, all that gliding, but he'd never been to a ballet. His first lessons with Betty Rogers had been primarily tap, and he'd learned other dance modes, like Spanish and modern, but never really ballet. *Ice* might be something new. If it wasn't something new for Broadway, it had to be for Buffalo.

Rehearsals were afternoons and evenings, whenever he could get everyone together. Everyone wasn't as professional as he was. And some of the kids had jobs, hobbies, other interests. He'd spend mornings scouring Buffalo for props, getting help where he could. He even went after ads for the program, although at this point no one was sure there was going to be a program. Maybe just a sheet with the title, his name as the director, the cast identified, the songs and dances listed. Opening night followed him around, sometimes like a friend, sometimes like a stranger he'd have to woo. He awoke from exhausted sleep one morning saying, "Ice, ice, ice." He wrote the words down, studied them on the paper, liked the way they looked and changed the single *Ice* in his working title to the repetition. Little things like that were important, although he wasn't quite sure what he meant exactly when he told the Student Council that the new title gave the show "tone." No one had questioned him, no one had objected.

Ice, Ice, Ice was an amateur musical extravaganza that Mickey, as a freshman, had proposed, in a much simpler form, to the principal at Hutchinson Technical High School, Martin Kuehn. He knew just how to do it. The music would be borrowed, but he'd write the book, design the scenery and costumes, choreograph the dances and direct. When a faculty adviser asked about constructing the scenery, Mickey said sets were to be on loan from the Sears display shop on Main Street, where his mother was a secretary, as well as from WGR-TV, the local television station, where he was a regular performer on *TV Saturday Dance Party*. Whatever carpentry the sets needed would be supplied by the workshop class. The costumes would be made by the Parent-Teacher Association. Everything else, Mickey said grandly, "would be supplemented" through his own "outside contacts." For example, the show called for a coed chorus. Hutchinson was an all-boys school. He'd solve that by bringing in girls from his dance class. He'd "send to New York for orchestrations."

Twenty years later, in 1978, at the age of thirty-five, when Mickey DiFiglia had become known as Michael Bennett and was working on a musical called *Ballroom*, he said, "At my blackest moments in high school I was set to become a bricklayer. Then I came up with the idea of raising money by putting on a variety show. I'm still doing that today! I cut classes, got homeroom and elevator passes to leave the building. I hated school except for English class. I did this show, *Ice, Ice, Ice*, then another one after that for another school I went to, Bennett High. I hardly ever went to class. All so *Ice* could make $150! We took in $3,000 but I spent $2,850 getting it together. And, by the way, it hasn't changed, hasn't changed at all."

Mickey DiFiglia had started dance lessons at the age of two and a half, at the insistence of his mother, Helen, who, despite the skepticism of her husband, Sam, knew Mickey "was different from the time he was a baby. He didn't act like, you know, normal, always moving, bouncing, struggling like." She had to fight Sam for the money to pay for the lessons (Sam worked at the General Motors plant and money was hard to come by), and she had to put up with slurs from his family about what she knew was Mickey's talent, "quicksilver feet." Yet after all the lessons and training, and Mickey's success in and around Buffalo, on the radio, on television, and his reputation as "an up-and-coming entertainer," Sam still "didn't think it was right, a kid as a dancer, his son."

As the opening night for *Ice, Ice, Ice* came closer, Mickey's excitement was like an electric current. When he thought about the 1,150 people who'd be sitting in the Hutchinson auditorium, he experienced a physical sensation, as though his nerves were sparking and igniting his blood. There'd be detailed pictures in his head and quick images. Sometimes he had no idea how either the pictures or the images had developed. He was thinking thoughts he didn't know he had, yet he was able to control them. In his own dancing he wanted to copy the loose, seamless ease that enveloped Fred Astaire in *Three*

Little Words and *Let's Dance*. (He could even remember seeing *Easter Parade* with his mother. She told him that, before he was born, Sam and she had seen all the Astaire movies together, and Mickey could dimly remember going to the movies with them, standing up because he was so small, resting his chin on the rim of the seat in front of him, captivated—if not irretrievably lost—in the images on the screen.) He also wanted to merge Astaire's free-flying grace with the equally surefooted but somehow more down-to-earth movement he saw in Gene Kelly and Donald O'Connor in *Singin' in the Rain*. He had trouble expressing what he sensed in these idols of his, but he hoped, when the time came, words wouldn't fail him. If they did, he'd dance out his thoughts. He'd think, hum, dance.

Late one night, in the narrow kitchen at 181 Florida Street, he had a sudden idea for the *Ice* finale. His mother was in bed, so was his brother, Frank. His father, as usual, was out with the boys, gambling, playing cards in a bar somewhere, probably drunk. Mickey didn't have much time left to make changes. Some in his chorus were slow learners. He'd have to simplify everything as much as he could.

Humming, he started dancing, his eyes following his feet across the worn linoleum. He pushed back the chrome-and-plastic kitchen chairs. He did a flat-heel turn, slid, did a step kick, then accelerated the movement. Imagining a skater whirling on a blade, he started to spin. He stopped, then began again. Dizziness became giddiness. He was unaware of breathing. He was inside a balloon, and the air itself—closed off—was exhilarating. He spun. Stopped. Took a breath. Spun.

He didn't hear the front door open and shut.

His father stood in his work clothes at the entrance to the kitchen, a black stare announcing his presence. Mickey saw the drunkenness before he heard it. He had been through this scene before. Browbeaten by his wife into a tacit acceptance of Mickey's talent, Sam for a while had given him grudging respect. For years he had complained about the money given to Betty Rogers, Norma Ferrara Gelose and Beverly Fletcher for dance lessons. But when Mickey started to earn money by dancing at weddings and parties, Sam paid him more attention.

Maybe Helen was right, maybe there was something to it—by which Sam meant something that could be turned to his own benefit.

Then Mickey had disappointed him.

In serious debt to the Mafia, Sam had the idea of selling an interest in Mickey's career to one of his Mafia friends. Sam would be bailed out of his losses in barter for a percentage of the kid's earnings, which weren't that great now, but *pazienza!* He'd keep the whole thing secret. With him managing his own kid, no one would be the wiser. So he had set up a meeting and Mickey did his stuff. The kid whirled, spun, kicked, slid, turned, a midget dancer. It was a real performance. A couple of things Sam could have done without, the little girl's bow at the end, but you had to hand it to him! It seemed a good bet . . . only the Mafia wasn't buying, didn't see the future. Sam didn't have an ace up his sleeve after all. The two guys he was counting on, Carillo and Nuccio, one picked his teeth, the other shook his head. The deal fell through. Sam felt a little humiliated. The guys looked at Mickey, then from one to the other, and Carillo said, "Ahh, *fata!*"

Now, here was Mickey a teenager rattling tap shoes, swishing across function rooms, bowing from the TV, and Sam was still in debt.

"You'll wear out the stinkin' floor," he growled. "You think this place is a dance hall? Why can't you play the drums or something like your brother. Gene Krupa I could take. *Jesus Christ!* Mama's boy. A little fruitcake."

"I took him to the dancing lessons," Helen DiFiglia says, "sat through all those recitals. Sam never did. Sam would only come in, stay a minute when Michael was on. See, Sam really wasn't interested. He had his cronies, his card games, his gambling. The dancing and the lessons, that was me. It was all right with Sam as long as we didn't bother him. And we didn't, very much.

"Later Sam was more interested. Later he'd drive Michael to club dates and television shows, and when he was on the radio. The first prize Michael ever won was singing on the radio, *The Uncle Jerry Show*, 'I'm Looking Over a Four Leaf Clover.' He wasn't even five years old. Later Sam was better about taking him."

In Buffalo on July 4, 1941, Helen
Ternoff, a plain Jewish girl in a big noisy family, went to a dance
with her girlfriends eight miles across the Peace Bridge at the Crystal
Beach amusement park. The Ternoffs numbered twelve. Both parents
had children from a previous marriage, father Benzion three, mother
Bessie four, and three together. Strictly raised by her mother, Helen
had an all-pervasive rivalry with her sister Dorris, whose blond hair
and peaches-and-cream prettiness she envied. To disguise what she
considered ugly-ducklingness—an open face that might have been
pretty had its roundness been completed by the arc of a chin—Helen
had developed an outgoing personality. And she was determined to
be smart. If she couldn't be as pretty as Dorris, she could be winning.
Her father cut her to the heart when warning her about bringing
boyfriends into the house. One nod from Dorris, a lowered lash, she'd
lose them! *Azoy geyt es.*

Crystal Beach was crowded and hot that night, seventy-one humid
degrees when Harold Austin's local band began to play, and hotter
still for Helen Ternoff when tall, dark, handsome Salvatore DiFiglia
asked her to dance and nuzzled his strong Italian nose against her
dark hair. She knew without asking that it was forbidden. As with
most things forbidden, the pull was irresistible. Even before she heard
his name, she knew the dark man fox-trotting her in his grip under
the flecks of light from the spinning crystal ball was "not her kind,"not
a nice Jewish boy. (Find yourself a nice Jewish boy, Mama had said,
so the family shouldn't worry.) Helen had been out with nice Jewish
boys. Now, at this moment, under the clammy mock-astral sky of the
Crystal Ballroom, on this airless Fourth of July, she was dizzy with
desire. The man knocking her knees was the goy. Not only that.
Salvatore, known as Sam, was the *Italian* goy.

Later, when Helen told her mother, Bessie, taboos echoed
through the big Ternoff house at 661 East Ferry Street. It was as
though a Borsalino had been hung on a peg next to the prayer shawls
and phylacteries, as though the boot of Italy had kicked a velvet matzoh
into a corner. Worse was yet to come.

When—some time after the Crystal Beach fireworks—Helen

told Bessie that she and Sam had eloped (there is no evidence they had) her mother's wrath was terrible, more crucifying than her love. Helen was banished, and she hadn't mentioned she was pregnant. Sam was stuck. Ruled by Sam's mother, Serafina (who, at ninety, would be celebrated by her grandson as a woman more distinguished than Katharine Hepburn), the DiFiglia household at 318 East Delavan showed the kind of unpredictable stoicism Sicilians reserve for potentially disruptive events, like marriage and murder. Sam would do the right thing. Helen and her fetus were given shelter. Sam joined the Navy. Helen gave birth at Buffalo Columbus Hospital on April 8, 1943, although among her papers is a birth certificate dated 1941, which she says her son "doctored for some unknown reason." There is a Buffalo wedding certificate dated September 5, 1942, with Helen's maiden name spelled Terrion. Although the Catholic Diocese of Buffalo has no record of a DiFiglia-Terrion—or a DiFiglia-Ternoff— marriage, there is a St. Francis de Sales parish certificate of baptism for Michael Bennett DiFiglia signed by Father T. J. Dunn and dated July 4, 1943. Either as final defiance against her Jewish background or as a tactic to claim a husband, Helen had agreed to raise her child Roman Catholic, telling her mother she and Sam had been married at St. Francis de Sales. Whatever *auguri* sailed through the DiFiglia house failed to reach the Ternoffs ten miles away on the far edge of the East Side. There, resentment and resignation were tempered with Bessie's relief. From my mouth to God's ears, at least the *kleineke* has a name!

Shorn of its soft Italian vowels, set up with two end consonants the equivalent of exclamation points, two-thirds of the name would later light up Broadway, London's West End and entertainment districts in twenty-one countries from Australia to Sweden, Israel to Japan. On the computer-activated wraparound marquee of the Shubert Theater off Times Square, 220 pulsating thirty-watt bulbs stutter-spell "Michael Bennett" from 10 A.M. to midnight year to year. The name continues to glow against the Shubert façade even as he slips into ravaged death at 2150 Camino Miraval in Tucson seemingly at the age of forty-four. The name continues on the marquee still, into its fifteenth year. Twenty-five million dollars (along with sums still being counted) figure in the last will and testament signed Michael Bennett DiFiglia on Saturday, May 30, 1987. Thirty-three days later, AIDS stutters through Michael Bennett DiFiglia's shriveled system, dousing all the lights at 4:50 A.M., Thursday, July 2, by which time perhaps sixty-five hours later forty-six years earlier Helen Ternoff had danced her first dance with Salvatore DiFiglia.

When Michael Bennett revealed childhood memories to his lifelong friend Robert Avian, what he dramatized was close to a Dickensian upbringing. Mickey's mother drained him dry, his father ignored him, his brother was an albatross. "I don't think she was a great mom to him," Avian says. "This is pop psychology, but I'm sure he was in love with his father and hated him. When he was a kid his mother made him do all the washing and ironing. He took care of his brother, took care of the house, cleaned it, did all that stuff, shopped, cooked dinner. And the first time he made a nickel, they retired and he supported them. I mean, they took, they just took. I don't think Sam understood Michael's accomplishment, but Helen did. She's like the Queen Mum now. Goes to all the shows, goes backstage, says hello to everybody. She has always done that."

Bennett confirmed similar memories to his longtime agent Jack Lenny, who says that Michael and his father "fought like cats and dogs. Big as Michael got, Sam wanted to holler him down." Further, Sam's high-stakes involvement with the Mafia was a constant debt his son paid off ("till the day Sam died Michael bailed him out").

In Helen DiFiglia's condominium at 2110 Ben Franklin Drive in Sarasota, which was bought in her son's name and left to her in his will, she refers to him only as Michael, never Mickey, never Mike. He hated Mickey, she says, "and never became, you know, a Mike." He was Michael Bennett. Seven months after his death, she was still making dinner reservations for herself and her guests in his name. She is Michael Bennett's mother. Her own life now as a widow is a reflection of her dead son's. At sixty-eight she's a prize pupil at Arthur Murray's, where she dances "one hour a day nearly every day." She and her husband Salvatore ("everyone called him Sam"), met at a dance. Dance was part of their lives. She loved it, she was "light on her feet," Sam "smooth as silk." She made her son into a dancer. She deserves credit for what he became. For the "bad part," was she "the only one responsible?"

"I'll never understand why he treated me so badly. Why he had to . . . to hurt me. He shut me out, shut Sam and me out. And at the end he wouldn't even tell Frank, his brother, his only brother. Oh, they were so close growing up kids. Michael used to take care of Frank for me; I worked as a secretary at Sears from the time they were little, Michael eight, Frank five. I was away so much.

"Oh, he changed, my Michael changed! Was it the drugs? Someone said he was an addict. I don't want to hear that. He seemed to . . . hate me. Almost I can't say the word. He didn't hate Sam. But the both of us and Frank—what? Embarrassed him? He was so hostile these last few years. And it's Gene's fault. And the doctor. I never believed in psychiatry. I knew from the beginning he was special, and I'm not just saying that because of everything that happened to him. The success. The Tonys. The Pulitzer. The money. That big East Hampton house. He was a colicky baby. He never walked, he bounced. He was hyper. The first year of his life I thought I was going to lose my mind because he never slept more than three hours at a time. Never ate! Never got him to eat anything! I was young and nervous and didn't know how to take care of him. I thought: If I can only get through this first year.

"Oh, he was colicky!"

Although there is a mystery to the Bennett that interrupts Michael DiFiglia's name, his mother claims she gave it to him because she knew he "was going to be special." Her parents were Russian Jews named Taranov. When her father landed at Ellis Island, hesitant but hopeful and speaking heavily accented English, he set down his bundles and his battered suitcase and spoke his name as clearly as he could: Benzion Taranov. The clerk promptly scrawled in his immigrant register the name Ternoff. ("It didn't make much difference," Helen DiFiglia says, "until later when the phrase 'turnoff' was around.") Ternoff later appears on documents as Terrion. At home Benzion Taranov was called Ben. Looking down at the infant in her arms, the twenty-three-year-old Mrs. DiFiglia wondered about giving him a middle name; Michael had already been decided upon. By itself Michael DiFiglia was nothing but a salute to the Italian side of the family. In Hebrew, *mikha'el* translates as "who is like God," but Helen DiFiglia only saw the name Michael as an honor to Sam's youngest brother, Michael, and the perpetuation of the family's roots in Sicily. If she was unconsciously trying to certify Michael's partial Jewish birthright by alluding to her father, Benzion, she doesn't remember it that way. All Helen DiFiglia remembers is that her special son "needed something extra."

Then she adds, "DiFiglia is a nice name if you say it right. Dee-feel-ya. Most people can't take the time. They say Dee-figg-lee-o or Dee-figg-lee-ah. Hard *g*'s. Frank hates that. Michael dropped DiFiglia I can't remember when. I think he officially changed it when he was starting out in New York and went with his agent, Jack Lenny. He was Mickey DiFiglia all through dancing school. My other son, Frank, changed his name to DiFilia. No *g*. I'm known as 'Michael Bennett's mother,' so I don't have the problem so much."*

Frank DiFilia says his mother made up the name. After Michael Bennett left Bennett High School in 1960, his junior year, Daniel Kublitz, a teacher, suggested that his student took the name in lieu of a diploma. Robert Avian says that Michael Bennett told him "a lot of conflicting stories about the name." Bennett is, however, on his 1943 birth certificate.

---

*Helen DiFiglia sometimes calls herself Helen Bennett although she has not legally changed her name. She has worked on various AIDS committees as Helen Bennett. She is quoted elsewhere as saying, "When my husband died, I even took the name Bennett . . . it made me feel more Jewish. After all, I had *given* Michael the name, I could take it back. But then it kind of became a tribute when he died."

How Salvatore DiFiglia felt when his son dropped the patronym, Helen DiFiglia doesn't say. She shrugs her shoulders. Was it another attempt by her son to disassociate himself from his past, or perhaps a subconscious barter because his mother had bypassed her Jewish heritage and raised him and his brother as Catholics? Had she first made that concession with Sam because it was the only way she could legitimize their baby son? It's possible, if not likely, that Michael Bennett's condensation of his name was his own direct repudiation of the father who seemed never to be present when he was a child, a long-hidden childhood memory worming its way through displacement to consciousness and revenge. Freud suggests that memory—precognitive, primal—hangs in the haze of years while the "practically unconscious" thoughts it represents belong to an advanced period of experience and maturation. Michael Bennett's ambivalence toward both his parents was triggered by the complex emotions of a disturbed and warring child, one clapped to his mother's ambitions and kept from his father's reach.

Buffalo winters are ferocious.

Clutching Mickey's mittened fingers in one hand, her pocketbook with Mimi's two dollars for the lesson in the other, Helen DiFiglia waited for the bus that would take her and Mickey from the East Side to Grant and West Ferry streets and the Betty Rogers Dance Studio, one flight above Smith's drugstore.

Snow smoked up from the empty streets. Mickey danced on the falling flakes, a little figure in the glass eye of a swirling paperweight. Helen wondered if he was trying to keep warm or simply repeating steps he had been practicing at home. She had thought about missing the lesson, but Mickey had gone into a rage as threatening as the predicted blizzard. Nothing was going to keep him from his flat-heel turns on the studio's wide, resined hardwood floor, where the sweep of space gave him a freedom to dance he could only imagine in the kitchen of the small apartment on Bryant Street and, later, in the cellar of the Perry Boulevard project. As usual, Sam wasn't home.

Helen dressed herself warmly in a worn coat, bundled Mickey in a jacket, drew a wool cap over his ears, warned him about losing his mittens and handed him his tap shoes in a brown paper bag. Out they went. She was going to carry him partway to the bus stop. He wouldn't hear of it. He was five years old, and had been "acting like this," Mrs. DiFiglia says, "from the time he was two."

Interspersed with performing, the lessons would continue until Mickey was fifteen, with maiden Aunt Mimi's "little extras" gradually becoming Helen's responsibility. ("I told Sam and his cousins, who were always asking why I was spending money on lessons, I told them what everybody else saw, the kid was talented, and he was going take tap and that was that!") Mickey slid along in front of the mirrors of the Rogers Studio, with Betty Rogers squawking ". . . five, six, seven, eight" above the twanging plunk of a Krakauer upright played by Millie LaPetnia. Later he saw his kinetic reflection in similar mirrors lining the studios of Norma Ferrara Gelose, Marie Flynn, Ginger Burke and Beverly Fletcher. Betty Rogers remembers Mickey as "talented and pushy; Mrs. DiFiglia was pushy too, your typical stage mother hauling that kid to every dance teacher in Buffalo, right up to Beverly Fletcher's in Niagara Falls." In dancing terms, Mickey and his mother were traveling, artistically "covering ground." Having learned tap, jazz and modern, he sometimes taught classes himself.

Helen DiFiglia's dreams for her son spun from her own sense of deprivation, then were further wound in the cultural aspirations she had discovered in the family of her best friend, Pearl Hock. Unlike her own mother, Bessie, Mrs. Hock took her children to concerts, to plays and occasionally to art galleries. Adding this to her own interest in movies, Helen DiFiglia felt that her son Michael (and later Frank) should go to concerts and plays as the Hocks had done. Her cultural experience was limited, but she'd learn, and so would her two boys. If Sam's shoemaker father was disappointed in his five sons, none of whom had gone to college, all of whom had settled into gambling, Helen was going to make the father of her sons proud. She knew Michael had talent. She was certain of it. If she was wrong about Michael's talent, well, then there might be something in Frankie . . .

Frank DiFilia was rushed off to dance class too. If Sam had trouble accepting one son flitting like a butterfly in the kitchen, he wasn't about to accept two. "Dad thought the dancing was . . . well, sissy," Frank DiFilia says, "and I wound up taking drum lessons. Dad had no frame reference. I was okay because he kinda had a Gene Krupa fantasy thing about me.

"Michael never seemed, you know, normal in the sense of being a child concerned with watching TV, or just playing. He was never at home doing normal kid things. Always gone, always working. Only time he was home was when he took care of me, cooked me dinner after school. Mom would come home from work, and Michael would go off to dance somewhere for money.

"'He was never a little kid, he was always older than his years. When I hit puberty Mom said I probably knew everything I needed to know about sex from hearing it on the streets but if I had any questions, 'Ask your brother.' In a sense Michael was my father because of the person he was and the person my father was. Dad was great with nice situations, but not interested in solving problems, or even giving guidance. Michael was a lot closer to Mom than to Dad. Perhaps too close. She and my father really didn't communicate on the same level about emotions, feelings, life in general. She may have had too adult a relationship with Michael when he was too young. She did turn to Michael because Sam wasn't around. And when he was, Sam wasn't interested."

Before Frank DiFilia was born, Michael Bennett had his mother to himself for four years. And with his father in the Navy for three of those four years, there was no one to rival him in her affection. For Helen DiFiglia this love child had separated her from her own family. She clung to him desperately, and set up an oedipal pattern that would determine his personality and color his life. The pattern has an almost clinical perfection: loving the child all the more intensely in the absence of the father, she both coddles and drives him. Her little boy will become a big man, and, in fact, while still a little boy he's earning money, showing signs of being the big provider he one day will become. She knows he's "special," but it is she who defines that specialness. She can't help turning her "special" little boy against his ordinary father, who, when he returns home from the service, is a womanizer.

By the time he was fourteen, Mickey DiFiglia had the makings of a local legend, a potential supernova among Mrs. Dunn's Little Stars of Tomorrow. (Mrs. Dunn, then eighty years old and an ex-showgirl, had packaged local talent for Sunday-afternoon entertainments at Glen Casino Park, a beer garden on the outskirts of Buffalo.) Mickey had made his recital debut at two and a half (one of six little boys in a luau number—some playing bongos—among twenty-two little girls in grass skirts). He had sung on the radio; had played Puck in a Studio Arena Theater production of *A Midsummer Night's Dream*; had danced his way from nightclubs to personal appearances at "private functions," including one harrowing moment at the reception following his Uncle Russell's wedding. In high school he showed the first signs of being the ruthless impresario he would later become (Jack Lenny once called him "the director/intimidator") when, virtually single-handed, he staged two full-scale productions still remembered in Buffalo to this day.

"When Michael's Uncle Russell, Sam's brother, was married, Michael of course danced at the reception," Helen DiFiglia says, in her condo where a pair of bronzed, beat-up "baby tap shoes" sit on a dresser in the bedroom. Moving behind the kitchen pass-through, she leans through it, like someone peering into the dark of a confessional.

"Michael started dancing at Italian weddings when he was five. He was the ring-bearer at Russell's wedding. Must have been six or seven. Well, it came his time and he was out on the floor, long pants, little half-jacket tuxedo, bow tie. He started his routine, and he was wonderful, he was always wonderful. He had these little mannerisms, I didn't know where he got them, little things he would do he was never taught, holding his head just so, his little fingers maybe daintily turned in, like a wink in his eye.

"He was dancing just fine, everybody applauding, and then he started to . . . spin.

"I'd seen him do it before, of course, flat-heel turns into a spin, circling the floor like a . . . like a top, a tiny little top. Suddenly he frightened me because I knew he wasn't going to stop! He was going to spin until he dropped. He kept going, going, making the circle bigger, bigger, pressing the people back, turning, turning. Then he seemed to tip, tip to one side, the way a top does when, like, it's running down? And for the first time in my life I knew he was . . . out of control. He couldn't seem to stop. I didn't know what to do. I grabbed a cousin of Sam, made him go out and stop him. Michael didn't really seem to know where he was."

Helen DiFiglia, too, seems like a top about to topple. Her words slow down. She sighs, shakes her head.

"He told me once that when he was performing, when he was on a stage in front of an audience, he really didn't know where he was, never heard the applause, never saw the people standing up clapping at the end. At the time I didn't understand, but after I danced onstage myself for the first time, here in November, at the AIDS benefit, I knew. I wasn't conscious of the audience either, the stage, the music, anything. I was in another world, just like Michael. They tell me the people stood up and applauded.

"Other times when Michael was a kid and he'd dance for people, they'd throw money—quarters, dimes, nickels—the Italian custom. I told him, 'Don't you touch any of that money! Don't you pick it up from the floor!' Because to me that was lowering himself. I wanted him to dance; I didn't want him to do it that way! So we always had one of our friends, or a cousin, go around pick up the money, then give it to us. God knows I needed it, needed it for his lessons, his tap shoes, his clothes. He was always growing out of his little tuxedos."

As much as Helen DiFiglia fantasized Mickey in the footsteps of Fred Astaire and Gene Kelly, whose movies she loved and would drag Sam to see—when they had the ticket price—as often as three times a week, she knew her son had to have "something to fall back on" if things didn't work out. Sam was a precision grinder at the Chevrolet Division of General Motors on East Delavan Street (he would work there until his retirement in 1977 at fifty-seven). Deprived of higher education herself, she sometimes envisioned Michael as an architect. Every time she had this thought, she'd see his "quicksilver feet." One way or another, she'd get him "up and out."

In company with his friends and a cousin, Mickey took an enrollment examination at Hutchinson Technical High School, and passed; his companions didn't. (Otis and Henman-Nelson IQ tests later tallied his brain waves at 117 and 121, respectively, placing him on the cusp of the High Normal range.) He entered Hutchinson, a college preparatory school specializing in mechanical technology, on September 4, 1957, and began a course designated building construction. Notching a slide rule, positioning an isosceles triangle, he spent long hours over a drawing board trying to concentrate on square roots, logarithms and quotients. He tried to keep his mind on the draft paper, on the neatness of his measurements and the possibility of architectural stress. Increasingly, he found he wasn't interested. All he really thought about was being a gypsy. (At first he thought the word "gypsy" referred only to dark, wandering people given to tricks and curses; then he discovered it also meant a dancer in a musical show.) He wanted to be a gypsy, to be in the theater and the movies. Right now all these thoughts were focused on the possibility of staging a show at the school.

Bored as he was with schoolwork, he found fulfillment in extracurricular activities. He was a cheerleader, a member of the Student Council and the Newspaper Club. He was also teaching a dance class after school and on weekends, as well as performing on television and at various hotel functions and club dates. Doing a number at one of these clubs, he suddenly had the image of himself on ice skates. The spin he was turning seemed as rapid as a scratch spin he remembered from a Sonja Henie movie. He wondered if a dance could really simulate ice skating, the stroking movements, the swift glide, the open sweep. The idea began to obsess him. It could really be something new.

During the first half of the 1958 term at Hutchinson, Bennett staged a variety show that so impressed the faculty that he was more or less given free rein to stage a later production which became *Ice, Ice, Ice.* In the frantic month it took to produce, he wouldn't—or couldn't—eat, sleep, relax. His mother would find him midnights, and later, pacing the living room, spinning out ideas, humming. His involvement was so complete, and cost him so much energy, that he flunked not only his building construction course but three others as well.

To pass the subjects he failed and to continue his education, Hutchinson required that Bennett repeat his sophomore year. Refusing, he transferred, as a junior, on September 10, 1959, to Bennett High School, where—despite a 77.9 percent (or C plus) average—he failed to earn a diploma. Immediately he became involved in masterminding another musical production. This time he ran up against an English teacher, Daniel Kublitz, the first of many competitive threats in his career.

Mrs. DiFiglia: "I don't know what it was about that Dan Kublitz. He must have been a frustrated actor or something. He was always so envious of Michael, and gave him so much grief."

Kublitz left the classroom and Bennett High School in 1968, and retired as a school administrator in 1982. He recalls "Mike as a loner," whose "odd speech, mannerisms and attitude were remembered by many of the students." Kublitz says, flatly, "Michael DiFiglia was not the greatest to ever hit Bennett's stage. He was rarely permitted—during his two years as a member of our variety shows—to take stage as a solo act. His partner was a girl named Wendy Pollack, who was the better of the two."

Explaining that the school expected its English teacher, who was also in charge of drama and speech, to be responsible for student productions (a yearly three-act play and a variety show), Kublitz fulfilled that role for almost fourteen years with "no extra compensation" because he loved theater. What he didn't love, and came to bitterly resent, was the later newspaper coverage when "the boy genius of the Big Apple" graced Buffalo with his presence. Michael Bennett was credited in interviews with directing and starring in the Bennett High School variety shows.

Whatever it was Daniel Kublitz did or didn't do, the DiFiglia variety show ran three nights and had audiences stomping for encores of "Steam Heat," the hip-swiveling, finger-snapping Bob Fosse number Mickey had lifted from *The Pajama Game*, the Broadway hit he had seen four years earlier in 1954 when he was eleven years old. He spent part of the next summer in New York studying dancing, and the next two summers scurrying up and down the synclinal ramps at the Melody Fair in North Tonawanda, where he came i ϲ Jack Lenny's attention. An apprentice one summer, he was a performer the next.

Returning for his junior year at Bennett High, he first dropped out of school on May 17, 1960, filling in the blank marked "Reason for leaving" on his dismissal certificate: "Age 17," his legal majority. That summer he danced the role of Baby John in a *West Side Story* tour put together by Jack Lenny. He dropped out of school for good in September when Lenny hawked him out of his homeroom for a production of *West Side Story* being readied to tour Europe.

Kublitz: "One day—this I vividly recall—Mike came into my office and told me he had the opportunity of playing Baby John in the road show of *West Side Story*, but he would have to drop out of school to do so. He was seventeen. I became annoyed, and told him that after the tour he would perhaps wind up in New York as a gypsy, slowly starving while trying out for some chorus boy part in competition with hundreds of other misguided kids. Stay in school, I suggested.

"He left school the next day, taking with him the school's name. Obviously I was wrong. . . . After *Chorus Line* took the nation by storm, a few teachers from Buffalo went to see him in New York. One finally saw him and was asked by Mr. Bennett, 'Is that asshole Kublitz still at Bennett?' "

Mickey DiFiglia was persuaded to leave school by Lenny, whom he had met in 1960 at the Melody Fair, a 3,000-seat summer theater specializing in star attraction musicals (John Raitt, Van Johnson, Anna Maria Alberghetti, Howard Keel, Dan Dailey in replays of *Oklahoma!*, *Carousel*, *The Music Man*). Lenny's involvement at the Melody Fair began in 1956 and lasted until the placed closed in 1980.

The "biggest talent" Jack Lenny ever met was Mickey DiFiglia. Jack Lenny's first professional job was in an act featuring four boys and three girls. It opened at Perth Amboy, New Jersey, on July 1, 1925. Exactly fifty years later, Lenny's prized client, now established as Michael Bennett, gave him an "elaborate sit-down surprise dinner at the St. Moritz, a hundred people, the Shuberts, Alex Cohen, Joe Papp, Alexis Smith, a piano player for cocktails, a string quartet for the entrée." The party was to celebrate Lenny's show-business odyssey from chorus boy to business agent, which lightly paralleled the more ambitious journey of his protégé. Early on Lenny had cautioned Mickey DiFiglia about his ambitions to become a choreographer, telling him to wait, watch, gain experience. Mickey waited, watched, gained the experience, collecting it like kindling and eager to strike a match. In time he would dance the flames into a reputation as director/choreographer, an innovator who created the first "musical vérité," who would be hailed both as the king of Broadway and as a genius, often to the ashes-in-the-mouth envy of other director/choreographers (Jerome Robbins, Gower Champion, Bob Fosse, Tommy Tune), as well as their one-hat counterparts (Harold Prince, Ron Field, Joe Layton, Onna White, Ron Lewis, Patricia Birch, Peter Gennaro).

It was at Lenny's party that Michael Bennett played the demo tapes of the CBS original-cast album of a show he had downtown at the New York Shakespeare Festival's Newman Theater. It was called *A Chorus Line*. In less than a month, at the 299-seat Newman, it was being whispered from Greenwich Village to Times Square as a substantial hit. It was scheduled to move uptown to the Shubert Theater on July 25, twenty-four days after Lenny's party, where it would become the longest-running show in Broadway history, and a gold mine. It would dramatically change Michael Bennett's life, convincing him, at last, that he was a wunderkind impresario, a role he would cultivate until he was forty, when he finally put away his red baseball cap, blue jeans and white sneakers for wing-tip shoes and expensively cut Italian suits.

To the accompaniment of the Marvin Hamlisch/Edward Kleban *Chorus Line* score, which punctuates a story line developed by James Kirkwood and Nicholas Dante from two twelve-hour rap sessions among a group of gypsies, Michael Bennett took sixty-eight-year-old

Jack Lenny by the hand, led him between the draped tables, off the carpet, out to the St. Moritz floor. Humming, Bennett faced, then embraced his puzzled friend, and danced him through the lyrics of the show's finale, "One."

> *This is what ya call trav'lling*
> *Oh strut your stuff*
> *Can't get enough . . .*

They danced like a father-and-son act, a pair of Astaire vaude-villians gliding, turning through an all-knowing pattern of time steps and step kicks as polished as the floor. All the way through Michael Bennett led, the spry young man pulling against the old man's spindly bones, the boy and the elder, the son occasionally spinning in front of the father. At the end Michael Bennett beamed and Jack Lenny wept.

Lenny: "When I met Michael we were putting together a *West Side Story* tour for the summer, places like Kansas City, Indianapolis, St. Louis, then up the summer tents to the East. Michael came in to audition. It was a lot like the audition in *Chorus Line*. He'd just turned seventeen, but he looked about fourteen. He was hired to dance Baby John.

"I wouldn't be telling the truth if I said I really knew how talented he was right away, that first day. But by 1964 when he did his first choreography for *Joyful Noise*, I knew he was some kind of a genius, knew he'd go a long way. We formed our business relationship in 1964. Even when the big guys tried to horn in, like the William Morris Agency, Michael stuck with me. I've been in the business sixty-two years, I'm eighty now, and Michael kept me on his payroll to the end."

When Mickey DiFiglia made up his mind that Buffalo was a dead end and he had to leave, Helen DiFiglia said she wouldn't let him drop out of school ("No way, José! Half the school year was over, he was to graduate in June"). Mickey persisted. He wasn't going to settle for becoming a bricklayer. Nothing like that. He wasn't going to shine bumpers at General Motors or stock merchandise at Sears. His classroom education had been worthless. All he cared about was show business. He had talent. His mother saw that. Dad didn't seem to care what he did as long as he stayed out of his way. Seeing herself in her son, Helen DiFiglia relented. He signed for the *West Side* tour, went to Europe and had his eighteenth birthday in Paris.

"After the tour he came back and stayed two days with us," Helen DiFiglia says. "All of a sudden he was different. He said he wasn't going to stay in Buffalo the rest of his life. Just like that it was 'Goodbye!' But at least I had him until he was of age. Or almost of age. I'd wanted him to get that high school diploma. But in his case it didn't really matter, although they still—to this day—call him a high school dropout. And he never had much good to say about Buffalo."

Buffalo, however, stayed with him, not only in the increasing responsibility he would assume in his parents' lives but as a metaphor for his own struggle and flight.

In *A Chorus Line* an upstate refugee named Bobby recalls growing up out of sync with his family. His father labels him a sissy, his mother doesn't understand him. Isolated and depressed, Bobby thinks about taking his life: "But then I realized—to commit suicide in Buffalo is redundant." (Although the line goes back to Mark Twain, there would be various claims that one or another of the original cast members said it first at one of the tape sessions that Kirkwood and Dante threaded into the musical's book. The bickering over the authorship of the line would become a small example of the backstage enmity that developed after *A Chorus Line*'s runaway success.)

There would be other Buffalo memories—"dancing ghosts," Bennett called them. Some were charming, some were cruel. None of them would ever be stilled.

"I remember when Desi Arnaz and Lucille Ball came to Buffalo," Michael Bennett said. "It was right before they did the TV series. I think they had a radio show at the time. My Aunt Mimi took me to see them at Shea's Buffalo. While the show was on, I was walking up and down the side aisle. I was eight years old and I thought: All I have to do—I'd seen Lucy on television, knew how she danced, and the kind of stuff she did—I thought: All I have to do is go up on the stage, say, 'Hello, I would like to dance with you,' and they will find it charming, and Lucy is going to go, 'Okay,' and she's going to do a time step, and I'm going to do a time step, and they're going to think I'm so wonderful they're going to want to work me into the act, and they're going to take me with them and I'll leave Buffalo and shuffle off forever.

"I paced up and down that side aisle trying to get up nerve to just go walk up the stairs. I thought that was my way out, my way to Hollywood . . . or someplace. I never did it, and I remember feeling disappointed I didn't have the guts, because it might have changed my whole life. Twelve, thirteen years later, maybe fourteen, I was choreographing a number for Lucy on *The Ed Sullivan Show.*"

The sweet promise lurking in the aisles of Shea's Buffalo was not without a bitter parallel. The same day Michael Bennett won the Pulitzer Prize for *A Chorus Line*, April 22, 1976, his father was indicted by the grand jury in Buffalo on six charges of gambling. Bennett learned of the Pulitzer in Toronto, where he was directing a *Chorus Line* touring company.

"The next morning he came back, and that day Sam was indicted for bookmaking," Helen DiFiglia says, with whining hurt. "Oh, let me tell you, the papers planned it this way! Here was this big thing in the paper. 'Pulitzer Prize Winner's Father Arrested.' Big deal! This reporter calls up, says to me, 'How does it feel to be the mother of a Pulitzer Prize winner and the wife of a bookie?' I said, 'If you have the gall—if you don't have enough sense not to ask a question like that, I don't want to talk to you!' He said, 'Lady, we don't care how you feel. You're news, and that's what we're after.' I hung up. From then on I didn't talk.

"I called Michael right away. 'Your father's in trouble.' In fact, I had to go out to the suburbs somewhere to pick Sam up at the police station. I ask Michael should we get an attorney to do something about what they're writing in the papers. He said not to, said they'd forget it. It was so stupid! What did that guy think I was going to say, 'It feels wonderful'? Oh they twist things. They'll write what you say but not what you meant. Michael always said, don't say much, say very little."

Bennett himself said a lot about Sam and the Mafia to his friends, even to some of his colleagues. He liked the drama it suggested. It gave drab Buffalo a glorious criminal glow, but it also filled him with fear. Imagining the curses and vendettas of his Sicilian ancestors, he often talked about visiting Sicily. Like a vulture, the Mafia beat through his thoughts, a threat out of his childhood that would trouble him the rest of his life, a story he would tell over and over, with increasing paranoia in each of its variations: "When I was a little kid my father tried to sell me to the Mob for a cut of my career. He owed them, I was to be the barter, and the Mob was to get a cut of my career.

"And then, by the way, there was my namesake, Uncle Michael? Murdered by the Mob. Shot in the head in his car, rolled down the street, dumped in the Niagara River."

CHAPTER TWO

Sweet Baby John
Eyes the Competition
(1960–1967)

Breaking out of Buffalo, saying goodbye to a past grimy with poverty and complaint and family problems that seemed far more difficult to solve than almost any entanglement he could imagine on a stage, gave Mickey DiFiglia a freedom he had envisioned but felt he would probably be denied. No longer would he have to put up with mockery when his father found him pirouetting around the scuffed linoleum on the kitchen floor. He wouldn't have to sit and listen to his mother choking out resentment over the narrowness of their lives, over her own depleted dreams. No longer would he have to block out her endless whine about Sam, her worries about Frank. He'd really miss his grandmother. There was something in her old heartbeat that drew him close and made him feel that perhaps she was the pulse of his talent. Serafina had mixed thoughts about her own sons, his uncles content with the numbers racket (and only in Buffalo), and she gave everything he did enthusiasm, approval (*"Mio bambino luminoso!"*). His grandmother didn't know anything about show business (how could she?), but that didn't matter. He and she understood each other. She believed in him with the same intensity he believed in himself.

There was similar empathy between Mickey and his cousins Joanne DiFiglia (daughter of Sam's brother Michael) and Elaine Celio (daughter of Sam's sister Grace). Sure as he was of the direction of his life, although unable to define it, he'd dream up "little plays" to entertain family and friends during a given holiday. Casting himself as the hero, Elaine as the heroine and Frank as the villain, he'd rehearse in the hallway or cellar, then present the play in the living room. Frank DiFilia remembers that his brother would "make everyone in the house pay to see the show." Whatever charm these little dramas created was short-lived. There was not much family warmth. Whatever feelings he engendered in his relatives were tangled on threads of envy, spite, resentment and jealousy, or simple disinterest in him and his "sissy" dancing. He wondered when the tangle first started. With the bickering of his parents? He could remember his mother shrieking at his father, his father raising his fist, shouting, *"Basta! Basta! Basta!,"* slamming the door and disappearing for a long time. Where did all the ill feeling come from anyway? He could remember himself as a baby being dandled up and down by his mother as though he were a dancing puppet, a sleeping, crumpled rag doll from her childhood she was trying to smooth out, reinvent, enliven. She did it all the time. When he automatically began tapping his feet to the rhythm of her clapping hands, he was never sure she was satisfied with his attempts. These little routines began with playtime delight, which suddenly dissolved. He wanted to please her, to keep her smile beaming down on him.

Later, in high school, a teacher said he was manic. At first he didn't like the word, it sounded worse than crazy—jiggy! real crazy! Then he looked it up in the dictionary and it fit. He thought he *was* pretty manic. Something whirred inside him—was that mania?—constantly recharging itself like a battery in Dad's Chevrolet plant. Was his mania, maybe, just temporary adolescent anguish, the anxiety of getting out, leaving, cutting off? There was supposed to be fear in that, but he had none. He couldn't wait to exchange the laid-upon responsibility of siding with his mother in every argument with Sam, of being saddled with Frank (who was okay as a kid brother, but who needed a kid brother, let alone one forced by their mother to compete with him?)—he couldn't wait to put all that behind and concentrate on a career, a Broadway career, maybe even a Broadway/*Hollywood* career. First, he'd become this hotshot dancer, then he'd become a choreographer, which was another word he looked up in the dictionary—again, it fit.

The scope of the ambition after that was a little unclear. He might be starting out as Baby John in *West Side Story*, but no one was going to call him Baby John for long. Most of the time in Buffalo he felt like Clark Kent about to fly over *The Daily Planet* skywriting the news of his real identity, except it was Broadway he wanted to inform. Buffalo had no idea of the accelerating star skipping along its bleak and boring streets. In his eyes his mother really didn't either. She pushed too hard. He came to think her pushing suggested her own panic and desperation. She'd bungled her life, had settled for less, for filing and typing at Sears, for a husband who strayed. Maybe he was going to end up like her, yearning, just yearning. In her harshest moments, his mother told him she had married a bum. Heightening the drama of his own birth, Michael Bennett would later actually say that his mother had been "knocked up by a Sicilian sailor," withholding the fact that Salvatore DiFiglia was a second-generation American. Helen DiFiglia sometimes softened her words about her husband. But when Michael Bennett was young he heard a steady recitation of his father's failure. Sam was content dividing his time between General Motors and bookmaking. He was satisfied punching a time clock and raking in the pot at the end of a card game. Helen projected far greater ambition for her son, just as she once had for herself. But, in her own insecurity, she had an unfortunate way of shortening the ambition's reach by sometimes suggesting it was beyond Mickey's grasp.

When he signed with Jack Lenny in 1960 to do the *West Side Story* tour in Europe, Michael Bennett was on his way and that was exhilarating. While he had no anxieties about what would happen as he left Buffalo, he did have a feeling of loneliness. The farthest he had been away from home had been New York, which had never seemed far because, by the time he was twelve, it was like Oz next door. In the summer of 1955, when he was twelve, his mother had allowed him to study at Sylvia Fort's School of Theater and Dance on West Forty-fourth Street, an experience that confirmed his Technicolor dreams about New York. The acrid sweet/hot smell of the subway in the summer, and the buzz of sound as he crossed and recrossed Times Square on his way from a dance class to a movie on West Forty-second Street, gave him a high he'd later equate with marijuana. New York mesmerized him. Years later, coming up from the depths of Pennsylvania Station on his return from an out-of-town tryout, he said he could sense "the energy down in the tunnel and by the time you got to the street it was like a hurricane."

During the formation of the European tour Michael Bennett met Robert Avian, who had danced the role of Indio, one of the Sharks, in a 1960 production of *West Side Story* at the Winter Garden. (*West Side Story* had first opened in 1957 and had run 732 performances.) Bob Avian was then twenty-two. Watching the young gypsies joining the company, most of them teenagers desperate to prove themselves, he was impressed with Michael Bennett. "He was this sweet kid, very gentle. But behind it was this—this magnetic drive. He was very, very ambitious."

Sensing Avian was someone from whom he could learn, Bennett responded to his friendliness. Avian knew the ropes and, just as important, he had solid footing in classical ballet, whereas Bennett's specialty had been tap dancing. At their first meeting, in an echoing rehearsal hall above Times Square, neither knew, of course, that their lives would become a symbiosis in which opposite temperaments found agreement and encouragement. "We're like husband and wife," Michael Bennett said, "all things to each other. We're family. Brother and sister, sister and sister, and we love and respect and trust and understand each other, and what could be better than that? And by the way, despite what everyone thinks, we've never been lovers. How's that for pure?"

At the start of the *West Side Story* tour Avian introduced Bennett to his "best buddy," Audrey Hays, who had danced the role of the Jets-sworn Velma in the 1960 production. Audrey Hays was approximately twenty-seven. She fell "head over heels" for Michael Bennett, who, according to Avian, "looked like a baby but he was around sixteen, seventeen." As the tour progressed through Europe, Hays and Bennett became inseparable, living together in tents they carried on their backs and which they would set up on a playground or *Platz* or any open space near the theater where the show had been booked. Baby John and Velma were beginning to look "as though they were married," and they continued to look that way when the company returned to New York. They found a cheap apartment in the Village, where, Avian says, "they lived like a nice, normal, happy little couple."

The happiness lasted two years, then cracked, the crack occasioned by an emotional rumble with a history stretching from the past to the future, and strong enough to splinter all of Bennett's heterosexual relationships. Unable to balance the demands of his career with domestic coziness, he fled the intimacy with Audrey Hays precisely the way he had fled from the embrace of his mother, precisely the way he would flee later from his wife, Donna McKechnie, and from his last female lover, Sabine Cassel. To him, women became succubi. In his dreams they were draining his talent. Avian says that every relationship Bennett ever had "was always *heavy heavy* duty with women—and with men!" Trouble usually erupted "when he started fucking around with other people." When the breakups happened they were "always high drama." When the time came to extricate himself from an affair, he would try to persuade a friend, an ally, someone else to deliver the message to the once beloved. Theater always came first. He looked upon outside emotional involvement as a hazard; personal commitments cut into the work.

Turning obsessively to work as his affair with Audrey Hays started to dissolve, Bennett was hired in the fall of 1962 for a show called *Nowhere to Go But Up*. Contracted only for the preproduction schedule, rather than as a later member of the chorus, he probed his way into the position of being Ronald Field's assistant choreographer, stepping over Patricia Dunne, who was nominally Field's assistant. Avian, who was in the chorus, witnessed the process and was amazed at Bennett's boldness. "Here he was nineteen years old, this little kid, and—zap!—he steps right into Pat Dunne's shoes. *All About Eve* time, right? He did everything he was asked and more! He wasn't shy at all about making suggestions. When it came to the stage Michael always knew exactly what he was doing, or, rather, where he was going. In a funny way, there was something frightening in that, the focus had so much intensity."

While Bennett was meeting new colleagues and making friends on *Nowhere to Go But Up*, specifically lighting designer Tharon Musser, who later became one of the technical wizards on his team, he was about to end the affair with Audrey Hays. She was driving him crazy. They were wonderful together, were really tuned in to each other, but Audrey seemed to resent any time he spent away from her. Their domesticity, which, at first, he craved, had become a distraction. Their silly little arguments were draining him. The only one who fully understood his need to keep himself focused was Bob. Bob clearly understood the pressure. Bob would help him. And the way he could help him the most, right now, was to tell Audrey it was all over. To add to his dismay, *Nowhere to Go But Up* seemed to be dissolving just like his love life.

But when Bennett went to Avian to enlist him as a go-between, he was further dismayed to learn that Avian was having second thoughts about a show-business career. Hearing Avian complaining about how quixotic it all was and wondering if he should become a schoolteacher, Bennett felt alone and vulnerable. His own feeling was that the whole trip—whether down brightly lighted roadways or along bleak ends, whether you were involved with a possible hit or a sure flop—offered nothing but opportunity. If a person had talent, real talent—as he did, as Bob did—all you had to do was to keep it flying under the proscenium. Protecting this talent—widening it, deepening it—took priority. Maybe the only way you could really protect it was by always putting it first, even before personal relationships.

Audrey was now too close, much too close, and he didn't know how to deal with her. Bob had to help him. There was just no way he was going back to the relationship, no matter what Audrey said or did. He persuaded Avian to become his emotional fall guy. Audrey

Hays, who was then in Philadelphia in a tryout of the Richard Rodgers musical *No Strings*, had her fears confirmed that her romance with Michael Bennett was over at the same time she learned that Rodgers intended to replace her in the show.

Refusing to return to the Village apartment he had shared with Hays, Bennett moved in with Avian, who had just found a new apartment, a $74-a-month, fourth-floor walk-up in Chelsea. They split the rent, $37 each. By now *Nowhere to Go But Up* was proving itself a disaster. Marking the debut of Dorothy Loudon, it opened November 10, 1962, at the Winter Garden, and quickly qualified as a pre-Thanksgiving turkey, closing after nine performances. It was Bennett and Avian's first flop together, but they didn't spend much time mourning. By the summer of 1963, Avian was in the chorus of *Zenda*, a musical with Alfred Drake and Chita Rivera, which was trying out in San Francisco and Pasadena, where it ultimately disappeared. By the fall of 1963, Bennett was in the chorus of *Here's Love*.

When Avian returned to New York after the failure of *Zenda*, he and Bennett set up housekeeping on a full-time basis. Dancing in choruses and earning money, they thought they were living in luxury. Two years went by. Close as brothers, Avian was "in absolute awe" of Bennett's determination and drive. "He told me he was going to become 'the second Jerry Robbins'; nothing or no one was going to stop him." Being in the chorus was a deliberate means to an end. Although there is no record of Bennett's contribution to *Here's Love*, he convinced the show's choreographer, Michael Kidd, to let him devise a "Rag Doll" number, which he then danced. Avian was "flabbergasted."

In 1964 Bennett was in the chorus of *Bajour*, which opened in late November and ran 218 performances. Edward Padula, who co-produced *Bajour* with Carroll and Harris Masterson and Norman Twain, remembers "the absolute excitement" of Bennett's audition. "He had an immediately personal style which you knew had nothing to do with the classical vocabulary of dance. He just stood out. He had a sense of theater about himself, and vivid—*vivid*—imagination.

He presented himself as this street-smart kid, I mean personally *and* in his dance movement. Very theatrical, very exciting to watch."

While dancing in *Bajour*'s chorus he auditioned and was signed for an NBC television show called *Hullabaloo*, a rather more sophisticated version of *TV Saturday Dance Party* from his days in Buffalo. Described as "fast-paced song, dance and comedy showcasing young talent from Hollywood, Broadway, television, nightclubs and recordings," the show featured rotating "celebrity hosts": Paul Anka, Trini Lopez, Frank Sinatra, Jr., Frankie Avalon, Annette Funicello, Dean Jones and Michael Landon. The Hullabaloo dance team itself numbered four girls and four boys. One of the girls was a gypsy, Donna McKechnie. Almost from the moment they faced each other in rehearsal, they became partners, McKechnie finding in Bennett "an exciting and tough—very tough—taskmaster," he finding in her "my most perfect, my favorite instrument."

"We were really whiz kids on that show," Donna McKechnie says. "I mean, we brought the Jerk and the Monkey to new heights! He and I were very popular as partners; got a lot of mail. Jack O'Brian thought I was the hottest thing since fire. The show was sort of a Hit Parade of Dancers, and I think it was the first musical variety show on the networks. The idea was to highlight the Top 40 songs, and the kids would dance behind some of them. All the big-timers were on it, Chubby Checker, Petula Clark, and it was one of the Supremes' first times on television. We were all Broadway-trained dancers and here we were having this great time pop dancing!

"Michael was so dynamic, really fabulous. And we worked so well together. He had all this strength in his dancing and—because I'd had ballet—I had this lyricism. He choreographed this one *Hullabaloo* number. It was complicated. But I understood it, got it right away, and he fell into this appreciation that I could do his work and interpret it. He allowed me a certain freedom, which, in a way, spoiled me, I mean spoiled me working with other choreographers—like Bobby Fosse—who were very specific about what you could and couldn't do.

"From the first *Hullabaloo* day I saw something in Michael; I guess he did in me too. I said to him, 'Well, gee, what do you want to be when you grow up?' Without hesitating, he shot back, 'A choreographer.' I thought to myself: Well that's nice; he knows the fate of most boy dancers in this business who don't have an education; this kid has a goal; that's nice to see. Only, *really*, I had no idea!"

The *Hullabaloo* dancers danced their way in and around the weekly vagaries of the Top 40 hits from 1965 to 1966. Well before the show went off the air on August 29, 1966, Bennett was sought out by Edward Padula to choreograph a new musical called *A Joyful Noise*, which Padula had conceived from a Borden Deal novel, *The Insolent Breed*.

Padula: "I remembered what a live wire he'd been in *Bajour*, and I remembered the kind of arrogant brilliance he had, and I just knew he could handle the dances. I was directing the book. *Joyful Noise* had a country-music score and it was simply way ahead of its time, which is one of the reasons it failed. We tried out on the summer circuit, got good notices, were well received, but out-of-town in the summer isn't Broadway in the winter. I was proud of the show. Every single contribution Michael made was simply wonderful. He understood everything about it."

In fact, Bennett's understanding was so perceptive that Padula eventually wanted him to take over the production as its director.

When Bennett had signed on as choreographer he brought along some friends, Baayork Lee, whom he had met at Sylvia Fort's dance classes, and Donna McKechnie. He had convinced Padula that McKechnie could play one of the featured roles, Jennie Lee.

But as *A Joyful Noise* pulled in and out of summer tents, cow palaces and makeshift auditoriums, its narrative defects became more and more obvious. Padula's book told the story of a wandering minstrel—John Raitt as one Shade Motley—who's a shade too noble to be true, a Eudora Welty hero without mud on his shoes. (Run out of a Tennessee town by a dyspeptic father protecting his daughter, Shade becomes a successful folksinger, only to return to Tennessee to wander again yodeling for the few, and far happier.) Bennett improved the choreography by hiring Tommy Tune and, according to Padula, "devising a sensational clog dance for him." Then he turned his attention to the book. "He really didn't know much about the Nashville country-music scene," Padula says, "but his instincts were dazzling."

At first the tryout audiences and the reviews were enthusiastic, but as work progressed the show started to lose focus. In the typical backstage swell of out-of-town hysteria there was talk that John Raitt was too old, that Donna McKechnie wasn't right, that the plot was saccharine, that the Mark Hellinger, where the show would open, was too big. All anyone backstage really knew was that *A Joyful Noise* had sensational dances and a hummable score by Oscar Brand and Paul Nassau. When Padula suggested to his backers that Bennett become the show's director, there was dissension. Padula's co-producer, Slade Brown, was enthusiastic but felt the need of a name director. Dore Schary, the Hollywood-Broadway director/producer/playwright, was brought in. At this point, the tour was almost over, money was tight. The Mark Hellinger opening night was only a few weeks away, its nearness terrifying. It was too late to give the narrative the kind of zest that was in Bennett's choreography.

Schary, unimpressed with Donna McKechnie either as a dancer or as an actress, replaced her with Susan Watson, despite Bennett's objections. Schary set about rewriting individual scenes and redoing some of Padula's direction. "He didn't help appreciably," Padula says. "There really wasn't time." Although there is no mention of Schary among those credited for *A Joyful Noise* in the 1966–67 *Burns Mantle Theater Yearbook*, which lists Edward Padula as director, the production in fact was finally directed by Dore Schary.

By August 1967, Bennett was signed to do the choreography for *Henry, Sweet Henry* ("I told them they were going to be a flop without me," he said). All this time Avian had been watching his roommate from the sidelines, astonished by the acceleration of his career. At this point Bennett asked Avian to become his second assistant on *Henry, Sweet Henry*.

Having graduated from Boston University with a major in both theater and education ("to have something to fall back on if Broadway didn't work out"), Avian wasn't sure he knew enough about choreography to be able to assist, but his friend's enthusiasm canceled his doubts. Although the Bennett whirlwind swept him up, Avian, who is almost serenely modest, kept his balance: "One thing about our success is that I never wanted to be Michael and he never wanted to be me. I never aspired to be a choreographer, or to be the star. That just wasn't in me. Michael had that distinctive A personality, and I liked being the stage mother. He was a control freak because he knew what he wanted and he knew he had to control everything to get it done his way. We had an interesting relationship because it worked so totally. A lot of people think we were lovers. We weren't. We couldn't have been any closer. We were closer than brothers. I knew everything about him, and we trusted each other."

Bob Avian knew his exact role was, at first, simply to be an adviser whose specialty was dance: "We'd watch a number and Michael would be going, 'Well, what do you think?' I'd say, 'I-love-it-I-love-it, but why don't you try coming this way, like on a diagonal.' And he'd try that. Actually I was an editor, that's the best word for it, and he responded to me instantly. We'd been really good friends up to this, and now we had this working relationship. Eventually our styles ended up playing off each other, my training in classical ballet, his in jazz and tap; we were able to merge them. There was never just a simple singular style in any of our shows. We could go from A to Z beause of our combined techniques, and that's probably our particular contribution to Broadway choreography."

After *Henry, Sweet Henry* opened in late October 1967, Avian stayed with the production as dance captain for the ten weeks the show ran. During this period Bennett was increasingly in demand for television. In 1968 he choreographed a Hallmark special based on *Pinocchio* and a Kraft Music Hall show called *Don Rickles' Brooklyn*. Avian became perplexed because he was put on the sidelines; Bennett wasn't seeking his help. Then "the real click-in happened" when Bennett was signed to do a number for Carol Lawrence on *The Ed Sullivan Show*, "a smasheroo with huge everything—sets! costumes!

lights! music!—and the whole shebang based on Michael's ideas."
While putting this production together, Avian began contributing ideas
of his own. After that, referring to themselves as Mickey Rooney and
Judy Garland putting on a neighborhood show in the backyard, they
called each other Mickey and Judy.

Despite Bennett's vacillating attitude about personal relationships,
during the time he was in *Bajour* he fell in love with a chorus boy
named Larry Fuller, who was dancing in *Funny Girl*. He met Fuller
one Thursday night at the Roxy bowling alley on Forty-fourth Street,
where weekly bowling competitions were held among the casts of
Broadway shows. Soon after the meeting, he moved out of the apartment he shared with Avian to live with Fuller.

A good-looking reddish-blond, Larry Fuller was intrigued by
"this smart little guy, five feet five, moles on his face, thin hair, not
much to look at but he had this sexual chemistry." The appeal had
deviltry in it, and "almost unbelievable self-confidence." Fuller was
twenty-four, three years older than Bennett, and, like Avian, a seasoned
gypsy. Bennett was smitten by Fuller's uncomplicated blond charm.
Blond men particularly thrilled him: "Over the years I've learned to
put up with the way I look, I've even come to like my moles, but
what I've always envied are the guys with a full head of hair, preferably
blonds—but not always."

The more they talked against the clocking clatter of falling duck-
pins, the more Bennett felt he could learn from his new friend. Each
night after the curtain came down on *Bajour* and *Funny Girl*, they'd
head for Joe Allen's or (occasionally) Sardi's to eat and to lose themselves and find each other in theater talk. They lived together in a
big old-fashioned apartment at 470 West End Avenue for three years,
Fuller expecting a one-to-one commitment in their relationship. He
had no way of knowing that intimate details of their life together
would later be used as dialogue in *A Chorus Line*. He knew from the
start that Bennett was ambitious. His discovery of the scale of the
ambition was as startling as—if less hurtful than—his discovery of
Bennett's promiscuity. His "high-flying little choreographer" was testing his wings in areas other than dance. Professing fidelity while

romancing the neighborhood, Bennett, to Fuller's knowledge, was "having affairs with three women and a man, all—in one way or another—important to his career."

Fuller: "This sexual chemistry he had, it worked with men and women. There was this routine he'd do, and now that I think of it, it was partly fun, partly sad. He'd stand in front of a mirror and tell you how ugly he was.

" 'I'm so ugly, I'm so ugly, I'm so ugly.' He'd say it over and over.

"I'd say, 'Oh, come on, Michael, you're not.'

" 'I am, I am, I'm really unattractive.'

"I'd say, 'Look, you're not a handsome beauty, no. You're not Tyrone Power, but you're a very attractive young man. You're sexually attractive. You're not beautiful, not ugly.'

" 'Yes I am. Ugly. Ugly!'

"Well, by then, I'd given in, and say, 'Okay, you're ugly.' And he'd go, mad as hell, 'What do you mean I'm ugly?!'

"But, you see, he knew he had this extra something. There wasn't much I could do about the promiscuity. It seemed to accelerate near the end of our relationship when his career was really taking off. When he first started fooling around, I asked to discuss it. I'd begun to think he was genuinely bisexual, and wanted to know exactly what the level of my competition was here because: 'You see, Michael, women have certain things I don't have and the other way around.' I wanted to know if he preferred men or women. It was that simple. What he said was: 'Not particularly. I enjoy them both.'

"We really broke up over someone called 'this beautiful man,' a dancer, Scott Pearson."

Time and separation have tempered Fuller's resentment. He talks temperately about his old lost lover, but still expresses amazement when Bennett's name is professionally linked with Robbins.

"After we moved in together, he got a job choreographing *West Side Story* for Donald Driver in Wallingford, Connecticut. I'd danced in *West Side* for Jerry Robbins, who, to me, was—and is—incomparable, omnipotent. When Michael told me his ambition was to be the next Jerry Robbins, I said, 'Oh, come on, Michael, you're good, but let's not aim ridiculously high!' I mean, to me it was blasphemy. He was pretty upset with me. Wallingford was the start of his reputation. His career took off after that and we didn't see much of each other after we broke up. He began circulating with a lot of important people, Freddy Brisson, Hepburn, Coco Chanel, Neil Simon, Hal Prince, flying to Paris, London, all that, and I was still hoofin' my way to nowhere."

More and more Bennett came to see Jerome Robbins as his model. Eight years before, when he was eleven, he had returned to Buffalo from a summer in New York with the steaming dance patterns of *The Pajama Game* percolating in his head, but it was the show's co-director, Jerome Robbins, rather than its choreographer, Bob Fosse, he was determined to emulate. In his own hands-on experience, he'd been impressed with the *West Side Story* dances, their kinetic energy, the way they reflected character and mood. Then, in the space of six months in the single year of 1964, he'd seen Robbins' direction of *Funny Girl* (for which Carol Haney had done the choreography) and Robbins' real signature piece, *Fiddler on the Roof*. (For a while the two musicals ran concurrently; *Funny Girl*, which opened six months before *Fiddler*, ran a little over three years, *Fiddler* nearly seven.) No one was better than Robbins. By 1975, after the rushing success of *A Chorus Line*, Bennett egoistically came to think he had surpassed Fosse, as well as the rest of his contemporaries. All except Robbins, who is known among dancers as God, as well as—with perhaps less genuflection—the Master. The Master's route to Broadway had been paved by George Balanchine in 1936—seven years before Agnes de Mille had woven the "coterie art form" of ballet into *Oklahoma!*—when Balanchine designed the first significant ballet for a musical, Rodgers and Hart's *On Your Toes*. Created specifically for Ray Bolger and Tamara Geva to Rodgers' music, and freely fitted to the plot, the ballet was called "Slaughter on Tenth Avenue." The following year Balanchine choreographed *Babes in Arms* and, in 1938, both *I Married an Angel* and *The Boys from Syracuse*. Then he gave up Broadway and went back to the School of American Ballet, which, with Lincoln Kirstein, Balanchine had founded in 1934, the year he had emigrated from Russia.

Robbins' expertise includes not only musical theater but serious drama on and Off Broadway. To Michael Bennett the extent of God's "genius" would remain out of reach, would fly farther still and accede to a purity of art beyond show business, when Robbins—shadowing Balanchine—turned *his* back on Broadway to devote himself strictly to ballet. The pinnacle of Robbins' commercial success is his direction and choreography of *Fiddler on the Roof*. Well before *Fiddler* became the fourth-longest-running show in history (3,242 performances), Jerome Robbins had defected from Times Square, forsaking the theater to become artistic director of the New York City Ballet and the heir to George Balanchine.

What Michael Bennett perceived early in Robbins' work was totality, all the sums of a given piece adding to a unified whole. While the Broadway musical had begun to redefine itself significantly after the charmingly easy entertainments of the 1920s and 1930s—by the Gershwins, Jerome Kern, Irving Berlin, Cole Porter, all of whom had roots in Viennese operetta and Gilbert and Sullivan—it took time for the subsequent *Scandals, Gaieties, Follies, New Faces* and *Vanities* to make way for what first became known as the serious musical and would later be labeled the concept musical.

Since change doesn't really happen *sponte sua*, even in art, the claims made for this or that breakthrough are hardly clear-cut. Yet, in 1943, Rodgers and Hammerstein's *Oklahoma!* would prove a landmark musical. Although sentimental and nostalgic, it had the guts (or perhaps just the savvy) to deal with unpleasant melodrama. For all its beautiful mornings and box-supper socials, *Oklahoma!* had a dark tinge to it, a reality strong enough to deal with paranoia, isolation and mistreatment. (So, of course, before it, had *Show Boat* and *Porgy and Bess*; even the seemingly easy *Pal Joey* had something to say about sleaze and corruption.) It was so tightly put together that Agnes de Mille's dances, bowing to the mime-and-show/storytelling discipline of ballet, were as intrinsic to the unfolding drama as the dialogue. Although later he would scorn the stop-and-go interruption of its hit songs, Michael Bennett liked *Oklahoma!*: "It was one of the first Broadway shows I saw that didn't have improbable people doing improbable things, like dentists dancing." He perceived in its structure the concentration of metaphor that Jerome Robbins would make an inescapable subtext to *West Side Story, Gypsy* and *Fiddler on the Roof.* As Bennett systematically worked his way from show to show—with suggestions to a choreographer here turning into a fully realized dance section there; with idle moments of dance chatter swept into dramatic statement—he was following the insights of Robbins.

Gradually, the insights would shade to his own, resulting in three concept musicals, *A Chorus Line, Ballroom* and *Dreamgirls.*

Gradually, he would think he had surpassed the master.

"Maybe my identity was a little screwed up," Michael Bennett said, "but I always knew what I wanted to do. I really wanted to become Jerry Robbins, I wanted to become this brilliant choreographer/ director in the 'theatahh.' I didn't really see myself getting mixed up in the writing of shows, the thrashing out of the book, the business hassles of becoming a producer, but all that has happened. Then when I got to the place where I wanted to be, a choreographer who could also surprise the world as a director, I found show business was dying."

When a new talent appears in the theater, word spreads fast but often with a slow follow-up, like a starburst misfired. Harold Prince had heard about Bennett's choreography for *A Joyful Noise*, then heard further confirmation of his talent in *Henry, Sweet Henry*. Prince also knew about "the kid's push," which sounded like his own. Prince had begun as a quick-running gofer to George Abbott—the legendary mastermind whose Broadway credentials cover the entire twentieth century ("Mr. Abbott," as he is reverentially called, is now 103 years old)—and had pushed himself from being a faceless assistant into the name-value ranks of producers and directors. By the time Michael Bennett was making himself known on Broadway, Hal Prince had long since been established. He'd produced *The Pajama Game* with Abbott in 1954, when Bennett was only eleven years old, and his early directorial credits included *She Loves Me* and *Baker Street*.

In 1966, the year Bennett choreographed *A Joyful Noise*, Prince's show was *Cabaret*. Prince, who talks in a periodically intellectualized rhetoric self-consciously flecked with sudden interjections and dropped diphthongs (to the chorus: "Hey, gang, you're gonna have to do that Brechtian crossover again"), was impressed with Bennett's dances. He summoned him to his office to discuss working together, although he had no specific project in mind and wouldn't have until three years later. He recalls that Bennett was "very, very eager; boy, was he ever!" When Prince suggested working together, Bennett's eyes blazed and he said, as though the two words were one, "Right/when!?" The grasping attitude reminded Hal Prince of himself reaching for the reins across George Abbott's galloping horses. It also reminded him of the time he had hired Jerry Robbins to back up Bob Fosse on the choreography for *The Pajama Game*. Fosse had had a reputation as a performer, a nightclub dancer, which didn't necessarily mean he could create dances for a Broadway musical. Robbins wasn't interested in pinch-hitting. He agreed to make suggestions and alterations in Fosse's work but didn't want credit for it, didn't want the additional billing. He wanted to be known as a director and didn't want to give "the theater community" the wrong impression.

"The first thing I found for Michael and me to do was *Company*, in 1969," Hal Prince says. "By then he was chomping on the bit to be a director. By the time we get to *Follies*, he wanted what Jerry wanted on *Pajama Game*. Only now I was the one who made the suggestion about sharing billing. That's how I got him to do *Follies*. I hired him as the choreographer, then as my co-director. I knew there was going to be enough work for the both of us. *Boy, was there ever!* I have to say that back in 1966, 1967, I'd never quite seen anything like the eagerness. It was almost . . . um, hostile? Ruthless maybe . . ."

For all the brashness, the drive toward accomplishment (which occasioned the sudden disruption in personal relationships), Bob Avian steadily sensed "a sentimentality" in his friend. "A lot of people think he was hard and ruthless. He was, in his way, but his work always had heart, the kind of heart he didn't show in his personal life. He wanted his audience to cry; if he could work that out of *Chorus Line* or *Ballroom* or *Dreamgirls*, he'd done his work. He looked for emotion even when it bordered on the sentimental. That's why *Follies* was so tough for him. It was cynical, hard-edged; it didn't offer much hope."

As corollary to Avian's evaluation of Michael Bennett, there are the resentful words of his brother, Frank DiFilia, who is a tall, thin, sallow replica of his father, Salvatore.

"Here is this man, my brother, who could create wonderfully honest theatrical experiences and, in his personal life, couldn't trust his own instincts to know what was right. That's my forte, trusting my instincts. Michael had trouble with people. You couldn't talk to him about much. No interest in politics or sports. I almost never saw him with a book. He didn't read except maybe thrillers, whereas I have a wide range of interests, read all the time, lots of topics, science, psychology, philosophy.

"There were only two things you could talk to him about: theater and personal relationships—that is, the personal relationships with people *he* was having relationships with. He always thought everything—the simplest thing—had great psychological ramifications. So everything became overblown. Like: Should he loan me a thousand dollars to pay off this debt or not? Is that going to make me beholden to him for life, is that going to make me less of a man? I wanted to tell him, just fuck do it! Loan me the money!

"Life is a series of experiences and one thing feeds another. He could be heartless. Sure, he was generous to Mom and Dad. With money. But he almost denied Mom his love as an adult. He would be loving and then there was something that would make him punish her."

Curled on a pillow under a window facing West Twenty-first Street, DiFilia's white cat unwinds itself. After arching its spine, it hops on DiFilia's desk, where it sits on a scattering of newspapers and *People* magazines, the only reading material in the room. Yawning, the glowing cat stares at a drab home-drawn painting on the wall. A single silk calla lily studies its dust in a cheap mirror hanging above a lidless Chock Full o' Nuts coffee can.

Remembering the burden of bringing up his brother, Michael Bennett once said, "I used to take care of Frank, I mean do everything for him, dress him, feed him, look after him. I had to. The only time I liked any of it was when I taught him time steps in the basement. We had a routine we did together, 'Me and My Shadow.' "

Mrs. DiFiglia: "There was no rivalry between my boys. None at all. Michael was the boss and Frank just let him take care of him as though he was his dad. Sometimes Michael was real mean to him. Like doing crazy things! Like he'd make Frank be the horsey and he'd ride him around the room. Frank would get very tired but Michael wouldn't let him quit. In a way I was glad when Michael left. Frank was thirteen at the time, and so dependent on Michael he didn't know how to find his way to the corner!

"Although Frank danced, he was not another Michael. He was more like a shadow. He could follow but couldn't create. 'Me and My Shadow' was so funny when Frank was learning it! Michael would change it every so often, do something different with a step here or there. And here was poor Frank having to follow his shadow. I could tell he didn't know what he was doing because I knew all the routines. Anyway, Michael would change it during a performance, they'd come off stage, Frank would give Michael this dirty look and say, 'Hey, you didn't do what you were supposed to!'

"Michael'd say, 'So what? You followed, didn't you?'

"Frank got so upset he decided not to dance anymore. I said, 'Fine, be a musician, take piano or something like that.' Later, of course, Michael got Frank a job with Joe Papp."

As though living out the role his mother had written for him because of her own lack of a dutiful, responsible husband, Michael Bennett would eventually take care of an extended, if not always intimate, family, getting jobs for particular members of the family, giving jobs to others, advising and controlling with paternalistic concern. And as his mother's chosen son, her indisputable favorite, he would, in the Freudian phrase of Ernest Jones, "keep for life the feeling of a conqueror, that confidence of success that often induces real success." Just as son would become symbolic father, the conqueror would become tyrant.

Mrs. DiFiglia: "Michael could be mean. He had this bad side. Maybe everybody has it. Sam had it. With gambling. I'm sure Frank envied Michael's success and talent, all that, but I'm also sure he never wanted to change places with him. He's very well adjusted for someone growing up in his brother's shadow."

Michael Bennett needed someone in his shadow. Out of a deep sense of insecurity, he needed someone with him at all times, someone who understood him, who didn't haggle or compete, whose needs and ambitions were less than his. That person became his surrogate brother, Bob Avian, whose "loyalty," Michael Bennett said, "keeps me sane."

What he saw in Avian's level friendship was complete faith, trust, understanding and total lack of moral judgment. Even when his actions were bizarre, like his relentless attacks on young dancers he was supposed to love and whom he referred to as "my family, my world"; even when he overdosed on cocaine and was secretly rushed to a New York doctor; or when he rationalized his seduction of the wife of one of his best friends, and the bitter, name-calling destruction of that friend's marriage in a Paris courtroom—he would look to Avian for support. It was given unquestioningly.

Given unquestioningly because Bob Avian thought Michael Bennett was a genius who needed to be coddled and protected. To Avian, standards of personal behavior didn't matter because Michael Bennett was special, Michael Bennett was the equivalent of a show-biz super-hero out of *The Music Man*, if not out of Nietzsche. And in Avian's view, he needed nurturing, needed indulgence. This catering created a hothouse atmosphere where arrogance flowered like nightshade, where ego spread like a voracious vine ready to suffocate anything in its path. At the same time that the indulgence allowed the artist to create art, it corrupted the artist. It would be responsible for something as human and compassionate as *A Chorus Line* while simultaneously withering the humanity and compassion behind the work itself. Reality and illusion would ignore each other, then merge in a power play.

Nicholas Dante, a self-described "sissy, faggot, old, old chorus boy and would-be writer," was caught in the *Chorus Line* cross fire. Sitting tall and hostile in a high-backed chair, he explains himself with pained honesty, the result, he says, of his Buddhist training and recent psychotherapy. He "chants" every day.

"Look, I was part of the inner circle before they fucked me over and refused me credit for *Chorus Line*. So much of *Chorus Line* is mine, outright mine! Sure, with contributions from Michael and Bob Avian. Jimmy Kirkwood wound up with more than I did, more money, credit, everything! I was responsible for Paul's monologue. That's my story! I was that faggot, that drag queen discovered by his parents. It all happened *to me*! I came up with the conceptual idea of the montage, and it says—right there, in every program ever printed!—'Conceived by Michael Bennett!' My idea! I was a dancer just like Michael, and of course he made me fall in love with him, got what he wanted out of me, then basically threw me out like so much garbage, the way he did with everybody except Bobby, who is, truly, a wonderful man.

"But maybe . . . MAY BE! . . . If you think about it . . . Just what if Michael hadn't been so indulged by Bobby? Think about that.

"I was with them one night in Bob Avian's apartment, and I'll never forget it. Just the three of us, and we were all stoned. Bob was outside on his balcony, Michael and I were inside talking, and suddenly he went off! I mean off! Out of nowhere he suddenly goes craze-eee! I can see him now, sitting against the wall, suddenly announcing how brilliant he is. 'No one can touch me! I'm the top! I'm the best! I know everything!' This is when we were working on *Chorus Line*, and I thought: He's telling this to *moi*!

"It was the first time I sensed, maybe, he was a little nuts. He kept it up and kept it up, how brilliant he was, how much he knew, how good he was.

"I went outside to Bob and said, 'Is she for real?' Bob laughed so hard I thought he'd fall off the balcony.

"The thing was, Michael began to believe it all, the genius stuff. I mean really, truly, deeply believe it. He wasn't a genius, puh-leeze! Talented, very talented. Smart, very smart. Seductive, very seductive. Manipulative, very manipulative. But a genius? Come on! But he really started to believe it. A lot of it had to do with him being stroked so much by those people around him."

CHAPTER THREE

Flops and Promises

(1966–1969)

Before Michael Bennett began to work on Broadway, there had been more than Buffalo and the European tour of *West Side Story* on his résumé. During a summer at the Phoenix Star Theater, he did new versions of *The Music Man*, *Bye Bye Birdie*, *The Pajama Game*, *The Unsinkable Molly Brown*; later, closer to New York, at the Oakdale Music Theater, Wallingford, Connecticut, productions of *West Side Story* and *No Strings*. The latter buzzed his reputation through Times Square from one producer's office to the next. His dances were nimble, spirited, remarkably free of the Agnes de Mille influence that seemed to be surfacing in the work of most choreographers. Young as he was, he was contracted to choreograph the pre-Broadway tryout of *A Joyful Noise*. Among the members of the chorus who would figure later in his life were three dancers, Scott Pearson, Baayork Lee and Tommy Tune. Pearson—described by Nicholas Dante as "the love of Michael's life, the only real one" —would be mentioned in Bennett's will; Lee, although badly treated, would choose to filter her memory and remember Bennett as her lifelong inspiration; Tune would abandon Bennett, lose his friendship, then tearfully reprimand himself after Bennett's death.

A Joyful Noise opened December 15, 1966, at the Mark Hellinger, and flopped after twelve performances, closing on Christmas Eve. The musical competition for the Tonys that year included *Cabaret*, *I Do! I Do!*, *The Apple Tree* and *Walking Happy*. The surprise among the nominations was Bennett for his *Joyful Noise* choreography, which lost out to *Cabaret*'s hefty fräuleins in black-garter-belt routines by Ron Field.

"*Joyful Noise* was at the Hellinger, which backs right up to the Broadhurst, where *Cabaret* was playing," Michael Bennett said. "I walked in—this was before the Tonys but the nominations were out—saw Ron's dances, then waited to see him. I knew Ronnie from *Nowhere to Go But Up*, always liked him and everything, and I thought the *Cabaret* dances were just wonderful. I waited around, Ronnie came, and I walked up to him and said, 'Darling, the Tony's yours, don't think another thing about it!' "

Ironically, this scene would be played out with dramatic variations sixteen years later when *Dreamgirls* fell victim to Tommy Tune's *Nine*, with Tune, a Bennett protégé, winning the 1982 Tony for best direction of a musical. The night before the Tony ceremony, Michael Bennett's paranoia, this time stimulated by the fear of an embarrassing public rejection rather than Mafia mayhem, led him to Ron Field's lower Broadway studio. Out of control, wracked, rheumy black eyes staring, he laid out his fears. He was the best, didn't Broadway know that? Tommy Tune was only where he was because of him. *Dreamgirls* was an innovation, *Nine* the same old stuff. If he had been arrogant after *Chorus Line*, hadn't he paid for his sins by giving the street a flop with *Ballroom*? His work was superior to everyone's. He had six Tonys and a Pulitzer Prize in his Central Park duplex to prove it; only Hal Prince had more. What was the matter with the theater community? Was it all politics? Was it all about money and not the value of the work? If it wasn't that, what was it? A fuckin' popularity contest? He was the best, he was the best, he was the best!

As coke and vodka choked through his system, noosing not freeing the terror, he vomited.

In the black/purple theatrical gloom of his studio, where light is

shaded and minimal, Field remembers that night with guilt and remorse. "I wasn't a good friend. He needed a friend and I gave him
a lecture on reality. He believed *Dreamgirls* would reclaim his reputation. Lo and behold, there's this weird musical at the 46th Street
Theater Tommy Tune did that was interesting and boring, then
brilliant and boring, and interesting again, and then boring/boring/
boring! Michael thought *Nine* winning the Tonys was a slap in the
face after what he'd given the street. 'I gave them my comeuppance.
Now I've given them the most fabulous, technically dazzling, entertaining musical! I've given them a star! I've given them everything!
And now—now!—they're gonna slap me again and give the Tony
to Tommy???!!!'

"I said, 'Whoa, Michael, easy, slow down. Maybe it's just Tommy's year. They haven't given him a Tony so far. Maybe they just
wanna support a new director. Maybe the little snobby touches in *Nine*
make it seem an important musical.'

"All I was saying was: Michael, get off it! So they give it to
Tommy. What does that have to do with your talent, your brilliance,
your contribution? But he didn't hear it that way. He heard it that I
wasn't supporting him. And you had to, you always had to support
him. Now I wish I'd said it all real different because it was one of
the last times we were alone together. All he wanted was sympathy
and I didn't have any sympathy. I mean, at this point, I was poverty-
stricken, and here was this rich friend of mine coming over *pishing*
because that year he might not get another few awards!

"Then, that night before Tommy won with *Nine*, I just tried to
give Michael the truth. I'd been telling the truth since 1978 after I
took est, but I hadn't learned how to tell it in a supportive way. It
came off like napalm."

When Michael Bennett earned his first Tony nomination in 1966
for *A Joyful Noise*, the nomination itself was enough. It meant he had
been noticed and applauded. Fifteen years later he was no longer that
naïve. Separate from the recognition the Tonys—like the Oscars, the
Grammys, the Emmys—mean money. Nominees are selected by a
panel of "theater people" (which, until recently, included working

critics), then voted upon by some 650 professionals (members of Actors Equity, the Society of Stage Directors and Choreographers, first- and second-night press lists). Supposedly the Tonys have to do with "distinguished achievement," but their history is as flawed as that of any other prize system. A lot of it comes down to politics. Bennett once suggested that votes could be whispered in favor of a production simply because the production employed more people than perhaps did its competitors. Bestowing a Tony—or Tonys—on a heavily populated musical could increase a show's run and keep said population at work singing and dancing for years. In the competitive marketplace of the Broadway theater, the Tony Award can be both a pat on the back and cash in the pocket.

Despite published remarks that he had no real interest in money, Bennett had vowed to become a millionaire before he was twenty-five. It was talk Bob Avian heard when they were working on *Henry, Sweet Henry*. Bennett had a businessman's acumen, although it wasn't always steady. When he wanted something badly enough that acumen could be undermined by his enthusiasm. The praise surrounding the Tonys was all well and good, something he needed emotionally, but gradually he came to see the awards as financial markers. Beyond that, he thought a collection of Tonys put him on a level of achievement where he was certain to be treated with respect. He expected more from the *Chorus Line* success than he ever got. He expected deference, the genuflection given Jerry Robbins. But, lacking Robbins' distant magisterial presence and his legend, Bennett found himself still being treated as a kid. Until he was forty, he dressed like a kid, unconsciously eliciting an adult-to-child response from others despite the sophistication of his insights. He could never understand why there were people over him, like the Shuberts, who could control him, and people in Hollywood for whom he had to audition long after he had proved himself. He was Michael Bennett! There were even writers—Tom Eyen and Treva Silverman—who could make his life miserable. Where was the allowance for his achievement?

"From his point of view," Ron Field says, "he was not only great and talented, he was also sweet and kind and wonderful, and it was amazing to him that people could still stick it to him, could still fuck him over."

"We're talking about theater people here," columnist Liz Smith says, separating gifted crazies from the canaille. "They're highly competitive. And hysterical. And paranoid.

"In some respects I think Michael had an inferiority complex. He wasn't comfortable out of the theater. He really didn't want to move out of his world, so he created this platoon around him, all these people who worked for him. If something happened in his world, if he was knocked or chastised or ridiculed, he'd react, sometimes react like the little boy he was. And he got to the point where he didn't know why he had to keep proving himself all the time. Some of that, maybe, had to do with the way he was hurt."

Disappointed but hardly defeated by the *Joyful Noise* failure, Bennett—1967's hot new choreographer—was signed for *Henry, Sweet Henry* by the show's producers, Norman Twain and Edward Specter. An adaptation based on Nora Johnson's novel *The World of Henry Orient*, which had been a Peter Sellers movie in 1964, *Henry* lasted for only eighty performances. Bennett contributed what was fast becoming his own spirited brand of dancing, nothing as defined as Bob Fosse's group-leaning-together-pelvic-thrust, yet movement flexed with originality and purpose. Bob Avian was in the chorus; so were Baayork Lee and Priscilla Lopez. Lopez would later be among the angriest provocateurs in the bitter backstage battle about who-owed-whom and who-did-what to make *A Chorus Line* the success it became.

As unpromising as the opportunities may have been in *Henry, Sweet Henry*, Michael Bennett again emerged from a flop—two in a row—with a Tony nomination for his choreography, but he lost the award to Gower Champion, who won for *The Happy Time*. (Champion also won for his direction.) Bennett knew *Henry* didn't have it when he read it. From the start he had a keen theatrical sense, and it became steadily keener and more sophisticated. *Henry* gave him the opportunity to work with some well-regarded professionals. He was open-eyed, cool, pragmatic, still learning and willing to learn anywhere, anytime, and from anyone. The production had a star lineup: George Roy Hill, whose background coupled theater and movies, was its director; Nunnally Johnson, who'd done movie adaptations of *The Grapes of Wrath*, *Tobacco Road*, and *The Three Faces of Eve*, had written the book; Bob Merrill, who'd scored *New Girl in Town* and *Take Me Along*, had done the music.

For all that, the production didn't mesh, but Bennett came away from the show with the glitz provided by his Tony nomination.

Next on his calendar, in 1968, came *Promises, Promises*, a musical with a book by Neil Simon adapted from Billy Wilder and I. A. L. Diamond's screenplay *The Apartment* and a score by Burt Bacharach and Hal David, a soft-rock/pop duo making their Broadway debut. Bacharach and David were greeted as though they were the incoming Messiahs of the Big Broadway Musical, which was then showing signs of stagnation.

In the 1940s and 1950s the principal creators of musical comedy on Broadway had been Irving Berlin, Rodgers and Hammerstein, Lerner and Loewe, and Leonard Bernstein, with Rodgers and Hammerstein the most prolific and the most copied. *Oklahoma!*, which had opened March 31, 1943 (nine days before Michael Bennett was born), had been followed by *Carousel*, *Allegro*, *South Pacific*, *The King and I*, *Me and Juliet*, *Flower Drum Song* and *The Sound of Music*, and each had been imitated by less gifted music makers. *The Sound of Music*, which appeared in 1959, marked Rodgers and Hammerstein's last collaboration as a team.

In the 1960s, with the arrival of a new set of names—Jerry Bock and Sheldon Harnick, John Kander and Fred Ebb, and, principally, Stephen Sondheim—the Broadway musical showed signs of moving beyond the easy rhythms and easier thoughts that had pretty much defined it until then. By 1964 the vague 1949 political conscience of Rodgers and Hammerstein's *South Pacific* had found harsh exposure in Bock and Harnick's *Fiddler on the Roof*, which boldly defied existing patterns by dealing with something serious, the suffering of Jews in

Russian *shtetls* and pogroms. Two years later, Kander and Ebb's *Cabaret* blasted the Third Reich. And two years after *Cabaret, Hair* brought public outrage full circle by raising a rock-'n'-roll fist against the war in Vietnam.

This willingness to reach beyond the conventional Broadway format for serious subject matter had a personal rather than a political precursor in the Kurt Weill/Ira Gershwin/Moss Hart *Lady in the Dark*, which, in 1941, used psychoanalysis as its topic. At a time when Times Square was given over to the snappy silliness of Rodgers and Hart, Cole Porter, and Irving Berlin, *Lady in the Dark* attempted to probe—in what Weill termed "three little one-act operas"—the traumas that lie behind dreams. Slowly but surely the Broadway musical was stretching its own limitations.

While many of the 1960s and 1970s composers were content with old patterns, Stephen Sondheim sought to widen the possible subject matter while deepening it with the essentially dour—but intellectually fashionable—philosophy of existentialism. He wandered into areas where song and dance hadn't stepped, sometimes tripping in his ambitious shuffle, once producing a masterpiece (1979's *Sweeney Todd, the Demon Barber of Fleet Street*). If Sondheim's end-of-the-world attitude reflected a specific brand of contemporary cynicism, it was an attitude Michael Bennett found dramatically accurate but unrelievedly sour. Sondheim songs undermine love much the way Dorothy Parker's quatrains did in the 1930s. His songs offer hope in shreds. Love is dumb as well as blind. "Till death do us part" is gone in the blinking of an eye. If children—love's offspring—suggest promise, first they must escape the inescapable shadows of a darkening world.

Bennett believed some of this, then filtered it through his need to give an audience "optimism or, at least, a little joy." He worked on only two Sondheim shows, *Follies* and *Company*, the latter one of Sondheim's better bitter scores. Bennett wanted to be part of the "content change" he saw in the Sondheim/Prince musicals but "without quite so much heartache in what the shows said." If the early composers—Jerome Kern, Cole Porter, Irving Berlin, the Gershwins—were compromised by light romantic sensibility, Bennett wanted to retain the sensibility but make it tougher, "not really acerbic but, well, wry." He would come to scorn "swinging the scenery" music like Jerry Herman's, particularly *La Cage aux Folles*, which he considered a bad joke. He was capable, however, of having "a real good time," with something like *Annie*. Although he admired moments in Andrew Lloyd Webber's *Jesus Christ Superstar*, and praised Hal Prince's direction of *Evita*, he disliked Webber's work. To make a given score do what he wanted—that is, to move and propel action —he eventually found himself—after *A Chorus Line* and *Ballroom*— heading toward the techniques of opera. Minimal recitative would tell an audience what it needed to know. Songs would carry the basic weight of character and story, emotion and thought. The Tom Eyen/ Henry Krieger *Dreamgirls* score was to be the end result of this re-finement.

In 1968, what Bennett liked about *Promises, Promises* was Neil Simon's book. If *A Joyful Noise* finally had been done in by its hee-haw sensibility and *Henry, Sweet Henry* by its gummy sweetness, *Promises* had a tartness to it. Here was a musical comedy in which the badly abused heroine tries suicide when the married man she loves refuses to give up his wife. Told directly, and with Simon's humor, Bennett thought the show had real potential. Signed only to do the choreog-raphy, he was alert to everything and constantly studying what it was that made a successful musical. He liked the *Promises* score even though he felt the arrival of the Bacharach/David team on Broadway had been oversold (as it turned out, this was their only show). *Promises* pointed to interesting new directions. While the music—more often than not—marked time in the plot, it had a kinetically crackling, now and then modulated vitality. The sound was accomplished by orchestra and balcony loudspeakers in tune with an impressive black box, an electric console—beaming with tiny lights—that mixed the musical means, then amplified them. In those days, an audio engineer, usually working under a gooseneck lamp at the rear of the orchestra, manned the machine. He played it like a harmonium, his fingers pianistically flipping switches, toggles, keys, knobs, buttons and dials to adjust the doo-wop and the waaa-waaas—decibel by decibel, moment to moment—within the reverberating shell of the proscenium. Innovative in 1968, the engineer and his magic boom box have long since become regular participants on Broadway.

"**M**ichael was the choreographer on *Promises*, and just that," Neil Simon says. "The show was working great out of town, but we were having some problems at the end of the first act. There was a lot of discussion about what needed to be done, the usual give-and-take among the creative people, and here was Michael looking like this kid on a college football team sitting on the bench and pleading with his eyes for the coach to let him in the game. He looked like he was saying, 'Gimme-a-chance-gimme-a-chance-gimme-a-chance!' When we agreed to give him the chance, his eyes went wide and he went to work like a shot. And the 'Turkey Lurkey' number he came up with didn't just solve the problem we were having, it was also a sensation.

"He was just an awful quick intuitive study, and he was fearless. That's why later I asked him to direct *God's Favorite*, the fearlessness."

Directed by Robert Moore, *Promises, Promises* ran thirty-seven months, during which there were road tours and a London production. It was Michael Bennett's first big success, although, again, his Tony nomination didn't pay off with an award (Joe Layton won for *George M!*). No longer simply "getting known," he was making money, and felt protected under the cold, beckoning, irresistible neon glare of Times Square by the warmth of the friends he had worked into *Promises*, particularly Donna McKechnie. After their time together as *Hullabaloo* dancers, he had developed a brotherly relationship with McKechnie, whose childhood life mirrored his own, and who was then seeing Ken Howard, one of the actors in the *Promises* cast. Later, when McKechnie and Howard talked about getting married, Bennett, no longer fraternal but, rather, frenzied Svengali to McKechnie's Trilby, broke up the relationship, going so far as to try to bar Ken Howard from the *Chorus Line* dressing rooms at the Shubert. In 1976, when Michael Bennett convinced himself he could be Donna Mc-

Kechnie's husband, they were married. The marriage lasted three months.

Nicholas Dante: "Oh, puh-leeze! Michael wasn't bisexual! He was as queer as a three-dollar bill, as the more charming fag-bashers among us usta say in Olden Times. I know why Michael married Donna, and I think I know what the last woman in his life was all about, that French lady, Sabine. I've heard all the fantasy stuff, and I *do* understand it. On a certain level.

"The fact is, he was in love with Scott Pearson. Michael was certainly going with him during *Promises*. I think Michael had a terrible time with his gayness. I don't think he was bisexual at all. I just think he hated being gay. When I heard he married Donna, I thought: Why is he doing this? The fantasy stuff, the Prince of Broadway Marries the Princess of Broadway? Well, part of him wanted that, and another part of him wanted to be just one of the guys. But Michael was as gay as I am. And, honey, I ain't bisexual.

"I think Michael wanted to be the Full Picture of the Successful Choreographer. I think he wanted to be able to sit with the Shuberts of this world—meaning people like Bernie Jacobs, who *is* the Shubert Organization—and have Full Respectability: 'Pay attention here. I'm as much a man as you are.' He didn't want to be perceived as 'that dancing fairy,' 'the twit choreographer,' didn't want to be interpreted as swish. In the past I used to think it wasn't a problem about gayness, that it just had to do with gaining respect. Now I see it *is* a problem of gayness. What else could it be if you need a more respectable, a more *complete* picture of you that doesn't happen to be true? I felt it was a public thing he was doing, getting married, associating with women. He had his emotional affection for Donna and Sabine, but I know it wasn't sexual. I could be wrong, but I know it anyway."

There is common agreement that Bennett had sexual charisma, a phrase that has perhaps come to replace the soul softness of simple "bedroom eyes." Whatever the exact nature of this sexiness, Bennett knew he had it, used it, then would modestly be "amazed" at how successfully it worked, notably in the dangerous games he played midway in his career with the Shubert's Bernard Jacobs. A number of women found him "very sexually attractive." But, from his point of view, the attraction was strictly calculated. Bennett once said, "My mother and all my women were cunts. After Sabine—that was it! I went back to boys. Less demanding. Not so many complications. And you don't end up buying them condos." The women in his life whom he wounded—Donna McKechnie, Sabine Cassel, Treva Silverman, Diane Judge—seem to have forgiven him. They talk about his "volatility," "his quick mind" and the steady "hype he got from show business."

Discriminating about work, he carefully chose opportunities in 1968–69 which were beginning to outline an estimable career. Less discerning about sex, steadily convinced that his talent (his genius) allowed him freedom, if not inviolability, he was openly promiscuous. Gaining power, achieving stardom added an electric charge, a sizzle, to the boyish magnestism. Romance and seduction became part of the game plan. When he won what he was after—by staring deeply, as only lovers, best friends or the completely disinterested do—whether it was to draw out a performance from a nervous chorus boy or from a privileged star; to perfect a writer's script; to polish a lyric, a tune; or simply to reach for a passing moment in an empty midnight— when he won what he was after, he'd start to hum. The hum came from a contentment—perhaps more accurately a boredom—achieved by winning.

Conquest as coda.

If he lost the game, he simmered with exclamatory hostility, spacing his words as though loading a rifle, then triggering a millisecond explosion. "DARLING . . . I TRULY DON'T CARE WHAT YOU WANT . . . I'M IN CONTROL HERE . . . THAT'S THE WAY . . . IT HAS TO BE!"

Defiance in defeat.

By the beginning of 1969, with *Promises, Promises* an established long run, Michael Bennett's reputation was golden. He was the newest, shiniest street-smart Broadway whiz kid. His credentials were falling in line with his ambition. Having danced in the choruses of *Subways Are for Sleeping* (1961), *Here's Love* (1963) and *Bajour* (1964), he had even proved himself a willing and reliable show doctor (without credit) on *How Now, Dow Jones*, *Your Own Thing* and *By Jupiter*. When a show was in trouble on the road or in rehearsal or preview, he'd answer almost any request for help. Doctoring is a delicate business. It's a kind of second-guess surgery, the equivalent of redoing—or undoing—someone else's operation. Sensing that his own work has gone unappreciated, the troubled show's original director may resent the summoned doctor. Sometimes, however, he may welcome a second opinion, even coming late (as it usually does). Bennett's youth combined with his brash insistence that he knew exactly what was wrong inevitably bruised some directors and cast members. To most producers, however, he was a wunderkind maven, if not an adolescent surgeon with remarkable healing powers.

Coming off the success of *Promises*, Bennett was signed as choreographer for *Coco*, an Alan Jay Lerner/André Previn musical, which was to star Katharine Hepburn as the legendary Gabrielle ("Coco") Chanel, who, at eighty-five, was still designing clothes in Paris. For Katharine Hepburn, who had begun her career in 1928 in a play called *Night Hostess*, it was her first appearance on Broadway in seventeen years and her first crack at a musical. (In 1952, directed by Michael Benthall, she had been the lead in Shaw's *The Millionairess*.) Although she was known for the jaw-thrust snobbishness of her Bryn Mawr speaking voice, it was not known whether or not that voice could sing. (In Paris, when Coco Chanel was told Hepburn was to play her on Broadway, Chanel exclaimed, *"I loved her as Ondine!"* Audrey Hepburn, not Katharine, was Coco Chanel's self-image, even though Chanel knew the musical would detail her 1954 comeback when she was seventy-one years old.)

Michael Bennett was similarly delighted to find himself positioned between two legends, although he expected trouble with both. Chanel was eighty-five, Hepburn sixty-two. He was twenty-six. Coco Chanel "fell in love with him" when he spent two weeks in her Paris salon researching her career, and learning how haute couture clothes were sketched, designed, seamed, a process not unlike his own intuitive methodology for developing the fabric of a musical. He became so immersed in the idea of the fashion industry that Chanel tried to persuade him to chuck show business and join her salon. With Katharine Hepburn the learning process was a personal skirmish between "two egomaniacs." Bennett ultimately outmaneuvered her. He did so, it seems, without her knowledge.

"If you're any good—and he was very good, very smart—you always think you know everything, which is what he thought," Katharine Hepburn says. "I have the same problem. Then, inevitably, it turns out you *do* know everything. A lot of people are pretty stupid; dreary, soppy things. I liked him because he wasn't a fool. He was stimulating. We were two egomaniacs who had sense enough to like each other. He had get-up-and-go. And imagination. A pictorial eye. Energy. Nerve to burn. He lived a day and a half in a day. Energetic people get a lot done. He got a lot done. Too bad he died. He was an extremely successful fella, but I didn't know him personally. I mean, he wasn't my great friend Michael Bennett at all.

"What you do have to remember here is that he was directing someone who had never done any musical work on the stage, had never done anything of that sort at all. Michael Benthall was the director. Michael Bennett did the musical staging and the choreography. I admired him, and Bob too. They were nice talented creatures."

Avian: "A show we felt was lousy, but knew was going to be BIG, and couldn't turn down the opportunity, *Coco*. A piece of *garbahhge*. Killed me, that show! We researched *everything*. Different modeling techniques. How fashion shows were done. Went to the library, ransacked newspapers, articles, columns, magazines, old *Vogues*. Learned that fifties models stood with hands on their hips, just so; in the sixties, a hand over the head, dead fish limp. All that kind of stuff. Different styles, attitudes, moods, poses. Then we choreographed it A to Z. Michael was always heavy into research. In *Henry, Sweet Henry* there was a hippie number, so we went down to Tompkins Park in the East Village, watching all these acidheads freaking out on soap bubbles, things like that.

"*Coco* was the big musical of the year coming up. Anyway, that was the hype. But of course it wasn't. Had it been offered to Michael later in his life, he'd have gone, 'No way!' But right then, he had to say, 'Well, it's Hepburn and Alan Jay Lerner and André Previn and this one and that one.' "

It was also a director named Michael Benthall, a friend of Hepburn. Formerly at the Old Vic, primarily a director of Shakespeare who had worked in opera, Benthall was ill prepared to manage a Broadway musical. As he more and more lost his way, guided though it was by Katharine Hepburn, he turned to alcohol for support. According to a member of the company, Benthall "really couldn't handle it." Competent at staging a small scene with two persons, when it came to interrupting the dialogue to include a number with singers and dancers Benthall dithered, dallied, then usually made dumb choices. There were times when Hepburn directed the two-person scenes involving herself. Benthall was bungling even the basic blocking. As Bennett watched him, he would make suggestions so to-the-point that Benthall, then Hepburn, began following them, then asking for more. At the same time Bennett was mapping out the show's choreography.

"He had his own musical sequences to do," Avian says, "then this burden of saving the director's ass."

In her own way, Hepburn was a burden too.

Handling an ordinary star personality would have been tough enough. Hepburn's stardom seemed to stretch from Plymouth Rock to Hollywood and Vine. Brusque, autocratic, superior, she walked with a stride that suggested the death of any creature unlucky enough to be in her path (from an ant to a buffalo). Having endured seasons—at the height of the Depression—when her name had become box office poison, when her private and public persona had a supercilious chill, it was too late, at sixty-two, to have any qualms about starring in a Broadway musical. She had picked the people around her because they knew what they were doing, and she was counting on her loyalty to pull Michael Benthall through. The other Michael was a toddler. She knew how to take care of toddlers—no matter how much talented noise they made. She'd insist.

"Hepburn couldn't sing a note, dance a step," Bob Avian says. "I don't think she had a radio in her house, *ever*!

"During preproduction we'd go in and there she'd be, carrying on, croaking out these songs, moving like a dinosaur. We'd put our hands over our ears and wouldn't know what to do. This is our Musical Comedy Star? Our Leading Lady? I mean, we were in despair, deep despair. Just as we were feeling like that, Hepburn had this breakdown, in a private rehearsal we had together, a small group of us. She said, 'I don't know who gave me the goddamn nerve to think I could do musical comedy. What kind of idiot am I?' She started to cry.

"Michael and I looked at each other. *She knows, she knows!* She doesn't have that kind of stupid ego to think she'll conquer it all!

"From then on we knew we had something to work with, her intelligence about her limitations. She was deathly afraid of it right to the end. There was a huge production number, 'The Money Rings Out Like Freedom,' which dramatized the whole Coco Chanel history—the clothes, the pants, the jewelry, the perfume, the whole business—built around Hepburn. She was supposed to walk into the number. But she couldn't handle it. So Michael redid it, sitting her on the edge of the stage like Judy Garland at the Palace, then having her play the scene with a young girl, to whom she said, 'Let me tell you the story of my career.' She was two feet from the conductor, and he'd cue her, 'Ta-ta-ta-ta-taaa.' The orchestra would go, 'Da-da-da-da-dummm," and he'd hammer out the beat, mouth the lyric, 'And the money rings out like freedom.' And Hepburn would do what she could.

"We were in the back of the house dying! It was amazing!"

Hepburn: "The truth is, I have always felt I helped enormously with *Coco*'s final effect. And part of the truth also is that Michael Bennett, finally, was able to make something out of me. Something musical, I mean."

What Hepburn was able to deliver in rehearsals was what the audience would finally hear, despite all of Bennett's tireless work. He knew the "something musical" would never be more than a Yankee clack. There was no silk to be skimmed from the sow's ear. By the last week of previews, he was worn down and dispirited. Trying to protect Hepburn all the time, making certain that she didn't get lost among *Coco*'s endlessly parading show girls, proved time-consuming and, inevitably, frustrating. Just the effort to be patient—and he *had* to be patient or, at least, pretend patience—took energy. Well aware of Benthall's drinking problem, he found he was refueling his own drive with vodka. He didn't really know what a nervous breakdown was, but something like that was happening to him. His emotions went up and down rapidly. He knew *Coco* was hopeless. One moment it wasn't so bad, the next moment it was "just shit." He kept losing the show's focus. Were the politics of pacifying Kate ruining the production? It wasn't his production anyhow. Was he blurring into a "professional crisis"?

Bennett's quick study of his star proved perceptive. She was very intelligent, very sharp, and she automatically took the opposite side of any suggestion he—or anyone else—made, even when it related to something as minor as a crossover. If he suggested she enter stage right, Hepburn would insist stage left. This little war of egos didn't surprise him (he being a Broadway Baby, she a Golden Legend), but it began to irritate him. Rather than slow down rehearsals, he'd give in. Hepburn's attitude was: "Ready when you are, C.B."—only she'd be both C.B. *and* the star. Bennett played along until he discovered how to manipulate her, a lesson he would use later with other people. If he really wanted her to come down the staircase on the left side, he'd say, "Kate, why don't you come down on the right?" True to form, she'd answer, "I'd rather the left." Bennett would say, "Try it your way."

Despite everything he added, Bennett knew that *Coco* was a zero. Style without content. He was just marking time in a vacuum. *Coco* was heavy, expensive and massing into an awful disappointment. It wasn't coming together; wasn't good enough; nothing was going to make it any better. The big mistake had been not to try out out of town.

Avian: "There we were on Broadway, and it's Katharine Hepburn in *Coco*, music by Alan Jay Lerner and André Previn! It's the first preview, with still a month to go before opening night, and *everybody* in the industry is there! The first preview really becomes opening night. You still have a month to fix it, and of course it's terrible, but by then the word is out and you're dead, buried, rotting!

"When Michael gets backed up like that, he springs. He really wanted Lerner to come through, and Lerner couldn't. Michael'd plead with Previn, 'Let's work on him, let's do this, do that.' But there just wasn't a director with any backbone, and Hepburn had her hands full. So Michael cracked."

By the last week of previews Bennett was in such bad shape that he holed up in his West Fifty-fifth Street apartment. One of the problems was that he hadn't had enough control over the production. He was still only the show's choreographer. While nearly every improvement he mentioned had been implemented, he felt powerless. In some ways he was glad that *Coco* really wasn't his, because it was so slack and ordinary. How would he ever get to be Jerry Robbins with something like this on his résumé? How many early flops did Robbins ever have? Many? Any?

He made it through *Coco*'s opening night on vodka and four packs of Marlboros. He watched the show with his head aching, holding himself together as though he were a piece of glass the ache was about to shatter. He was sure he was having a nervous breakdown. He'd hide the shards by going to London. In London, his immediate distress was invaded by an old retaliatory terror from his past: imagined threats from the Mafia.

Coco opened at the Mark Hellinger December 18, 1969, and ran nine months, hardly long enough to pay back its $900,000 investment. For the time Hepburn was in it, it was virtually standing room only, with its top ticket price then the highest on Broadway, $15 in the orchestra. (Dramas were selling at $8.50.) When Hepburn left, after the Saturday-night performance August 1,

1970, and was replaced by Danielle Darrieux, the box office nose-dived. *Coco* straggled along for nine more weeks, then collapsed.

If Hepburn's performance was dim, sometimes close to guttering out, she was still the show's candle. She attracted the customers. Despite her backward sense of song and dance (the *Sprechstimme* honk of her voice, two left feet), she gave *Coco* the tough engine Chanel probably had to make speed on the fast runways of high fashion, although one critic said her "heads-up, wiry performance suggested a tennis champion instead of a dress designer." She also gave it her own brand of Yankee responsibility. When *Coco* hadn't paid off by the end of its run, Hepburn agreed to do the road company. Michael Bennett remounted the production and, with George Rose repeating the role of Chanel's financial adviser, the tour opened in Cleveland January 1, 1971.

Avian: "I mean, an admirable lady. She had this sense of deep responsibility to it as a project. When we played the Dorothy Chandler Pavilion in L.A., they had to set up folding chairs in the aisles. You just couldn't get into these joints to see her. The show reclaimed its investment. The checks were rolling in, Michael and I were in shock, going like: We can't believe we're making money on this, and it's so terrible!

"There's a funny story about Hepburn. She's very opinionated. Thinks she knows everything. *Says* she knows everything. And, of course, everything has to go her way. Her town house on the East Side is next to Steve Sondheim's. Get this! She's doing *Coco* at the Hellinger, and he's writing the score for *Company*. They're both home, and he's playing the piano, playing the piano, playing the piano. Hepburn throws up her window, leans out with a broom, sees him at the keyboard, taps his window with the broom and shouts, 'Shut up, shut up, shut up! Stop banging that goddamn piano!' "

CHAPTER FOUR

Keeping Company
(1970 . . .)

"Choreographers—a lot of 'em—give off considerable enthusiasm; at the same time, they like crisis and stimulate conflict. They feed off the tension," Hal Prince says. "That's very odd to me. I'm not happy unless I'm happy, and I'm not happy working with actors unless we're all having a real good time. The sheer love of contention seems to me counterproductive.

"Michael liked crises and drama behind the work. Sure, we had difficulties between us, more on *Follies* than *Company*. His main problem was that he didn't expand himself, didn't really look beyond the theater to the other big worlds out there. His cop-out was planting himself in show biz, staying there and using the theater over and over as a metaphor. He didn't travel enough, fill up enough, read enough. On the opening night of *Company* I gave him a dictionary—ostrich-covered or some damned thing—and he took it as a joke. I didn't mean it as a joke."

It was not books Bennett turned to for his education, or for his inspiration. (For relaxation he read pulp and spy thrillers, Jacqueline Susann, Judith Krantz, Robert Ludlam, John le Carré.) Instead, drawing on his feelings and intuitions about people, he would analyze all his personal interactions and learn from them. From the time he was a little boy, he had been forced to listen to his mother, often about matters he was too young to fully understand, and he had developed a manner of seemingly intense concentration which, when needed, could mask his wavering interest and allow him to think of something else without his inattention being detected. By staring hard, he could appear to be engaged. Later, when power radiated around his presence like an electric fence, he lost his shyness about showing his disinterest and he'd sometimes hum in the middle of a conversation, the hum usually a melody from a show tune. The learning experience was always show business.

"*Coco* taught me a lot of lessons," Michael Bennett said. "What came out of working with Katharine Hepburn—and I adored her, by the way—was the need to make people up on that stage do it the way I saw it, whether they felt they could or not. Actors aren't dancers, dancers aren't actors necessarily, but this is the Musical we're talking about here, folks, and it's moving closer and closer to reality, and acting and dancing—or acting and movement—have got to become part of each other, and now I will teach you all how we are going to do it, ready?"

Among other things, the experience with Katharine Hepburn taught him the art of intimidation. There were times when you had to rant and scream, and there were times when you could set up an exchange and bargain feelings back and forth. You reached beyond the person's name—and, in the case of Katharine Hepburn, the attitude attached to it—and established trust, maybe intimacy. It wasn't really trust—and it was unlikely to become real intimacy—because you were doing it for a reason. You wanted something in return for the embrace of your stare, the warmth of your willingness to share. Kate had to be led like that, being Katharine the Great; with others, you could always rant and scream.

Elaine Stritch and Barbara Barrie were the objects of his ranting and screaming through the rehearsals of *Company*.

"We were rehearsing *Company*," Elaine Stritch says, "doing the 'Side by Side' number, and Michael really began to get a little Auschwitzy. We'd been rehearsing that fucking thing until everybody was ready to fucking drop. There's no energy left, none, kaput! He's screaming, hollering, furiously mad. He gets up on the stage—he always loved to perform—and says, 'What I want you to do, step by step, muscle by muscle, is . . .'

"And he starts the number, does the whole thing, all of it, and everyone except me bursts into applause. 'That's the way I want it done.' And he stands there a second, glaring.

"I said, 'Michael, lemme me tell ya something. That was wonderful, just terrific! You did it just once, and you NEVER have to do it again, right? This will all be over. You'll do a nice new show later, pussyfootin' your way into the hearts of millions and millions more people sittin' out in the audience, and you will NEVER think of 'Side by Side' again.

" 'What I'm tellin' you, Michael, is, we're left here to do it eight times a week, and if we did it just as you showed us, *the way you want it done*, we'd all be dead in the stretch!'

"He just stared at me. I said the trick of the week was making it *look* his way without really doing it. He said I'd have to convince him that was possible. I said, 'If it wasn't possible, I wouldn't be in the theater.' In dramatic acting you can't do *Virginia Woolf* every night rippin' and roarin', so why should musical theater be any different?"

By common agreement of those involved the "Side by Side" number was an example of Bennett's "genius." Dealing with a cast of basically nonmusical performers, he couldn't seem to explain to them the spirit the number needed. "Everyone was trying to be professionally honest," Hal Prince says, "and these were actors first, singers and dancers second, if singers and dancers at all." Analysis on what the number meant became information without stimulus. No one seemed able to musicalize the thought in Stephen Sondheim's lyrics. (When another song referred to "a piece of Mahler," Sondheim said later, Elaine Stritch thought he meant "a piece of bread from a specific bakery.") Bennett's problem as choreographer was to get the actors to move gracefully, to act as if they were musical.

The number just wasn't working.

Then Bennett had an inspiration and he bounced it off Sondheim. This was a musical circling love and marriage. Although children, and their education, had nothing to do with the plot, Bennett's plan was to suggest that the cast open the circle and imagine themselves members of a Parent-Teacher Association who are about to do a show, possibly a benefit. He and Sondheim developed the premise. The actors were to think of themselves as ordinary New Rochelle PTA people singing and dancing. He and Sondheim then attached this identity to show business by giving the actors straw hats and canes. As it turned out, the PTA idea, a good example of Bennett's theatrical insight, set a style the cast could manage. It also added a sense of humor and preserved the essence of the musical numbers.

Stritch: "Whaddya mean, PTA? They never told me that. They wouldn't dare. I'd have quit. It was some PTA meeting!"

Although *Company* has perhaps been overshadowed by the far greater popularity of *A Chorus Line* and *Dreamgirls*, it remains a landmark musical, as much from Bennett's contribution as from those of Prince and Sondheim. Eighteen years later it says as much about anomie as any contemporary musical, and with a perception so polished it reflects loneliness as clearly as seeing ourselves in the *Chorus Line* mirrors. *Company* is about disconnectedness, as Sondheim once put it, "the lonely crowd syndrome." Robert (Bobby), the central character, is a thirty-five-year-old bachelor terrified of commitment and equally terrified of "being alone." With surgical detachment, he analyzes the marriages of his friends, desperate to learn whether or not the advantages outweigh the disappointments, an analysis Michael Bennett, who was then twenty-seven, would later apply to his own life. Unusual in its structure, *Company* substituted relationships for plot, had a disaffected hero, used fourteen characters who doubled as chorus and had a message so pingingly accurate that it was easily mistaken.

Company was written by George Furth, an actor who had known Sondheim. Originally, the script comprised seven one-act plays which Furth had intended to produce with Kim Stanley playing the lead in each of the seven plays. Sondheim and Prince had been contemplating a musical about modern marriage. Although not all of Furth's seven plays dealt with marriage, some did, and he became the librettist for what became *Company*, a first attempt at writing which launched his career as a playwright and scenarist. Sondheim dramatized the script with fourteen songs. Prince directed it seamlessly, as Bennett "motivated the characters' movements" against the hard, glinting urban splendor of Boris Aronson's apartment-world set, a high-rise chrome, glass and steel box suggesting other boxes and complete with smoothly running elevator.

When Bennett was first approached about doing *Company*, he was dazzled again—without showing it—by names, specifically Hal Prince and Stephen Sondheim. He had never met Boris Aronson, the scenic designer. When he did, it was a meeting of like minds. Bennett expressed some hesitation about Furth's script. He wasn't sure how dance could be worked into it. Prince, knowing Bennett's relationship with Donna McKechnie, added a lure. Would he do it if McKechnie was hired and given a featured spot? Absolutely.

Avian remembers *Company* as "a very happy experience." Prince and Bennett "bounced off each other." In particular, the set model meetings between Bennett and Aronson were high points (as well as a hands-on technical education). "For Michael just hearing how Boris came up with his ideas, how he had a series of skyscraper photographs and how that developed into his set! And Boris really flipped for Michael. He'd show him a little sketch, and go, 'Dees is wot I'm going to built from to do my next show.' Michael would go, 'I understand, I understand.' And he did understand. Their connection was fabulous. Michael would sit in front of Boris' models and stare for hours and hours, Boris standing behind him, smiling."

Dean Jones, a minor movie star who, as one reference has it, "usually plays well-behaved fellows," was cast as *Company*'s to-be-or-not-to-be marriage-worrying Hamlet. Chosen as much for his bland appeal as anything else (an appeal that had made him a Crayola hero in several Disney movies in the mid-1960s), Jones replaced Anthony Perkins, who had first been announced as *Company*'s star. Perkins withdrew to direct Bruce Jay Friedman's *Steambath* Off-Broadway. Although Prince and Bennett drilled Dean Jones into a solid performance, Jones didn't have the confidence, or stamina, for Broadway. Further, he wasn't able to overcome the possible indication that Bobby's marital worries evidenced latent homosexuality. Jones didn't want to be associated with any of that.

As early as *Company*'s pre-Broadway opening in Boston, the subtext's sibilant whisper was being bullhorned as statement. The *Variety* review stated: "It's evident that . . . George Furth hates femmes and makes them all out to be conniving, cunning, cantankerous . . . As it stands now [*Company* is] for ladies' matinees, homos and misogynists." Peculiar as that comment proved to be, the show was later troubled by a misconception about its message. Cold hard truth is often mistaken for cynicism when it's simply the cold hard truth. *Company* may—or may not—have had homosexual allusions behind its motivation. But there was nothing allusive about what it was saying. In the steady emotional bombardment of daily life, intimacy—in simple friendship as in complex marriage—is difficult. Despite the difficulty, it's worth the effort.

Dean Jones panicked. Playing even a faintly perceived homosexual might damage him in movies. He might never again get another *That Darn Cat*, *The Ugly Duckling* or *Monkeys Go Home*. If fairies were thought to be fluttering forth more and more, and less and less being swatted back, they still weren't allowed to fly through family movies. Fairies at the bottom of Disney-tilled gardens were the asexual, old-fashioned magical kind. Jones's career after *Company* might be in jeopardy. And as life imitating art would have it, he happened to be in the midst of a divorce. To add to the terror of playing someone who might be interpreted as a closeted gay, he risked being considered anti-marriage. Stating that he was "unsatisfied" in the role, he fled the cast five weeks after the show opened and was replaced by Larry Kert.

Company's implicit homosexual theme threaded through Michael Bennett's life. Donna McKechnie says that Bennett's homosexuality wasn't an issue at the start of their relationship, admitting only that "it might have been later." She sees herself and Bennett as dancing darlings who took a spin on marriage and got lost in its whir.

"After Michael and I were divorced in 1977, I used to say, in a silly, quippy way, 'We ruined a good friendship by walking down the aisle.' Marriage seemed right, then. Michael and I had gotten closer and closer from the time we were *Hullabaloo* dancers down to *Company*, then—out of nowhere—he broached the subject of having an affair. I wasn't interested, and told him that after all these years he was more important to me than that. I was the one who said, 'Marriage or nothing, it has to be that serious.' He simply said, 'Okay.'

"I had my own problems with intimacy, but Michael's were far greater. The problem was his fear of closeness. It was very painful to witness someone you love unable to give back on a certain level, unable to have enough self-love to be able to take . . . without suspicion.

"The intimacy we shared in the work we did together, well, that was an intimacy most people can't achieve or, maybe, just don't have the chance to achieve. How many couples work together? Long before we were married, we shared a fever about Broadway and dance. But then, I guess, marriage became more important to me. I wanted kids. Michael didn't. Michael was all about work.

"He came to resent me bitterly."

Part of what McKechnie says is contradicted by a lover who had preceded her in Bennett's affections.

"When Michael and I were living together he told me he had had an affair with Donna. It was over four years before they got married," Larry Fuller says. "After they got married, I asked him why he did it, why didn't they just live together, and he said, 'Because she wanted to be married, and I loved her and wanted to give her that.' That was his explanation. Who knows what lurks in the hearts of men and women? I also think he felt the marriage was good for his public image because he was at a certain point in his career. But I don't think it made a damn bit of difference. If he could create musical theater that made everybody money, the people around him wouldn't care if he was sleeping with a horse."

Company was the first concept musical Bennett worked on. It wasn't to be just another evening of Broadway schmaltz and glitz. Unlike anything he had done before, it had something to say. If it was, first, entertainment (which is what the Broadway musical had to be), it was, second, statement. It was psychologically candid. It detailed warring impulses, and wasn't afraid to be sour. Prince directed the Furth-inspired drama behind Sondheim's score with some trouble, but not much. Meanwhile Bennett and Avian were having daily hassles with the limitations of their "nonmusical cast," particularly the sequences with Elaine Stritch and Barbara Barrie. "There was a lot of screaming," Avian says. "Elaine and Barbara really didn't want to be doing this stuff, because they didn't understand it."

Wincing at the memory, Avian gives it the perspective of laughter.

"There was Elaine and the first preview.

"We were in the fourth row. The show is bumping along, the audience doesn't seem to know what's going on. Elaine gets to her 'Ladies Who Lunch' number, playing it as one of her five hour takes. She gets up on the table, goes, 'I'd like to propose a toast / Here's to the ladies who lunch . . .'

"Suddenly there's this 'Aaahhhggg!'

"One hand flies to her mouth, fingers hinge between her lips, and she's going, 'Gggrrraaahhhggg!' The conductor sees she's in trouble and he mouths the lyrics to her. Elaine's other hand reaches down her throat. She's still making this strangled sound. Now she's rubbing her makeup. Mascara leaks around her face. Now she's really gargling. We're sitting there dying! The whole half of the song goes by before she picks up the lyric and starts singing. She gets it back, only now she's, like, this mess.

"When it was over, someone said, 'We understand you getting nervous, Elaine, blowing the lyrics, but why'd you stick your hands in your mouth?' Elaine said, '*I was trying to find the words.*' "

From chaotic incidents like this, *Company* was built. While Bennett was having difficulties with the cast, he was aware that Prince, using his suggestions, was steadily refining the show's abstractions, steadily and effectively balancing the elements. Avian says the process "was an eye-opener." When audiences started walking out during the Boston tryout, there was no backstage panic. No one (with the probable exception of investors) got upset. The work kept going: editing, rearrangement, addition. Sondheim wrote new songs. The ending became the opening of the second act. By the time of the New York premiere *Company*'s narrative and Sondheim's score had the hard, fast gleam of Aronson's set. Avian says *Company* "changed what Michael thought the musical could be and do." It proved to be groundwork for *A Chorus Line, Ballroom* and *Dreamgirls*.

Company opened April 26, 1970, and ran through January 1, 1972. Having cost $530,000, it made a profit of $245,000. It won the New York Drama Critics Circle Award as Best Musical and six Tonys, including Best Musical (to producer Hal Prince), Best Director (Prince), Best Book (Furth), Best Score and Best Lyrics (both to Sondheim, his first Tonys) and Best Scene Designer (Aronson). Nominated in other categories, it lost out. Bennett's choreography was thought inferior to Donald Saddler's dances for the revival of *No! No! Nanette!*

Already, with Prince and Sondheim, Michael Bennett was revving the motor for another show.

Bennett: "I've always had a problem between shows. I don't know what to do. I like skiing but the last time I went was about five years ago. I don't know much about it. I love it, but it's not like I say, 'I'm sorry, I won't be in for two months because I'm going to Gstaad.' When I married Donna I thought things would change. They didn't. I'd like to become less compulsive about work but I don't know how. Right now the idea of taking six months off appeals to me. Not to do anything, not to have to know the answers to a lot of questions. I went to Paris once for eight months. I mean,

I really needed it, to get away from New York. There was nothing I had to do, and I thought it was time to live on the Continent and find out what that was all about. If you were to ask me what I did for eight months in Paris . . . I went to the museums every Tuesday. They're áll closed on Tuesday!"

CHAPTER FIVE

Hostility in Loveland

(... 1971)

In San Diego during the 1970 spring road tour of *Promises, Promises*, Michael Bennett unexpectedly produced a vinyl-bound script from his suitcase. In his usual manner of first minimizing something major by making it seem casual (the phrase "by the way" was a steady part of his speech), he flung the script across the hotel room he was sharing with Bob Avian, saying, "By the way, darling, here's our next show."

Still caught up in *Promises, Promises*, Avian had had "only the vaguest thoughts about the next show." Flipping through the script, here and there skimming the dialogue, he found it was a murder mystery. The idea of working on a murder mystery seemed very odd to him. Wasn't their partnership in the musical theater; weren't they really about song and dance? Was Michael about to get them involved in a whodunit? Why?

Avian's questions began to cluster as he read the script more closely. By page 38, he thought he was lost in a loser.

"I go strictly by the gut. Stories I get or don't get," Avian says. "I'm reading and not understanding a word. The story is rambling, obtuse. I go, 'Michael, this is going to end your career!'"

"He goes, 'Honey, we're doing it anyway because it's Hal and Steve and Boris, and it will involve us, and we'll all figure it out, and make it a beautiful, beautiful show. By the way, not just like that, it will take some time.' I go, 'You're going to have to tell me what it's about.' "

Despite Avian's continued hesitation, Bennett insisted that the script had potential, although he too had serious reservations about some of it. He was impressed that Prince and his pals considered it worth doing. Back in New York, after smoothing out the technical problems—the placement of lights, the movement of sets—on the *Promises* tour, Bennett and Avian were part of the group assembled in Prince's office to discuss the new project. By now Avian knew that what he had read in San Diego was an early draft. Written by James Goldman and musically dramatized with five songs by Stephen Sondheim, it had been under consideration by David Merrick and Leland Hayward in 1966 as *The Girls Upstairs*. Merrick had wanted to produce the show by himself, but Sondheim had forced the Hayward partnership and Merrick didn't like the arrangement. Striking back, he agreed to it but refused to help with investors, a task that fell to Hayward, who faulted.

Three years later *The Girls Upstairs* was optioned by Stuart Ostrow, who hired Joseph Hardy as its director. Rehearsals were announced. What seemed to be looming for Sondheim in 1969 were two musicals in the same season, *The Girls Upstairs* and *Company*. It was not to be. Squabbles developed among Sondheim, Goldman, Ostrow and Hardy, and Ostrow backed out. Sondheim, who has a reputation for being a slow, painstaking worker, was agitated by the prospect of simultaneously scoring two shows. He wanted to complete *The Girls Upstairs*, then turn to *Company*. He prevailed upon Prince, who had read one of Goldman's first drafts, to read the latest draft. Pushing *Company* first, Prince agreed to produce *The Girls Upstairs* next. He'd hire Michael Bennett as his co-director and choreographer.

Almost immediately the murder-mystery plot was killed off, and a plot paralleling sad careers and sour marriages was devised.

Goldman had developed a working idea for the show from a

paragraph in the *New York Times* about a Ziegfeld Follies reunion among a group of old show girls. The image of once glamorous beauties blooming in fantasy, then withered by the rust of reality, had a Proustian redolence for Prince. The metaphor suggested the show girls' specific lost innocence as well as the rubble of an almost forgotten era.

The story opens with the old Weismann Theater about to be razed for a parking lot and a reunion being held on its stage for the now middle-aged and some nearly-elderly "Weismann Girls," who, thirty years ago, had paraded and posed in glittering costumes and monumental headgear. As the old performers meet and remember the past, the narrative pivots around two Weismann Girls in particular, Phyllis Stone (played by Alexis Smith) and Sally Plummer (Dorothy Collins), and their husbands, Benjamin Stone (John McMartin) and Buddy Plummer (Gene Nelson). Once full of love and promise, both marriages mirror the short-lived arc of the women's careers, the marriages and careers further reflecting life's inevitable disappointment and decay. All of this was played out on the spectral sweep of Boris Aronson's crumbling set, which moodily evoked a cobbled past and an unclear future. The set was the cracked shell of the old Weismann Theater, littered, angled, with its roof open to the sky, and waiting for another swipe of the wrecker's ball. Like the lives it mercilessly laid bare, it suggested abandonment, torment and fear.

During the revisions *The Girls Upstairs* was changed to *Follies*, the new title suggesting both an image of show girls stalking the stage and an exact definition of the word "folly" in the sense of lives being tricked by a "lack of . . . normal prudence and foresight." As it turned out, the production fulfilled Webster's fourth definition: "an excessively costly or unprofitable enterprise."

At the first *Follies* meetings Avian began to notice a new aggressiveness in Bennett. A steeliness had been part of the determination from the beginning, but now there was a combative certainty added to it. The steel had been tempered. In competition with those who had already proved themselves, Bennett would give them a run to the wire. He might not have the academic credentials but he was as smart as anyone, at least anyone on Broadway. His head was full of ideas, some pellucid, some allusive and just waiting to be shaped. There were times when he yearned to express himself better, yet—even when he wished his vocabulary had longer, stronger words—he knew there was something appealing in his direct talk, as well as in his occasional nasal mumble. He was developing a method of getting what he wanted out of people by enlisting their help in whatever it was he'd present to them as first his, then their common problem. It seemed possible to him that he could draw whomever he wanted to his side. He was learning that "people always want something." If you gave something back, you gained a measure of control.

At the *Follies* meetings, whatever lingering insecurities Bennett may have had about being in the presence of his more experienced betters were replaced by his acceptance among them. In his own mind he had proved himself on *Company*. Now, again, he had been sought out. He was twenty-eight. His colleagues were thirteen years and more his senior. Stephen Sondheim was forty-one, Hal Prince forty-three, James Goldman forty-four, Boris Aronson seventy-one. As a contributor in the often arduous give-and-take of getting a show together, he knew he had narrative ability when it came to storytelling, a skill he had gained mostly from watching movies and imagining how they were constructed. He had an eye and an ear for dramatic placement. He also knew about thought processes and, more or less, how they developed. He had learned at least part of that as the little-boy-in-long-pants father confessor to his mother, the mother who had relied on him for advice and guidance when his own concern should have been where the next Mars bar was coming from. He had intuitions that sometimes frightened him, like his early perception that his father's careless attitude coupled with his brother's weakness somehow strengthened his own inner resolve, his own will to accomplishment.

In the early *Follies* discussions Hal Prince would sit at a long table with his colleagues to his left and right, scripts on the table or on laps. A scene would be blankly read aloud, with Sondheim, defending himself as "no singer," banging out the scene's requisite score and straining to musicalize his lyrics. ("Steve doesn't play or sing very well," Avian says, "and when he'd read his songs I never had any idea what they were about. They sounded so awful until you really heard somebody sing them.") There would be considerable discussion, then argument, then battle. Bennett would listen attentively, agree or not agree, then strike with his own perceptions.

From the beginning he was worried that *Follies* was going to be "hard-ass cynical," and he kept pitching for a more human—an easier—approach ("Darling, the world isn't all black, it's mostly gray, with light; sometimes, by the way, a lot of light"). Prince and Bennett had agreed that the approach would be nonliteral. It was to be a "memory piece," bitter hurts reflected upon years later. Its theme was to be the folly of living in yesterdays. In the division of duties, Prince was directing individual scenes, Bennett was shaping the overall concept as well as the choreography and the musical numbers. One of his most memorable ideas was to contrast the showgirls of the past, who were ghosts, with their current selves by having the ghosts costumed in black and white, their later transformations in vibrant color.

Avian: "Michael would make all these incredible suggestions, and I'd think: How does he know all that stuff, where does it come from? I mean, it was like he had this unbelievable knowledge, except it wasn't learned. It was innate with him, intuitive. I'd sit very quietly, the dummy in a corner, and just watch him. Here he was with these heavyweights, handling himself with such assurance. Here he was— like from Day One—proving himself!"

As the meetings and the subsequent rehearsals went on, the battling was almost nonstop. If *Company* had been occasional warfare (with Bennett yelling orders, browbeating Elaine Stritch, hurling a chair at Barbara Barrie), *Follies* became a ceaseless war. But this time most of the far-reaching artillery was exchanged between Bennett and Prince. Whatever rage Bennett may have wanted to displace onto his performers was held in check by their age (it would have been like beating on his mother). The cast had some nearly-elderly and elderly troupers, like Fifi D'Orsay, Ethel Shutta, Yvonne De Carlo and Mary McCarty. In fact, the story of *Follies* was more or less written around the specific personalities of these so-called "old dolls."

Bennett and Avian researched the intended milieu of Goldman's book by attending reunions held by old showgirls, some of them actual Ziegfeld Follies alumnae. Over a year, in one decrepit hotel after another, Avian says, they "met a lot of sad old people showing up years later to remember their glorious past, what a short shot it was." Bennett spent time visiting Boris Aronson, describing the various hotels and their inhabitants, contributing his own ideas to the developing scenery. All this was kept secret from Prince, who had had an earlier son-to-father relationship with Aronson, which Bennett was afraid he, in his own enthusiasm, was usurping. Like a boy with his own cutout toy theater, he'd play with Aronson's models for hours on end, trusting him and Avian to keep it all quiet. *Follies* had enough trouble without added jealousies and resentments.

Rehearsals were slow and agonizing, one of the reasons being the hard-breathing age of most of the cast, yet the Equity-established rehearsal period of five weeks for a musical was met. The scene was like a nursing home. No one would have been surprised had a gofer been sent out for Geritol, an aluminum walker, a pacemaker or all three. Everything was done to keep the elders happy. Ethel Shutta, then in her eighties, wasn't impressed by any of it, certainly not her own sudden call out of retirement or the attention given her. She'd take things at her own tempo. Understandably, the tempo had slowed since *The Passing Show of 1922*, when Shutta brought the house down in a parody of Eugene O'Neill's *The Hairy Ape*. When Sondheim came in one day with a song he had written expressly for her, "Broadway Baby," a razzle-dazzle vaudeville turn, she said, "Thank you, sonny, this'll be swell." When Bennett started to work her through the song, he found she had only enough heartbeat for about twenty minutes at a time. He'd say, "Okay, Ethel, let's start." Ethel would say, "You'll just see what I do here!" She'd stomp into the lyric, do a single chorus and be ready for a nap, repeatedly telling him, "That's enough for today, huh, sonny?"

Fifi D'Orsay, who had played the Palace in 1932, when she was twenty-five, flitted through rehearsals, a gray coquette still on the wing. Cooing, fluttering feathery eyelashes, calling everyone Chickipoo, D'Orsay was sure her French-Canadian charm, which she passed off as genuine Parisian, would make up for her failing memory. She had trouble remembering a single line. The simplest of Sondheim's lyrics left her blankly looking for a nest. Nearly everyone except Alexis Smith and Dorothy Collins, the show's leading ladies, undermined Bennett's—and everyone else's—patience.

At first Michael Bartlett, the old-timer hired to play Roscoe the emcee, had a minimal assignment, a simple crossover. As the show developed, Bennett felt the scene needed three lines of expository greeting, a welcome to the audience. He talked the lines over with Bartlett, who was terrified by the prospect but willing to try. The first night the lines were to be spoken before an audience, Bartlett walked out on the stage and was stricken by stage fright. His lips tasted like sand, his mouth went dry. The words he had repeated over and over to himself suddenly were gravel. Gagging, he managed to mouth, "Well . . . howwww rrrrr yyyyy—" before stumbling into the wings. The audience was dismayed. Was this part of the act?

And then there was the problem of Aronson's severely raked stage, which some members of the cast expected to pitch them into the orchestra. (Then they'd really need wheelchairs.) Feet rickety, eyesight dim, alone in echoing space, they were in a no-man's-land without railings. Extra stage managers were hired just to get the old folks on and off. Leaning close to a stunned ear, a stage manager would whisper/shout *"Now!"* and push Ethel Shutta—or Fifi D'Orsay—on her way. Off they'd totter, leaving a muted "Thank you, thank you" in their prayerful wake.

Avian: "And then there were the ailments and the accidents. Opening night Gene Nelson's knees fell apart and he couldn't do his big number, 'The Right Girl.' Later his son got hit by a truck. And before that, out of town, it was one disaster after another. Not a night went by that someone didn't forget lyrics. Yvonne De Carlo blowing 'I'm Still Here,' Gene Nelson going up on 'Buddy's Blues.' Every night! Michael and I would sit there watching. About every twenty minutes there'd be a train wreck. In Boston we'd run out of the Colonial Theater across the street to the Public Garden, gulp some air and go back in. It was death-making!"

One of Prince and Bennett's suggestions during the early stages of *Follies* was to have Boris Aronson's set constructed at the Feller Scenic Studios in the Bronx so the cast could familiarize themselves with the general rake and the steps and platforms. The *Follies* cast were bused to and from the Bronx every day. A few weeks later— by bus, train and plane—cast and crew were shuttled to Boston for a break-in engagement at the Colonial Theater.

And *Follies* hit the fan.

Avian: "The first preview tells you everything. That's when you sit in the house with the audience all around you, and you're not fooled by anything. It's all gotta be real up there on the stage, and you can't lie to yourself. At the technical rehearsal—with the sets and lights and costumes perfect and working smoothly—everything had looked beautiful; at the orchestra rehearsal eveything had sounded fabulous. But this is it!

"Michael and I are sitting on the right, Hal, Steve and Jim are on the left. It begins. There's no intermission. Michael and I shudder through the show; we're not sure the audience is getting it. The curtain comes down. Michael turns to me and says, 'It doesn't work, it just doesn't work.'

"We head up the aisle to the lobby, meet Hal and Steve and Jim, and they're jumping up and down, and Hal is going, 'It works! It works! It works!' Michael doesn't say a word. And now I know we're in for big conflict. BIG conflict!"

The conflict would be stoked by artistic disagreement ironically coupled with the closeness that had developed between Prince and Bennett. Their professional difference of opinion became warped by a personal relationship which was hardly free from a sense of competition. While the Master (Prince) was willing to show the way to his Protégé (Bennett), he wasn't about to be overtaken. The objectivity in this or that criticism about *Follies* lost force when it knocked against emotional spite. Onstage *Follies* was about show girls bitterly trapped by the past. Backstage it was about two directors vying for the future.

From the beginning in Boston, and through the end of the Broadway run, the basic trouble with *Follies* was the book. It was bleak.

Whatever hope it offered to an audience was small, having to do with little more than desperate survival—although, in the theatrical age of Samuel Beckett, survival in itself would seem enough to some. While *Company* had been perceived as a cold show, its accuracy about modern-day relationships gave its cynicism a zest, a kind of brittle post-*Pal Joey* sophistication that has come to be far more honest than the calculated sentiment of Rodgers and Hammerstein. But the perception within *Follies*, the tangle of past and present, could be more easily ignored than seen, as in *Company*, as a paradigm. Nostalgia is notorious for vaporizing hard facts. Filtered through selective memory, what really happened "back then" often has only the evanescence of dream. Yet for all its romanticized realism, *Follies* could be seen as the distortion of a particularly disgruntled (even nihilistic) vision shared by its creators. The piece was thematically confused and the Goldman plot itself wasn't very clear, although it would be sharpened after the Boston tryout.

Performed without intermission, *Follies* concluded with a show-within-a-show section called "Loveland," during which all the characters' illusions were stripped away and then: bitter chaos. In one of the most shattering moments outside the realm of opera, where heroes and heroines are known to go mad at the unsteadiness of a glissando, Buddy Plummer has a breakdown brilliantly simulated through Sondheim's atonal music; it's a stark Sondheim high point, perhaps outdistanced only by the reach of madness in *Sweeney Todd, the Demon Barber of Fleet Street*.

"Loveland" had seven Sondheim songs plus an ensemble number featuring the show girls of the past as the Spirits of First Love, True Love, Pure Love, Romantic Love and Eternal Love. The reference to Federico Fellini's 1965 film *Juliet of the Spirits* was deliberate; in fact, the head and upper torso of a Greek goddess used in Fellini's film was transformed by David Edward Byrd into the *Follies* logo, a square-jawed beauty wearing a psychedelic headdress with *Follies* marquee letters perched above her forehead against a blunt aureole of Peter Max stars. A branchlike rupture—beginning at the base of the letter *e* in the *Follies* title—splits the whole left side of the goddess's face, temple to chin.

Avian: "The opening-night reviews in Boston were good, except for the book. But the contention between Hal and Michael really started after the first preview. Hal was adamant that everything was fine, and Michael was just as adamant everything wasn't. It wasn't open warfare—they were still working well together, with Hal at least listening to Michael's point of view. When the reviews came out, Michael thought he was being backed up. But Hal's pretty arrogant about critics, so he didn't pay much attention.

"Michael had two approaches. He wanted Steve to rewrite the show as an opera, or he wanted to bring in some other authors. He wanted the characters to be likable. But Hal thought *Follies* was about not making sense, that it was about craziness on the part of some of the characters and the world beyond them. Michael said that just wouldn't work because you don't like the people.

"Well, the conflict got real hot, burning.

"It got to the point where Michael was so depressed that he stopped going to meetings. Hal called a production meeting one night in a Chinese restaurant in Boston. I don't remember the details, but Michael wouldn't go, and he sent me to represent him. Hal, Steve, Jim and Ruthie Mitchell, Hal's assistant, were there. Hal said, 'Where's Michael.' I said, "He's not coming. He's very unhappy, depressed, and doesn't want to be here.'

"Hal started *screaming* at me! I said, 'Shut up!' He started attacking Michael. I can't even remember what it was about, but he was yelling. I said, 'You can yell all you want to. I'm not Michael, so just cool it or I'll walk out too. I have nothing to lose here.'

"He and Michael got angrier and angrier, and some of that anger had developed from their personal relationship. Ultimately Hal knew the show wasn't working. But by this time they weren't in sync anymore as a team. If their relationship had continued, they might or might not have overcome the show's problems, but they proably would have come out of it being friends."

Prince: "We didn't have a major falling out. Michael wanted to bring in Neil Simon to help with the book. There is a moment when I remember saying to him, 'Michael, you know what? We're co-directors but I'm the producer. I retain that edge. And I can say no. And the answer is no.' For a few days we didn't talk. He was genuinely pissed off. I think at the time he thought I'd prevented the show from being the popular success it could have been."

Although Bennett talked guardedly about his relationship with Prince, whom he mostly admired, he resented his control. He wanted that kind of power and influence too. Time and again he said that his psychoanalyst, Dr. Emmanuel Feurer, questioned him about his need for control, probing him to explain it to himself. "I like fantasy," Bennett said, "and my analyst tells me I can't stand not to be in control. I know I can't control life—look at my own! I can't control Israel and Egypt. But I can control 'Come to the theater tomorrow.' I can control that. And it's a wonderful place."

Prince: "Look, being a director is a great expression of personal will. You go in, and all your colleagues are sitting all over the place, and you put up or shut up, sink or swim, it's all those clichés. Michael and I worked good together. We never had an argument about how the space was to be used in *Follies*. He was somewhere doing all his numbers, I was somewhere doing all the scenes. And when we conferred it was usually straight to the point. Michael was much younger than I was, which was always interesting for me because you knew you were seeing things through the eyes of someone younger, and that's significant, and it directly relates to my own years with George Abbott when I was a kid. I think it's very good if you can have that.

"But, you see, there was a real limitation to Michael.

"I don't think Michael had much . . . perspective. If he thought I was responsible for *Follies* failing, for not bringing in Neil Simon, for not adding jokes and making it popular, well, that not only frustrated him, it also seemed to rein him in, curtail him, hold him back. I remember having a discussion with him and when I said, 'When are you going to realize a show is a show is a show, and there's another show where that came from, and *that life is not your last show?*'

"Last time I saw Michael was six, seven years ago. He called up, said, 'It's been too long.' I think I was rehearsing *Evita*. Anyway, we were chatting, and the only thing one remembers from the conversation is that he asked had I heard of AIDS. I said, 'No, what is it?' Then he told me this extraordinary story about a choreographer friend who was on the road and had called him about his lover dying of this thing called AIDS in the hospital. The friend wanted Michael to look in on him. Michael went to the hospital, then kept going regularly, saw this person slipping away. One night, to keep him company, he slept by his bed on the floor. He said it was horrifying. Sleeping on the floor like that was a very Michael thing to have done. He was enormously generous and all that.

"I guess, maybe, the last time I saw him was backstage at *Doll's Life*. But I really ceased knowing him soon after *Follies*."

CHAPTER SIX

Just Let Me Do It My Way

(... 1972)

Mrs. DiFiglia rummages in a closet in the bedroom of her Sarasota condo looking for a family album. *A Chorus Line* and *Dreamgirls* posters hang on a wall next to a snapshot collage of her husband, Sam, her sons, Michael and Frank, relatives and friends, all peering above the battered, bronzed "baby tap shoes." "It's not a shrine," Mrs. DiFiglia says.

In the living room a soulful, studied airbrushed photograph of Michael Bennett faces the dining area. Dark eyes staring above a mustache and thin beard, moles on his face softened, he's seated sideways on a canvas director's chair smoking a cigarette, his chin angled on wrists crossed over the chair's post. He's nineteen. His black eyes command the room. Twenty feet away a blue Star of David is affixed, at eye level, to the glass door opening onto a cramped porch.

Leafing through the family album is the equivalent for Helen DiFiglia of Proust's madeleine and tea. For a moment she hesitates. Scraping skeletons in closets, sensing indiscretion, she sometimes whispers. She whispers wonderment at "having been too close" to her first son. As memories accelerate, she's unable to resist the whir. Like Sally Plummer and Phyllis Stone in *Follies*, Helen DiFiglia wonders if she married the right man. When she talks about her husband, Sam, his gambling, his infidelities, and her gradual, withering discovery of the "welfare other woman" who bore his child in 1974, her voice scurries as though words were sticks and stones to break her bones. Rage— as much as fear—makes her run; running, she may outdistance both. Michael is momentarily offstage. Not for long.

"Sam always, always tried to compete with Michael. He took acting lessons once in New York—this was after he retired, and he really wanted to become an actor, can you believe it! See, I was alone with Michael for a couple of years while Sam was in the service. All of a sudden this man comes home—I mean, Michael knew his father, we had visited Sam in Pensacola. All of a sudden this man comes home and takes his mother away. Michael and I were very, very close. We had a one-bedroom apartment, and he slept in my room in a crib. All of a sudden, here's this man! And we're moving Michael out, y'know, and Michael feels kinda, well, a little envious. The day Sam came home, Michael was so upset! It also happened to be his birthday, he was hyper anyway, running, running. Well, that day my husband came home from the service, Michael was spinning crazy through the apartment and tripped over a stool, split his head wide open. We had to take him to the hospital. He bled and bled; had the scar until the day he died.

"He was just so excited that day. He was two years old and he didn't know what to make of this man. And all of a sudden I think they both started to resent each other from that moment on. I don't know, I couldn't feel that kind of resentment towards my son, but I'm not a man, I don't know how a father feels. Sam was proud of him, bragged about him constantly. They had a good loving relationship when they were together, but when they were apart . . . well, the resentment was always there."

Donna McKechnie says that Bennett's parents "fought all the time" and that he seemed more concerned about his father in these battles than about his mother. Sam, the gambler whose cards never seemed to pay off, whose occasional strikes never lessened his debts, must have had mixed feelings about his son's success, the son who'd always been a nuisance, his taps rattling in the kitchen when Sam had a hangover. It was easy enough to step around him when he was a baby, to ignore him. As galling to him as Mickey's interest in dancing was, he gradually sensed that the kid had something salable that, one day, might be as valuable as a full house. But he really wasn't sure. By the time Mickey was making it as Michael Bennett, Sam wished he's been closer to him when he was growing up. Maybe then the DiFiglia name wouldn't have been eighty-sixed, maybe then it would have been up in lights.

The first Broadway musicals Mickey worked on didn't impress Sam, but *A Chorus Line* really got to him. It might have been a series of stories about kids in show business, but he saw the gamble of their lives as the gamble of his own. He also knew that the show really was a grand slam that would take care of him and Helen for the rest of their lives. Night after night he'd come home and put the *Chorus Line* album on the turntable, make a drink, sit, listen. He'd have another drink and another, and play the album over and over. At first Helen would listen with him, but she hated his drinking and soon became numb to the music. Numbness gave way to annoyance. She'd start shouting. She didn't care how moved Sam might be, what the lyric was, she'd rage through "What I Did for Love," turn off the sound. Sam would rage back, turn the sound on, make another drink, turn the sound higher.

And in her lifelong pattern of desperation, Helen DiFiglia would seek out her son for help. No matter what time of the night it was, she'd call him and complain. She'd try to get Michael to speak to his father. Sometimes Sam would take the phone, sometimes he'd refuse. In the background Priscilla Lopez would be singing "Kiss today good-bye / The sweetness and the sorrow . . . and point me toward to-morrow."

McKechnie says there were other family entanglements.

"We had similar backgrounds. We both came to New York as young kids, early teens. And we both had this double thing of trying to please one side of the family or the other. Michael found religion confusing. He always went on and on about being half Jewish, half

Sicilian. I guess for a while he was brought up predominantly Catholic. I was raised Presbyterian and Lutheran. Each of us had the feeling we didn't belong, that we were different. I thought I was the black sheep. Just the idea of being a dancer was a sin. Michael didn't have that yoke, but he had others.

"His father was this very attractive, very Italian guy. Michael always had this macho thing, or pretended he did, I was never really sure. He couldn't understand what women's liberation was all about. He'd say, 'What do women want? Just ask me. They want to party.'

"One night we went out to dinner with his father and a cousin. I'm there with these three Italian men at Frankie and Johnny's. It's a pleasant evening, big steaks and drinks, all that. After dinner they say, 'Let's have a nightcap.' I assume I'm to be included, but Michael says, 'We'll put you in a cab.' I say, 'You'll whaaaattt?' This was like two weeks after our honeymoon, and right then I had this feeling: This isn't going to work. Put me in a cab? PUT ME IN A CAB!!!

"Michael was so different in the company of men, particularly his father. He'd become this macho Italian dude insisting the women walk three paces behind him. Like he was trying to show Sam something . . ."

Frank DiFilia thinks his brother envied their father's handsomeness and his masculinity.

"At Dad's funeral, and Michael directed Dad's funeral like he directed everything else, he insisted the organist play 'Me and My Shadow.' It was a number we'd danced to as kids, and Michael just decided on the spot that Dad had loved it. I don't remember if he did, but it was touching to hear it in a church. It was theatrically great. In Michael's mind 'Me and My Shadow' tied all three of us together. I think maybe he even thought of himself as Dad's shadow even though he couldn't really emulate him as a real man."

Having learned some of the tactics of backstage warfare he needed to win complete control, vowing never to find himself a mere platoon sergeant again, Michael Bennett came to regard *Follies* as a bivouac. Proud of his work, he was bitter. He would build from the experience, as he had built from *A Joyful Noise* to *Company*.

What bothered him most—imploding nervous breakdowns he'd try to defuse with four packs of Marlboros a day, marijuana, vodka, Quaaludes and, finally, cocaine—was interference with his talent. Canny as a collaborator, he'd make concessions only to get his way. When that didn't work, he'd become enraged. *How dare he—or she —or they—not listen!* If the rage met its match, if he met an ego as flamboyant as his own, he'd retreat, disappear. He was convinced that Prince's rigidity in maintaining *Follies'* thematic hopelessness ruined the show's chance to be a popular success; he was convinced that *Follies* could have remained true to itself had there been some break in its bleakness.

Prince won the battle and lost the war. On Broadway and on a subsequent road tour that was cut short, *Follies* lost $700,000. Bennett didn't gloat; he was too involved. He regrouped. Analyzing his credentials with the same precision he used to break down a scene, and consciously following the pattern of Jerome Robbins, he decided it was time to become a director proper. He'd can the music, hang up the dancing shoes and take on a straight play. What interested him was a George Furth script about tangled family relationships, in the center of the tangle a manipulative mother. The script's original title, *A Chorus Line*, was subsequently changed to *Twigs*.

By now Bennett had become incorporated. He was president— with Avian as vice president—of Plum Productions, Incorporated. As whimsical as the Plum name was, so too was its president's apparel. After the high-heeled, bell-bottom, loose-shirt fashion of the late 1960s, Bennett began to dress in sneakers, khakis and sweatshirts, the casual image given playful semblance by a visored (usually red) baseball cap. He would often conduct rehearsals and meetings without removing the cap. The cap, which hid his thready hair, became his signature, a deliberate comic scrawl. He knew the cap and his clothes, in combination with his small physical frame, made him appear to be a little boy, just a kid. The hard, knowing stare boring under the visor suggested otherwise.

Avian: "Tommy Tune came up with the name Plum Productions. Michael said one day there's going to be this big basket on the top of the building with a plum, a banana, a pineapple, a kiwi, and we're going to call each of our different companies after a different fruit. Sounded pretty funny, but the fact is we did have Tangerine, which was for the restaurant/bar in the building at Eight Ninety Broadway, and we did have a division called Tangerine Productions.

"Later we went to the name Quadrille, as opposed to another fruit, when John Breglio and Sue MacNair became our producing partners on *Ballroom*."

Bennett decided that Plum Productions' first financial involvement would be the Furth play, which already had a single producer, Frederick Brisson, who had planned on financing it alone. Since it was going to be Bennett's first assignment directing a straight play, he felt that he and Avian should make it a double first by coming up with 25 percent of the operating budget, which was $250,000. As with most Broadway investments, there was risk. Beyond Bennett's enthusiasm for the script and his belief in himself, there was simply no way of knowing if there would be an eventual payoff. While it was true that millions could be made in the theater, it was equally true that you could lose your shirt. Although Bennett lacked the slippery card instincts of his gambling father, part of the appeal in backing a Broadway show was the pure speculation, the guesswork. There was drama in uncertainty—even when it came to money.

Avian: "Michael and his big mouth, right? So, okay, now we're producers, and our responsibility is to raise a quarter of the investment. Which, then, wasn't that much. Michael didn't have any money qualms at all. He'd been watching Hal. We each put our own money in it, and just about got it back."

George Furth, whose plays had become the basis for *Company*, sent Bennett the *Twigs* script when he and Avian were vacationing on Malibu Beach. Avian read the script and wasn't particularly impressed with Furth's story about a crusty old woman who, late in life, legitimizes her three daughters by marrying their father. But Avian was impressed, yet again, with Bennett's self-confidence, his lack of hesitation in taking on a straight play. And he was beginning to understand Bennett's need for total control. The *Follies* lessons were anything but folly.

"I was still not quite sure why we were doing this. *Follies* to *Twigs*?! Even just saying it didn't sound right. But I figure, well, okay, this is: Michael Gets His Feet Wet."

At the beginning the play was in five parts and had five women characters. Rosalind Russell, Brisson's wife, was interested in doing it but, at this point, was suffering from rheumatoid arthritis. Bennett started reading actresses—Elaine Stritch, Cloris Leachman and eventually Sada Thompson. Knowing exactly what he wanted, and how he wanted to proceed, he made quick eliminations.

"Elaine read for us," Avian says, "and bounced off the walls doing Elaine Stritch. Cloris came in letter-perfect. I wasn't there when she read, but Michael told me later—and he told Cloris the same thing—that he wouldn't have anything to do if she played it. He wanted to do it with someone he could mold. He wanted to do it his way."

Auditioning Sada Thompson in Stratford, Connecticut, where she was appearing at the American Shakespeare Festival in *Mourning Becomes Electra*, Bennett found the actress he was after. He knew intuitively that he and Bob and she would work well together. He knew, too, that Sada Thompson would make it exciting for him because he could greatly increase her reputation.

Bennett: "I really cast Sada because she confounded me as almost no one has confounded me, ever. I'd seen her in *Marigolds** as that nasty woman—that awful, bossy mother—then met her at a party somewhere and just couldn't believe this nice, warm, easy, comforting woman standing in front of me was the same person I'd seen on the

*Paul Zindel's *The Effect of Gamma Rays on Man-in-the-Moon Marigolds*, which was produced Off-Broadway in 1970.

stage, and I knew I *had* to work with her one day. I wanted to make her a star, a real Broadway star."

"George Furth wanted to have a reading of the play for Michael to hear it and to decide what to do," Sada Thompson says. "It was after the reading that Michael thought of having one actress play all the women, but he wasn't positive. George had seen me in *Marigolds*, a few months before I did *Mourning Becomes Electra*. When Michael told him I was to read—there'd be a bunch of us, Jimmy Coco, Barnie Hughes, Mary Louise Wilson, Lois Smith—George had said he didn't think I was right for it. I'd done other readings in various manifestations of the script years before, always as a favor to George.

"When Michael really made up his mind that one actress would handle all the roles, he offered it to me and I thought it was a joke because there had been no hint at the reading at all. They had called me at Stratford and Michael and Bob and Freddy Brisson—in a limo a block and a half long—came to see me. Freddy had never seen me, didn't know me at all. We got a couple of Stratford actors, sat down, read the play, and Freddy offered it to me."

Furth's original five-part script was pared to four. The four parts—two in the first act, two in the second—are united by the relationship among the female characters and by a continuous time sequence that begins at 9 A.M. on the day before Thanksgiving and ends twelve hours later. The women are three sisters, Emily, Celia, Dorothy, and their mother, Ma, each a distinct individual. One is a middle-class divorcée, one a drudge married to a dolt, one a happily married suburbanite, and then there is Ma. Ma is a spit in the eye at motherhood and all its sentimental muck. As it turns out, Ma's less than cherished daughters are all illegitimate.

Furth's inspiration had been Ruth Gordon, whom he had once approached about playing the roles. When Gordon suggested the play be directed by her husband, Garson Kanin, Furth, hesitant about working with "a team," backed off. Later, when he suggested Ruth Gordon as a possibility to Bennett, Bennett said he didn't admire her. When Prince had considered doing the script, Thelma Ritter had been his choice. Later, odd as it seems, Elizabeth Taylor would hold a movie option on the material for a year. Produced by CBS, *Twigs* subsequently turned up on television with Carol Burnett, diminished, stripped of its humor.

Avian: "We had a lot of trouble in terms of making it come together. George did a lot of rewriting and switching around during the tryout in Wilmington, but it all seemed pretty modest to me. Then we open in Boston and suddenly we're this *tremendous hit*! We were all stunned. I mean, it had seemed, like, just this little play, and suddenly . . . !"

If acting is a dark mystery (as great acting is), Sada Thompson lights candles when she starts down its beckoning path. Thompson is a schooled technician, and her training is balanced with inspiration, with what she mysteriously calls "connective tissue." A first reading is followed by a second, then a third. Then comes memorization. Even after the lines have been learned, their nuances refined, Thompson keeps the script in her dressing room, in sight, on the makeup counter. Before every performance, she enacts a private ritual. She thumbs through the pages quickly, her fingers sometimes scrolling down lines or tapping a particular word or phrase. She covers the first scene to the last, glancing at and touching her own dialogue as well as the dialogue of the other characters. At a loss to explain this process, she says simply that she somehow absorbs the play's energy through the pages of the script. Bennett understood this "connective" intuition, this link with resources having more to do with accumulative experience than with strict technique. He used it himself.

Thompson: "Michael was a very young man when I met him. Considering the extravagance of his nature, I found it amazing the way he worked with Bob—the absolute lack of ego. He had a strong ego but it simply wasn't challenged in his association with Bob. There was such generosity in the give-and-take. I never saw people work like that before. Liz Smith said something at the memorial service that seemed to me so true about Michael. He could make everybody feel they were his best friend. It wasn't false. He just gave himself to you so generously. He wanted things from you too. It was complementary. If he thought you had information he wanted, some view on life, he'd home in on it. He had about half more life in him than other people. He was so absorbent, extra alive, every part of his being, his brain, his skin! Everything in him just drew in information, then reflected it back at a rate, really, that I had never encountered before. I loved every minute of working with him."

In addition to shaping Thompson's dramatic talent through four different characters, Bennett had another challenge, an echo of sorts from *Company*. The script called for the second sister, Celia, to do a song and dance. Years before, Celia had a bit in a movie. When a friend of her brutish husband comes to visit, her husband suggests she do her stuff. While the number lasted only a couple of minutes, it took Thompson "forever to learn." Every time she thought she had it, Bennett would applaud her and then suggest a refinement. There were so many minute alterations that Sada Thompson jokingly forced an agreement out of Bennett and Furth, a signed note saying, "There will be no more changes."

"Michael knew how to find the talent, the core in you that was different, unique. Also, he had a strong physical imagination. He could tell you how he wanted things to look, then he'd help you find acting hints—or choices—within the physical image. He was one of those people who have a stage up here." Sada Thompson places her right palm against her forehead. "His spatial sense, and his use of it, was very important."

All through the preparation and production of *Twigs* the working relationships were smooth. But for Michael Bennett there was one element missing, excitement. He was challenging himself as a director, but where was the tension associated with musicals? There weren't as many people around, not as many problems, not as many opportunities for him to mesmerize and mastermind. He was shocked when he called Tharon Musser to do the lights and she said she was busy and recommended David Segal. He was shocked even more during the tryouts in Wilmington and Boston when no one flew in from Broadway to see what was going on. Had it been a musical, he'd have been besieged by friends and associates, then clocked and chronicled in the press. It was as though no one was watching!

And something else was happening.

If he had always been in awe of writers, the awe was steadily lessening. George Furth, by his own candid admission, was first and foremost an actor. He hadn't started writing until he was thirty-seven, and considered it almost a hobby. It wasn't a priority. He wasn't driven.

Furth once told Michael Bennett: "When I get bad reviews for a play I've written, I think they're probably right. But let me get bad reviews on my acting and I'm ready for the asylum. I don't have any illusions about writing. I don't do it every day. It wasn't what I was trained at, or what I'm even skilled in. It's certainly not literature or anything; if it is, that's accidental. What I do is good tape recording of what people are talking about. No more."

So, with Furth, there wasn't any real conflict. The work was agreeable, almost effortless, as it was with Sada Thompson and with the other actors and the technical crew.

There was, however, a scorching showdown with Frederick Brisson. Upset by what he considered Bennett's adolescent arrogance, Brisson confronted him in a room at the Ritz Carlton during the Boston tryout, and began yelling. He, after all, was the principal producer, no matter the arrangement with Plum Productions.

Brisson was then fifty-eight, the son of an actor knighted by the kings of Denmark and Sweden. He had been married to Rosalind Russell since 1941; had been a manager and producer in London since the 1930s; had produced movies; had co-produced *The Pajama Game* with Robert Griffith and Harold Prince, and had other Broadway credentials, including *Damn Yankees, New Girl in Town* and numerous plays.

If Brisson's specific complaint against Michael Bennett has been forgotten, his rage has not. The fury behind his words that night in the Ritz suggested, "I'm-not-asking-you/I'm-telling-you, kid, and you-better-listen!" He delivered his rage, and stalked out of the room.

Michael Bennett stood there, very still.

Looking at Bob Avian and George Furth, he said, very slowly, "I feel so sorry for him . . . because he'll never work for me again."

Avian: "So we're a smash in Boston, come to New York and start previewing. Opening night isn't far off, and we've sold two tickets and they're *not* for opening night! We're trying to get people into the theater. Hundreds of tickets in my hands, I walk up and down Forty-fourth Street, Forty-fifth Street, stopping anybody I knew. 'What you doing Saturday night? Want to come to the opening of *Twigs*?' All of us are calling people, buttonholing friends, handing out tickets. We open. Get great reviews. Run nine or ten months. Sada wins the Tony Award for Best Actress in a Play. It's the '71–'72 season, the same year *Follies* is on and wins eight Tonys, with Michael getting two, for co-direction with Hal and for his choreography. We do a *Twigs* tour. We almost pay off. And Michael really is now 'a Director.' "

Twigs opened November 14, 1971, at the Broadhurst, and ran eight months.

Thompson: "We toured and did better than we did in New York, particularly in Chicago. The tour gave Michael the chance to mount it again, and to do what he had always wanted: to have the characters do their changes right before the audience. Wardrobe, ribs, makeup, hair, all of it came out front. He'd been thinking about it a long time, and knew how to do it.

"I didn't see Michael frequently enough after *Twigs*. I didn't know much about his private life. We had dinner a few times. I was up to that wonderful black apartment he had before he moved to Central Park. He told me the reason he wanted to do Furth's play was to work with actors, because he hadn't worked very much with them. He thought the experience would help enrich the musical, make it deeper, better. He caught on so quickly with actors, had so many fresh ideas. He worked so well with all the men.

"I don't think people understood Michael, and I don't think he entirely understood himself. He had to force himself to socialize. I think he felt a stranger in his family, and nothing had ever really changed that feeling. I don't know whether he pushed people away. I don't really know about Donna. They seemed happy to me. I was never pushed away. But then, I can't claim to have been truly close.

Not that he would have kept anything from me. One night—I was working in a stock play but had a little flat in Sutton Place—we had dinner and walked back to the apartment. We stopped off at one of those pocket-handkerchief parks overlooking the river, and he told me that wonderful story about his father wanting to become an actor. He wanted to have it written as a play or a movie. I can't remember the facts, but I laughed so hard at the way he told it.

"Most of the time he ran around in his little red baseball cap and sneaks and work clothes, as though always ready to go to work. As seductive as he was, one of the things about him was that he never seemed to be putting you on, never seemed to be lying. His interest was intense. He wanted to hear you. So many people try to hide all that. I felt this tremendous closeness to him whenever we were together. We talked about everything, puzzling, strange, knock-you-down/get-up-again, beautiful life. I had the impression he didn't read much, but he *knew* things. He never seemed to get over that point in his teens when you have to open every door to see what's behind it, who's behind it.

"Michael and Bob were so patient with me learning the musical number in *Twigs*. I was slow, oh so slow! And I had to count under my breath. But they would just take it, make me refine one phrase over and over and over. Infinite patience! The joy of getting one phrase was obliterated by the terror of adding a second phrase, then a third! They drilled and drilled. Finally, I got it.

"When we left New York for Detroit on the tour, I was to meet them at the airport. I'm always early for planes, Michael was always late. I was standing waiting, and I saw them coming down one of the immense corridors. They saw me but didn't pay any attention. Michael was in this red coat, a little hard to ignore, and I kept my eye on their approach. They walked all the way down the corridor, suddenly dropped their luggage, nodded to each other, started to run and did this big grand jeté in the air right in front of me!

"That's how I see them still, up in the air, clicking their heels!"

Dancing in an airport, free-falling through space, may suggest nothing more than a whimsically spontaneous image. But like most things Bennett tried, it developed out of a concept, here a concept of himself and Avian as nearly airborne as the jets leaving the runway. Kenneth Lipper, Bennett's neighbor in East Hampton, says choreography was a method of control and he used it all the time. Choreography, after all, plots steps and tells people how to move.

"He choreographed everything, every moment of his life right up until the moment he died. He even controlled his death. My wife and I saw him in Tucson a couple of days before he died. When he first knew he had AIDS, he said he wasn't going to die suffering, he'd kill himself. Midway through the struggle he changed his mind. He started discussing death as though it were a play in trouble on the road, and he was determined to beat it. He'd submit to anything, any drug, any treatment before, as he said, 'they pull the shades down.' He became an absolute gladiator, taking on everything, all the suffering, all the indignities.

"He was *so* controlling. He couldn't stand *not* to be in control. He talked to Evelyn and me about his doctors. He had us in stitches! He'd walk in to be examined, the director, the genius, and he'd immediately sit on a lower stool so the doctor would think he was the one controlling the examination and Michael was the submissive subject. He said, 'Otherwise, if we were on the same level, looking at each other eye to eye, he would know I was still the stronger.'

"The doctors had to believe they were the controllers. Michael choreographed it that way."

Donna McKechnie feels the need for control was a cover for insecurity, almost the reverse of what it seemed.

"When Michael wasn't playing games with people, it was as though he didn't know how to act. He was the one who wanted out of the marriage, and it hurt me a lot. I was willing to try anything, and certainly I didn't want to fight about it. He felt guilty and hurt. But instead of saying, 'Hey, you hurt my feelings, and you did this and this, and I don't understand why you did this and this,' he simply withdrew. His way to survive was to lose himself in work. Not dealing with his hostile feelings enabled him to put them on me. So he found a reason for the work to continue, and not to see me, not to speak to me, to seal himself away. I couldn't get through Bob Herr or any secretary at Michael's office at Eight Ninety. They wouldn't let me talk to him.

"And the hostility continued long after the divorce. At one point . . ."

McKechnie stops talking. She sits still for a long, reflective moment.

"At one point I wasn't working. I had arthritis, a lot of physical pain, and he didn't know it. He was in rehearsal, and it was as though he felt guilty the public wasn't seeing me continue my career. So . . . he began saying I had drug problems, serious drug problems. I had three friends who were journalists. They told me this is what Michael was putting out about me. One of them, who knew me better than he knew Michael, and knew it wasn't true, was going to reverse the story. He said, 'I'm going to waste him away here.' I said the best thing was to ignore stuff like that.

"But it was all so devastating. It hurt me so much.

"Once, shortly after this, Michael called about having me do something in Las Vegas, and he was so nervous. I could hear it in his voice when I didn't give him any resistance. I said, 'Thanks for thinking of me,' and after that I tried not to call him so often at Eight Ninety. But, of course, there were times when I had to.

"Michael felt he had to protect himself all the time, so he put himself in Bob Avian's care. He had all these other people around him too. The last time I saw him was the reunion when *Chorus Line* broke the record. He had two bodyguards! I went, like *'Huh?!'* The few times I tried to reach him at Eight Ninety Bob Herr would treat me like, 'What is this in reference to?' When it gets to that point, years later, and you have to explain yourself . . . I said, 'It's personal,' even though it wasn't. You had to explain yourself to Bob Herr so he could relay it to Michael. Then it would be up to Michael to determine whether or not he wanted to—or could—handle it. I guess people just sometimes run away with their power. . . .

"The last time I went back to dance Cassie, Michael took it as a supreme compliment; it meant something very personal to him, although that's not why I did it. He was so happy I was back. We had lunch and he was very solicitous. I mentioned something about my own feelings in being back with the show and he said something really cruel."

McKechnie stops abruptly. She takes a breath.

"He said, 'Well, you'll probably do it every ten years.'

"He was saying that was all I'd ever do, Cassie in *Chorus Line*. I went limp. I felt the old sting and thought: Wait a minute, something's going on here. It's not me. I didn't do anything. He's fighting against his hurt feelings. The hostility is his way of defending himself, his way of protecting his creativity. Michael always had access to his irrational self. And that's not easy to be around."

CHAPTER SEVEN

Seesaws and the Lure of a Good Hot Meal

(1972–1973)

The promise of making a musical with mass appeal catches the light above Times Square like a shiny lure and, like most lures, it's catch-as-catch-can. For all the glittering long runs—the *Fair Ladies, Dollys* and *Fiddlers*—the theater is a dark and dangerous sea. As relentless and deadening as the news most often is from season to season, until recently there always seemed to be musical teams courageous enough for the risk. During Michael Bennett's Broadway tenure the news that *Kelly*, a musical about a gambling man who jumped from the Brooklyn Bridge, ran a single night in 1965 and lost $650,000; that *Dude*, the follow-up by Gerome Ragni and Galt MacDermot, who had written the runaway hit *Hair*, ran sixteen performances and lost $746,000; that old hands like Harold Prince, trying to push entertainment into art, were not earning profits for investors, wasn't much of a deterrent. Tallying losses like these, Brooks Atkinson, the prominent newspaper critic of the era, wrote: "The big successes proved that Broadway was a great place in which to make a fortune but a poor place to make a living." Zeroing in on the 1972–73 season, *Variety* added up fifty-eight productions, thirty-five of which failed.

But the lure lures on. While new musicals are always risky, investors sometimes feel safe when a property has a history, such as *My Fair Lady*, the song-and-dance version of Bernard Shaw's *Pygmalion*. In 1969–70 Joseph Kipness, nominally a restaurateur, and his partner, Larry Kasha, produced *Applause*, a Tony Award-winning adaptation of the movie *All About Eve*. Two years later they were involved in *Seesaw*, a musical derived from William Gibson's hit play *Two for the Seesaw*, which had co-starred Henry Fonda and Anne Bancroft. From the beginning, the *Seesaw* troubles were monumental, but Kipness and Kasha continued to feed money into the production, close to $1,000,000 by the time of the out-of-town tryout at the Fisher Theater in Detroit.

An emotional man, Kipness had been nicknamed Cryin' Joe. His tears ran rivers when he saw his money running down the drain; *Seesaw* was draining him as though he were the Mississippi. In the midst of his tears he sent a call for Michael Bennett's help. Kipness thought that Bennett was the only person who could solve *Seesaw*'s problems, *"Oy what problems."* He knew that Bennett was frequently called in as a doctor when a show was ailing out of town. He had heard he had helped Neil Simon. He persuaded Bennett to go to Detroit. Bennett saw the show and decided it was hopeless. "He thought it was garbage," Avian says. Bennett told Kipness no, Kipness started to cry. Embarrassed, Bennett said he didn't have time, had other prospects.

Awash, Kipness said please.

Bennett said no.

Knuckling his wet eyes, Kipness said it was Bennett's duty to the theater, to the American musical.

Bennett said no again, and again.

Cryin' Joe Kipness then said, "I'll do anything/everything/anything you ask, anything!"

And Bennett gave in.

Avian: "At the beginning of all this Michael thought Kipness wanted him just to doctor the show, fix it up a little. He'd done a lot of doctoring, usually without any credit, sometimes without even being paid. But Kipness wanted more than Michael's doctoring.

"Before we'd seen it, I asked Michael what he was looking for, since we knew—or assumed—there were lotsa problems. I asked what the bottom line was. He said if he liked the story, cared about the characters, he could forget everything else. The potential had to be there in the story, but if the score happened to be terrible that couldn't be overlooked. The *Seesaw* score was by Cy Coleman and Dorothy Fields, and Michael thought it was a plus."

Adapted from William Gibson's slight but charming two-character play, which had opened in 1958 and run 750 performances, *Seesaw*, during its early tryout, was anything but slight and charming. Directed by Edwin Sherin, it had Ken Howard in the Fonda role and Lainie Kazan miscast in the Bancroft part. Lainie Kazan was supposed to be a dancer named Gittel Mosca desperately in love with Howard, a straitlaced lawyer from Nebraska named Jerry Ryan. The first problem was that, more swollen than svelte, Lainie Kazan didn't look like a dancer, didn't move like a dancer and, other than stretching her muscles to a fixed rhythm, couldn't dance. But she was a belter, and there were some Coleman/Fields songs to be belted. This was her big Broadway break. Maybe the hop/skip/jump footwork beneath her ample bosom and hips wouldn't matter.

Aware of her size, if not her limitations, Lainie Kazan, at the start of rehearsals, promised to shed forty pounds, saying she'd have the promise typed into her contract. So many other matters were being worked out, neither Kipness nor Kasha bothered to check the document carrying her signature.

Michael Bennett took one look at Lainie Kazan and decided she had to go. As a director, never mind as a chorus boy who had struggled to the front of the line, there was no way he was going to move hefty baggage across the stage pretending it was arabesque and flight. Whether in repose or in the air, dancers have a look, a manner, and no amount of rehearsal would be able to instill the look or manner in Lainie Kazan. She was out. And Bennett told Kipness, who, if he didn't cry, cowered. Kipness was aware of the problem with Kazan, but was incapable of dealing with it. Kazan and director Sherin had been at each other's throat. In fact, *Seesaw* had lost the backing of Columbia Records (which was to bring out the cast album) when a Columbia representative witnessed a name-calling brawl between the would-be star and Sherin.

At first Bennett started to work with what he had. Robin Wagner was the show's scenic designer. It was the first time he and Bennett worked together, and they responded to each other immediately, each beaming off the other's intelligence and professionalism. Bennett also got along well with Ann Roth, the costume designer. He did not get along well with Michael Stewart, who'd adapted Gibson's script. The beginning between Bennett and Stewart was placid enough, but as Bennett began exercising his control by reaching into areas where Stewart thought he didn't belong, Stewart balked. Who the hell did this kid think he was? He wasn't a writer. A director suggesting a line change here or there was one thing, but this nervy little kid was trying to *rewrite* the whole book! Stewart called him on it and Bennett responded that *Seesaw* was now *his* show; check with Joe Kipness. Michael Stewart quit.

In a hectic period beginning in January 1973, Bennett then began the time-consuming and costly task of reauditioning the entire chorus, which, given inflation, simply wouldn't even be considered today. He fired over half the chorus. Then he fired half the principals, including Lainie Kazan.

Bennett: Sorry, Lainie, but I don't think you're right for Gittel.

Kazan: Why?

Bennett: You're supposed to be a dancer . . .

Kazan: I dance.

Bennett: Not good enough. You're supposed to be this modern dancer, and you're . . .

Kazan: I'm what?

Bennett: You don't read like a dancer to me. You're supposed to have this number, "Tutu in Tights," and you look . . .

Kazan: I look WHAT?!

Bennett: Ummm . . . big.

Kazan: What do you want me to do, cut off my tits? I'll do it, I'll do it!

If he felt compassion for this desperate-to-prove-herself woman sitting in front of him, he showed none. If he had to be ruthless and cruel to shape *Seesaw* into something that wouldn't damage his developing reputation, he'd be ruthless and cruel. He'd do anything he'd have to. Maybe it was impossible to be successful and nice. He wondered if George Abbott had gone through his career having everyone love him; surely there were bodies in his wake. A press agent who worked for Bennett says that he was "always driven and ruthless but that's what it takes in the theater these days."

Admitting that she has blocked out the details of her dismissal from *Seesaw*, Lainie Kazan says, "Other than the death of my father, I can't think of a more painful time in my life. Michael's cruelty to me, his hostility—just talking about it, reliving it! He was so devoid of humanity, so very, very cruel. It was borderline sadomasochism, something dancers have when they turn directors. It cost me, *it cost me!*"

There's a glottic catch in Lainie Kazan's voice.

"I was in bed for two years after this. There are things I don't remember, can't remember. My marriage failed. I lost my home. I had a six-month-old child. I was financially desperate. I thought my career was over. I was in and out of hospitals, I broke my leg, had blood clots in my lungs. *Oh . . .*

"I'd been in the business eight, ten years and *Seesaw* was to be my big break. It was a perfect vehicle for me. When I first read about it, I was pregnant with my daughter and I called Cy Coleman. He thought I was right for it and it all began so idealistically. I work differently from some actresses, internally, and maybe my rehearsals were a little slow. I'm slow to rise but once the cake is baked I'm fine. I got there and I was good, very good. But the reviews were mixed and then the panic started.

"Various directors were brought in. Ed Sherin wasn't about musical comedy but he was wonderful. The show was a small, intimate piece then—it was like what *A Chorus Line* became. It had stark lighting, little scenery. I wore jeans and a T-shirt. It was very personal, all of which was Ed's concept. Michael Bennett came in, fired everybody, made it all balloons and hogwash, then later stole the show's original concept for *Chorus Line*.*

"I don't remember him firing me, the details. I do remember he took over unbeknownst to me. I was the leading lady and he wouldn't look me in the eye. He began by redoing all the musical numbers I wasn't in. My instincts were shocked, but nobody was saying anything. Larry Kasha kept telling me nothing was wrong. Then after about three days—maybe it was a week—I got a call from my manager, Ray Katz, who told me I was out. He said Michael hoped I'd be a *mensch*—that was Ray's word—and stay through Detroit. Michele Lee, who's a friend of mine, was to replace me. I went to talk with Michael and he refused to see me. Avian set up a meeting for the next day and then—if I remember clearly—Michael called that off saying he was stoned and couldn't function. He came to see me closing night in Detroit. He had fired twenty-six people during the intermission. Supposedly I was being fired because I wasn't a dancer. Well, neither was Michele."

Kazan recalls getting a weekly settlement from the producers but says it ran only "a couple of months." Again apologizing for her memory, she says that she sued Larry Kasha over her contract and he brought her before Actors Equity on a number of charges including "being late several times and other failures." She says she had lost twenty-five pounds by the time Michael Bennett appeared on the scene. While she and Ed Sherin may have had disagreements, they ended friends. Beyond Bennett's brutalization of her, Kazan is certain he used their experience for the Cassie/Zach relationship in *A Chorus Line*.

"Michael had blinders on his vision. He was very, very selfish. The trail of blood and dead souls he left behind him! I never mourned when he died."

---

* A complaint by playwright James Lipton and composer Cy Coleman that they had once discussed with Bennett a musical centering on group therapy—an idea that could have resulted in *A Chorus Line*'s "original concept"—resulted in a lawsuit that was settled out of court.

Tilting *Seesaw* so that 80 percent of its weight fell off one end, Bennett began balancing the show with his own ideas and his own people. He added Baayork Lee and Thomas J. Walsh to the chorus and brought in Tommy Tune for a featured role. Lainie Kazan was replaced with Michele Lee, whom neither Bennett nor Avian had worked with but who came with the reputation of being talented and a fast study, "a real whiz who works like crazy." Lee, who was Kasha's idea, had made her Broadway debut in a 1960 David Merrick revue called *Vintage*, and by 1967 had gone Hollywood and been pretty much forgotten.

While the show's old version was still running evenings and matinees in Detroit, reconstruction began. Robin Wagner threw out his original realistic design (this was not a show that needed real bricks, Bennett had told him) and came up with the equivalent "of a straight musical concept out of an MGM movie." Cy Coleman and Dorothy Fields eliminated numbers, wrote new ones. Choreography was changed. Supervised by Bennett, Tommy Tune developed a tap dance that miraculously decoded the arrhythmic legalese of a court document principal in the musical's plot.

And with Michael Stewart's defection, Bennett took on the process of writing the show himself. ("Darling, I've done dances for everybody, directed Kate and Sada, directed with Hal, and now it was time to write, perhaps not like Molière but we'll see. I always thought writers were different, something about them, but for years Neil Simon has told me you just sit down and do it. So I sat down.") Although he is officially credited with the script, Bennett admitted that nearly everyone in the cast contributed. And he called in Neil Simon. Talking with Simon on scenes and characters, he learned that writing could spring from "a process"—rather than, as he had always thought, from "some deep indefinable talent," and, in particular, that writing for the theater "just meant getting lines of dialogue down on paper." A play could be made as his grandfather had once made shoes. The hard work of exchanging dialogue—and refining it during the exchange—could make up for inspiration. Even then he admitted, however, that "a certain attitude, a tone" was automatically struck

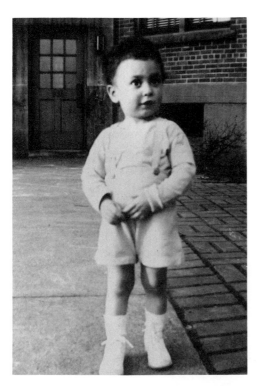

Michael Bennett DiFiglia, age two.
(Courtesy of Mrs. Helen DiFiglia)

Mickey DiFiglia, age ten, struts his stuff. His idols were Fred Astaire and Gene Kelly. *(Courtesy of Mrs. Helen DiFiglia)*

An early chorus line: Mickey DiFiglia is the bongo toddler (first row center) in his Buffalo debut recital in 1945. *(Courtesy of Mrs. Helen DiFiglia)*

Teenager Michael DiFiglia executes a figurative leap from Buffalo to Broadway. *(Courtesy of Mrs. Helen DiFiglia)*

Michael Bennett, as a twenty-three-year-old newcomer, rehearses 1966's *A Joyful Noise* with star John Raitt and producer Edward Padula. *(Van Williams, Courtesy Billy Rose Theatre Collection, New York Public Library at Lincoln Center)*

This portrait of nineteen-year-old Michael Bennett hangs prominently in the Sarasota condominium of his mother, Mrs. Helen DiFiglia. *(Courtesy of Mrs. Helen DiFiglia)*

Follies comes under the scrutiny of its co-directors Harold Prince and Michael Bennett during rehearsal in the spring of 1971. (© *1987 Robert Galbraith, Courtesy of Mrs. Helen DiFiglia*)

Sada Thompson and Michael Bennett during a reading of George Furth's *Twigs*. (© *1989 Martha Swope*)

In 1972's *Follies*, Michael Bartlett, the Emcee, makes his way across the stage as Alexis Smith, Ethel Shutta and Mary McCarty (left to right) perform a number. (© *1989 Martha Swope*)

Michael Bennett holds his diploma, which he was given retroactively by Buffalo mayor James Griffin (left). Behind Bennett are his parents, Helen and Salvatore DiFiglia. *(Courtesy of Mrs. Helen DiFiglia)*

Living up to the Broadway/Hollywood legend, the director marries his star. Michael Bennett and Donna McKechnie at their marriage on December 4, 1976. *(Courtesy of Mrs. Helen DiFiglia)*

Jean-Pierre Cassel and his wife Sabine were the witnesses to the marriage of Michael Bennett and Donna McKechnie in Paris in 1976. *(Courtesy of Mrs. Helen DiFiglia)*

After the runaway success of *A Chorus Line*, Donna McKechnie and Michael Bennett were a well-publicized part of the Broadway scene from 1974 until 1976. *(UPI/Bettmann Newsphotos)*

In *Coco*, when Michael Bennett discovered Katharine Hepburn couldn't carry a tune, he had her speak-sing lyrics to Gale Dixon in "The Money Rings Out Like Freedom." *(Billy Rose Theatre Collection, New York Public Library at Lincoln Center, Friedman-Abeles Collection)*

The climactic waltz sequence—under a spinning crystal ball—in Michael Bennett's *Ballroom. (© 1989 Martha Swope)*

Eivind Harum, Michael Bennett and Donna McKechnie during a recasting of
A Chorus Line. (© *1989 Martha Swope*)

Staring into the house, Michael Bennett
interrupts a *Chorus Line* rehearsal to take a
question from a colleague in the orchestra.
(© *1989 Martha Swope*)

The *Chorus Line* cast waits for Michael
Bennett's next directorial move. (© *1989
Martha Swope*)

James Kirkwood and Michael Bennett during the making of *A Chorus Line*, which Kirkwood co-authored with Nicholas Dante. *(© 1989 Martha Swope)*

United in *A Chorus Line*'s victory, Joseph Papp, Michael Bennett and Donna McKechnie. *(© 1989 Martha Swope)*

Joseph Papp and Michael Bennett during *A Chorus Line*'s Off-Broadway rehearsal at The Public Theater. *(© 1989 Martha Swope)*

Michael Bennett stands before the grand piano in his elaborate office complex at 890 Broadway. (© 1989 Martha Swope)

Bernard Jacobs, Michael Bennett's self-described "surrogate father," and Bennett at an after-theater party. (© 1989 Martha Swope)

When *A Chorus Line*'s 3,389th performance made it Broadway's longest-running show, Michael Bennett crowded the stage with 332 *Chorus Line* veterans. (© 1989 Martha Swope)

when a well-known writer's name appeared among a musical's list of credits. But right now he would mostly write *Seesaw* with a little help from his friends.

First reading the Gibson play, then the Stewart script, he drew a rough amalgam between them in his head. He was reading and rehearsing around the clock, and the old show was like an attic floor scattered with forgotten notions and useless objects. He would blue-pencil speeches, then entire scenes, sometimes using an idea from Gibson to fill out one of his own or to overlay a piece of business from Stewart. Just as he had done all those years ago in high school with *Ice, Ice, Ice*, he was constructing his own play, tapping it together with a cobbler's hammer. Emboldened by his associations with George Furth on *Company* and *Twigs*, with James Goldman on *Follies*, he found his meetings with Simon, as infrequent as they were, the most stimulating. By his own example, Simon demolished the image of the writer as a soulful cousin of Shakespeare and O'Neill. Writing was lonely but it didn't have to be done in cold cottages or stark shacks. It could be done in restaurants on napkins, the napkins stacked and pressed out later. But it was perhaps best accomplished in an office or a study. Bennett admired Neil Simon without reservation. He and Simon had shared the same day in, day out work ethic, the same professional dedication.

By the time *Seesaw* had been reassembled in its final rehearsals in New York, it was an entirely new show and its program read: "Written by Michael Bennett." The first run-through, according to Avian, "was quick and snappy and great," but the response to the first preview at the Uris Theater, two weeks prior to its opening, was halfhearted. "It just wasn't so hot and more work was needed," Avian says. Among the audience at the not so hot preview was Michael Stewart, who eventually stormed out of the theater with rage, resentfully telling anyone he met, "They've ruined it, totally destroyed it, it was never meant to be this kind of show, it's awful!" This tantrum gyrated within show-business circles. *Seesaw* was now rumored to be in as much trouble as when it had started. Although tears again ran down Joe Kipness' face, the money suddenly dried up. There was an order barring further changes. Kipness retired with his Kleenex and Bennett opened the show in a still unperfected state.

Seesaw opened March 18, 1973, and became an immediate critical success. But the day following the first-night standing ovation, Kipness and Kasha thumbtacked a closing notice on the backstage bulletin board at the Uris. There simply wasn't enough money to print the opening-night huzzahs in the newspapers, to say nothing about flashing thirty-second spots on television. *Seesaw* had begun as a $750,000 enterprise and had escalated $400,000 over budget, which included $200,000 for Michael Bennett's changes, as well as a weekly check of $3,000 to Lainie Kazan (for the run of the play) because, as Cy Coleman said, "Kipness had been too gallant to put the weight clause in the contract." Coleman, Stewart, Fields and Kasha had been splitting the payment of the $3,000 among themselves.*

There was a hardscrabble effort to raise money to keep *Seesaw* running. Beseeching friends and relatives, Kasha, Kipness, Coleman and Bennett scratched together enough money for a television commercial. Fields contributed $30,000. Then a masterful publicity gimmick almost turned the trick. Given the musical's New Yorky beat (Tommy Tune's statute tapping number was being referred to by one of its lines: "The late great State of New York"), Mayor John V. Lindsay was persuaded to appear onstage during a number set in Times Square and called "My City." His assignment was to watch an assortment of so-called Neighborhoood Girls strut their stuff. The press coverage resulted in a boost at the box office. *Seesaw*, after poorly attended previews, finally began breaking even. Then, as though spooked by the seven-performance disaster of *Via Galactica*, the musical that had preceded it at the Uris, *Seesaw*'s successful run, which was stimulated by two Tony Awards (including Best Book), was interrupted when the production was forced to move from the Uris to the

---

*Lainie Kazan says that Kipness paid her "under the table" until the suit was settled, then adds that she remembers being paid the $3000-a-week settlement only "for a couple of months."

Mark Hellinger. Even when a long-established hit shifts from one theater to another (forced out by a prior real estate transaction), there is a risk of losing an audience. Although there was a subsequent Philadelphia/Boston tour (with added improvements by Bennett), *Seesaw* never earned back its investment.

Avian: "After doing all these shows we had no money, very little. *Twigs*, then *Seesaw*, no money. *Follies* never sent a check because they were losing. Right after *Seesaw*, Michael doctored *The Good Doctor* for Neil. We went to a New Haven matinee, and I said, 'Can we really fix this?' It was such a dry piece. Neil had brought us in because the play had some musical sequences. Before Michael showed up, everything the director and producers had thought wasn't working, they'd thrown out; everything they liked, they'd kept. Michael said he wanted to see what they'd thrown out. And he put it all back and *threw out* what they'd kept!

"This is Michael and his fixing!

"No one really ever knew what they were getting into when they'd ask him to help. When you'd ask Michael to fix a show, he'd say, 'Put Act Two first.' And I'm not joking! He would put Act Two first. But he always knew what he was doing. To this day Liz McCann credits him for helping out on *Dracula*, the Frank Langella one. He was also called in by Tommy Tune on *My One and Only*—what a bitter experience that turned out to be!

"Anyway, after *Seesaw* we were living pretty modestly. No nest egg. Even as a chorus kid I kept a certain amount of money in the bank, but now everything was pretty low. I needed a new oven and knew where I could get one for two hundred dollars, and I'm going, 'Oy, God, what am I going to do? I'm breaking my back and getting nowhere.' Michael started talking about doing this little show about dancers, down at the Public Theater. Joe Papp was going to back it for us, and we'd get a hundred dollars a week for the next year, and I said, 'Perfect, I'll do it, but if it doesn't work out, I'm going to become a schoolteacher. I can't afford this, and this show is going to be my final, ultimate gamble.' Michael looked at me and said, 'Whenever you work for the money, it doesn't work. When you do it for love, it works. We're doing this one for love.'

"So we had our first *Chorus Line* workshop. Then there was an interruption—or maybe it was after the second workshop. We did *God's Favorite* for Neil. We did *God's Favorite* because we wanted to eat."

Early in 1974, before Bennett signed for Simon's play, he was briefly involved as the director of Herb Gardner's *Thieves*. The cast included Valerie Harper, Dick Van Patten, and Richard Mulligan. The play's theme centered on the anonymity and anguish of 17 characters living in urban soullessness, in this case in New York City. In its Boston tryout, *Thieves* was a wobbly mess with dialogue of streetside pretentiousness ("It's 2 A.M. in Manhattan, honey-babe, and everyone's looking for Peter Pan." "Living is for staying alive"). The comedy was trite, the performances—notably by Valerie Harper—were trying.

Even before the first Boston performance, Bennett had begun to think *Thieves* was thin and not going to work. Before the tryout was over, he quit and was replaced by Charles Grodin. In a commercial sense, Bennett was proved wrong. *Thieves* ran 312 performances on Broadway. By the time it closed in 1975, Bennett was immersed in *A Chorus Line*, which would open in preview Off-Broadway three and a half months later.

CHAPTER EIGHT

Fixing the Book of Job
(1974–1975)

"**M**ichael was just the kid choreographer on *Promises*," Neil Simon says, "and he said to me, 'I really should be directing this,' and I thought to myself: Boy he's got a lot of chutzpah. Nothing fazed him. It wasn't that he thought Bob Moore was doing a bad job directing. He just felt he could do it. I said something like 'Wait'll you get some experience, kid.'

"Next thing I knew he was directing *Twigs*. I thought he did a terrific job for a play that wasn't all there; he really pulled it together. So, by this time, I guess I wasn't surprised at anything he did. He got me to come in on *Seesaw*, and my recollection is I didn't get paid. He'd replaced someone else, and wanted me to help. He had me to dinner with Cy Coleman and Joe Kipness, and there was Kipness tearful about how we all had to help each other. I remember Kipness saying that anybody who came to help got highly paid, including Michael. Anyway, sometimes it's not about money. Sometimes you just like the challenge.

"In about here—1973–74—I'd written *God's Favorite*. It was an unconventional play for me. I really never thought it was going to be a success. I'd written it in some frenzied outburst of anger to rationalize my wife's death at the age of thirty-nine. The humor was very black, and I wanted someone new to direct it, and I got Michael. Let me tell you, he was wonderful. And let me tell you, he was responsible for making one of my recurrent nightmares come true . . .' "

God's Favorite, Neil Simon's fourteenth Broadway production, is not one of Simon's better plays. It examines the Book of Job in an update involving eight characters, principal among them a rich businessman named Joe Benjamin. It's set in a palatial estate on the North Shore of Long Island, and Act Two is designated "The Holocaust after." As in the biblical Job, a string of disasters—strictly personal despite the Holocaust allusion—befall the characters, the string itself so tightly drawn it strangles credibility. Joe Benjamin was played by Vincent Gardenia, with Maria Karnilova as his wife and Charles Nelson Reilly as a quirky, haloless angel doing God's (or somebody's) bidding. The technical crew included the lighting designer Tharon Musser, who would later recall that Michael Bennett "used to bug the hell out of me with questions about gels and shading and this and that, like he *had* to know in a way no other director I had worked with before had to know."

Simon: "I had this nightmare. I dreamed I'd written this really successful play, it could be *The Sunshine Boys*, *Plaza Suite*, anything, and I'm in Europe, and I see the play is in a European production somewhere, and I go see it. I walk in, go down the aisle, and there's my play, only now it has twelve musical numbers somebody has put in. Sometimes in the nightmare the director is Mike Nichols. I say, 'What have you done to my play?' He says, 'Don't you love it?' I say, 'Take them out, take them out!'

"Then I wake up in a cold sweat."

One day, close to the Broadway opening of *God's Favorite*, Simon was to supervise Bennett's rehearsal at the theater Simon owned, the Eugene O'Neill, where *God's Favorite* had been booked. He had told Bennett he'd be present for the 10 A.M. call but had been delayed. When Simon hadn't shown up by 4:30, Bennett—assuming Simon wouldn't make it at all that afternoon—took the opportunity to insert "a musical interlude" he'd been thinking about for a few days, a kind of gospel hoopla to punch up Simon's essentially downbeat narrative. He told the cast what he wanted, gave them some lines to holler, had someone simulate a gospel rhythm on an upright piano. *God's Favorite* suddenly had a choral frenzy not found anywhere in its script.

When Simon opened the outer lobby door, the gospel rap rang in his ears. For a moment he thought he'd stepped into the wrong theater. *All God's Chillun Got Wings* was being revived somewhere close by. Here? This theater? Was there singing in that? Could be . . .

Impelled by the racket of the ascending "Hallelujahs," "Amens" and "Lawdy Lawds," Simon crossed the lobby. As he opened the door to the orchestra, the swell and rattle sounded like a Baptist Sunday morning in Georgia. Making his way down the dark aisle, Simon knew he hadn't mistaken the theater. He recognized the cast. There were Charles Nelson Reilly and Rosetta LeNoire down on their knees, and almost everybody else! Flailing but ecstatic! "Hallelujah! Razza, razza, razza! Praise de Lawd! Lawdy Lawd! He'p us save our house, save our son, Lawd, Lawd!"

There, off to one side, was Michael Bennett whooping it up like a deacon.

Simon walked to the lip of the stage and stood aghast, eyes wide as plums behind his circular glasses.

In the middle of the heavenward musical climax, Bennett suddenly turned and saw Neil Simon. He clapped his hands and grinned. "Don't you love it, don't you just love it?"

Simon waited until the gospelers gradually petered out, until their ad-lib petitions had fallen to earth like burst balloons. He said slowly, "Michael . . . take . . . it . . . out. It's not amusing, that's not what my play's about."

Out it came.

There was no tension behind Simon's command, and no tension at all throughout the rehearsals. Simon had a complex commitment to *God's Favorite*. The script was a memorial, really, to his wife. In his mixed feelings of fear and hope ("two-thirds fear, one-third hope"), he knew it wouldn't work as a play. It was simply an experience he had had to filter through the catharsis of his work; that was something he had been doing all his life, even before his first play, *Come Blow Your Horn*, in 1961.

Avian: "The rehearsals were very funny. At one point I was asked to read the part of the ingenue—this crazy, weird girl—because the actress playing her was sick. I was very nervous, but I went for it. For the whole first week I was this girl, and Vinnie Gardenia was my father. Vinnie was so sincere, and I was just as sincere back, going, 'But, Daddy, Daddy, Daddy!!!' We were screaming, laughing through rehearsals. It was such a good time.

"And then, as it usually is with the theater or can be, the play starts falling downstairs. We go out of town and Act Two is not working, not working at all. The curtain comes down and Neil wants to close it, forget it. 'Let's just stop. It's the wrong kind of pain for a comedy. There's no way we can fix it. It's the story of Job and when you're dealing with blindness, houses being burned down, I can't make that funny.' Michael and Manny Azenberg, who was producing it, convinced him we could still do something with it. Neil can go right to that place of depression, crash hard, and the next day recover. He said, 'Okay, but it'll never be a hit.'

"He was right. It ran six months. And we didn't make any money."

In Buffalo, meanwhile, Salvatore and Helen DiFiglia were undergoing a series of secret disasters that rivaled the troubles of the Benjamins in Simon's play, if not the pain and penalty found in the Book of Job. Five months before *God's Favorite* opened, Salvatore DiFiglia called his older son to tell him "a guilty secret." For some time now he had had "a certain lady friend," Mary Coniglio, whom he had been seeing "fairly regular." Of course, Helen didn't know. *Can you just see that! She'da killed him!* It wasn't just that Sam needed his son's confidence about "somethin' on the side that's been kept pretty quiet." There was something else. Mary Coniglio had just had a baby, his baby, a boy, his third son.

The baby—Michael Bennett's illegitimate half brother—was soon to be christened Salvatore Coniglio, again the father's name swept away. Having confided in Michael, then Frank, Salvatore DiFiglia was determined to keep the information from his wife as long as possible. As long as Helen didn't find out, life—Sam hoped—could go on as normal; of course, he'd "take care of the kid."

Frank DiFilia says his mother "didn't stumble upon it until years later." Living out the melodrama, Mrs. DiFiglia says she heard it two ways: "from a close friend" and "directly on the phone from that tramp Mary Coniglio, who my husband met in a bar." Michael Bennett later gave the melodrama a Sicilian spin by arranging a double burial ceremony when his father died in 1983, the dual arrangements kept secret from Helen DiFiglia until the last minute. Honoring Salvatore DiFiglia's death, the first ceremony was for the immediate family; the second for Salvatore DiFiglia's mistress and his nine-year-old illegitimate son. Temporarily installed in an aboveground vault, which Bennett described as "this big, sleek, shiny filing cabinet," DiFiglia's body was visited by two sets of mourners and keened over twice. Helen DiFiglia was present both times.

God's Favorite opened December 11, 1974, and ran for 119 performances. By the time it closed, March 23, 1975, Michael Bennett and Bob Avian were involved in "this little show about dancers at the Public Theater" that would change their lives. Bennett would spiral from relative backstage anonymity to stardom, the spiral circling so that reality and fantasy, control and mania would blur exactly the way they had blurred when he was slapping heels and toes against the floor and spinning toward dangerous midnight at the wedding of his Uncle Russell.

CHAPTER NINE

All I Ever Needed Was the Chance to Dance

(1974 . . .)

Michon Peacock was furious, a fury that had been developing since 1966, when she came to New York from St. Paul to dance on Broadway. Dancers worked their asses off, almost literally. Disciplining their bodies, they trained like athletes. If you were serious about a career, every day was a physical struggle, and it never got easier. Even when it seemed like fun achieving the high that came from sweating your muscles, swerving energy through your body when kicking above your head, soaring on the ecstasy of being—even briefly—airborne, even when it seemed like fun, it was grueling hard work. And physical pain was only one of the penalties. You got used to that even though the sting was always there, a blister both physical and psychological.

What was more difficult to accept, what caused psychic injury far worse than sore toes, tender insteps and torn muscles, was the common assumption that all dancers were dumb. Then there was the constant rejection, the endless auditions ending with a brusque "Thank you—next, please?" Or "You're not exactly what we had in mind at this time." *At this time? When, then?* The rejection was perhaps inevitable. But why did it have to be coupled with being considered disordered, unintelligent and inarticulate?

Michon Peacock had been in four shows. None was a hit, although one ran six months Off-Broadway.

After happily dancing in *Seesaw*, she had a bad experience that set off a diffuse yet politicized inner rage. In company with Carole Bishop, Thommie Walsh (formerly Thomas J.) and other dancers, she "was steadily humiliated" by Tom Eyen on a show of his called *Rachael Lily Rosenbloom and Don't You Ever Forget It*, which closed in previews at the Broadhurst on December 1, 1973. Why were dancers treated like dirt? Why did they put up with it? Was the promise of —maybe—being a star worth the humiliation suffered day in, day out? How many really got the chance to break out of the chorus and shine? How long did the shining last anyway? Every Broadway dancer had been brought up on the promissory myth in the movie *Forty-second Street*, as well as within the enveloping images of Fred Astaire and Ginger Rogers, and the fantasy of *The Red Shoes*. And, sure, every dancer knew the Carol Haney/Shirley MacLaine story, the ambitious understudy with ready-to-rattle tap shoes going on at the last minute in a principal role. But what happens if the breaks don't come? What happens when your energy drains, when you just can't do it anymore, when a glissade, a plié seem like a challenge? What happens when art becomes arthritis?

What Michon Peacock was thinking, as she danced with her friends in *Rachael Lily Rosenbloom*, had a kind of unfocused revolutionary zeal. Apolitical she might be, but she wanted to improve the dancer's lot. Actors Equity provided protections, work rules, compensations, all that. Michon Peacock was interested in something less practical, something humanistic. She wanted to improve the dancers' image, wanted to repair what she perceived as a backstage grievance: ridicule and prejudice, maltreatment, if not sadism, at the hands of directors, playwrights and even some choreographers.

How do you do that?

Well, first, you collect your dancer friends, then you talk, exchange secrets and confidences, find out if others think and feel as you do. If the rap turns into group therapy, well maybe there'd be solidarity in that. Perhaps the feeling of being alone would abate; perhaps the terror of not making it, of not being a star would lose its power when confronted by a group, when a community (however small)—rather than a single frightened individual—challenged the myth.

Clear in her intent, unclear in her method, Michon Peacock had grumbled her thoughts to Michael Bennett during and after *Seesaw*, which, as it happened, closed its disappointing ten-month run seven days after *Rachael Lily Rosenbloom*. She didn't know whether she wanted to start a repertory company for dancers or what. All she really knew is that she wanted to improve the situation.

"Michael called me New Year's Day 1974 to come see him, and Tony Stevens and I did," Michon Peacock says. "When I told him what we had in mind he said he had an idea not dissimilar from ours, and he wondered how many dancers felt the same way we did. It was decided we'd get some people together and have a rap session. Tony and I weren't sure at all about what we were doing. When we called people, we didn't even know whether or not to mention Michael was involved. Involved in what? And, also, we felt some dancers would feel vulnerable and not come if they knew Michael was going to be present.

"I knew a fellow Buddhist who worked at the Nickolaus Exercise Center near Third Avenue, and we used that space. We met either January 11 or 12, about twenty-two of us, and Michael provided the food, the booze, the joints, the drug of your choice, whatever. First we danced, then we talked. We created this rectangular circle, sat around and explained our lives from, like, kindergarten. Hours later we were up to about the age of twelve.

"The next session was early in March. We knew we had to crack the twelve-year-old barrier and get to New York. Most of the same people were present, although some weren't, and there were about four newcomers. It was all pretty amazing, a catharsis. Dancers in the room who hated each other or who were simply competitive, well, those relationships changed enormously. Between the two sessions Tony and I had gone to Michael and he had told us he wasn't sure what the first session had been worth. He'd suggested at the first one that there might be no outcome, that all the talk might wind up being a magazine article, an outline for a movie, a book. We were CRAZED! *All this life in a book!*

"Then, I don't know, Michael went to work on *Thieves,** the play with Marlo Thomas, and Tony and I decided we had two projects. Project A: devise a show for dancers where dancers did everything, produced it, wrote it, acted it, did the scenery, costumes, lights. Project B: keep taping material for Michael, for what specific purpose we didn't know."

Nicholas Dante, who was present at the Third Avenue session, corroborates Peacock's recollections.

"Michon had talked to me and another friend, Tony Stevens, about seeing Michael. She was extremely vague about what she was doing, didn't really know whether she was asking for advice or what. All she really knew was that she wanted to help dancers develop their other talents. It really wasn't about: What do you do when you can no longer dance?—although, okay, yes and no, it was about that. She and Tony went to see Michael. I didn't go, the first time.

"The timing was very important here. Michael had directed *Twigs*, then, I think, *Seesaw*, and was itching to get back to working strictly with dancers. He wanted to do a show, so the meeting served a dual purpose. He listened and said, 'I don't know what you're asking. What do you want me to do?'

"He suggested Michon and Tony get some dancers together to talk. He wanted them to set up the meeting. He didn't want to because—since he knew most of the dancers, had worked with them—he didn't think they'd be honest if they knew he was going to be there.

---

*At this stage in the development of *A Chorus Line*, Bennett had been involved in the pre-Broadway tryout of Herb Gardner's *Thieves*. After Charles Grodin took over the play's direction, he recast Valerie Harper with Marlo Thomas. *Thieves* opened at the Broadhurst April 7, 1974 and closed January 5, 1975.

"This is where I came in, at the first session, and told my story . . ."

A Chorus Line, Scene 18.

Zach: I really like the way you dance . . . What made you start dancing . . . ?

Paul: . . . my father loved movies. And he'd take us all the time. He worked nights and he'd come home and take us to Forty-second Street. And we'd come out of one movie and go to another and another movie—I don't know why—but I loved musicals.

Zach: How old were you?

Paul: Seven or eight.

Zach: On Forty-second Street?

Paul: Yeah—it was a trip.

Zach: Go on . . .

Paul: I'd have to move down front—'cause I couldn't see—I wear contact lenses now . . . I'd move down front and these strange men would come and sit beside me and "play" with me. I never told anyone because—well, I guess it didn't matter . . . From seeing all those movie musicals, I used to dance around on the street, and I'd get caught all the time. God, it was embarrassing. I was always being Cyd Charisse . . . Always. Which I don't really understand because I always wanted to be an actor. I mean, I really wanted to perform. Once my cousin said to me, "You'll never be an actor," and I knew she was telling me this because I was such a sissy. I mean, I was terribly effeminate. I always knew I was gay, but that didn't bother me. What bothered me was that I didn't know how to be a boy. One day I looked at myself in the mirror and said, "You're fourteen years old and you're a faggot. What are you going to do with your life?" . . . By that time I was in Cardinal Hayes High School. There were three thousand boys there. I had no protections anymore. No homeroom where I could be charming and funny with the tough guys so they'd fight my battles for me. Like when I went to small schools. I liked school. But my grades got so bad. Even if I knew the answers to questions, I wouldn't raise my hand because I would be afraid they would laugh at me. They'd even whistle at me in the halls. It was awful . . . just awful. Finally, I went down to the Principal's office and said: "I'm a homosexual." Well, it was Catholic high school at around 1962 and at the age of fifteen you just didn't say that. He said: "Would you like to see a psychologist?" And I did. And he said: "I think you're very well adjusted for your age and I think you should quit school." So, I did. But I really didn't want to. I couldn't take it anymore. See, when I quit school, what I was doing was trying to find out who I was and how to be a man. You know, there are a lot of people in this world who don't know how to be men. And since then, I found out that I am one. I was looking for the wrong thing. I was trying to learn how to be butch. Anyway, I started hanging around Seventy-second Street, meeting all these really strange people. Just trying to make friends that were like me. So that I'd understand what it was that I was. Somebody told me they were looking for male dancers for the Jewel Box Revue, you know, the drag show. So, I go down to audition. Now, from all those years of pretending I was Cyd Charisse, I had this fabulous extension. And they said to me: "You're too short to be a boy, would you like to be a pony?" I said: "What's that?" And they said: "A girl." "What do I have to do?" "Show us your legs." "But I have hair on my legs." "That's okay, come on upstairs." So I went and they hiked up my dungarees and they put on a pair of nylon stockings and high heels. It was so freaky. It was incredible. And then they brought me back downstairs and they said: "Oh, you have wonderful legs." I said: "Really . . . Terrific . . ." It's so strange thinking about this. It was a whole lifetime ago. I was just past sixteen. Anyway, then there was this thing of me trying to hide it from my parents. That was something. 'Cause I had to buy all this stuff. Like, ah, shoes to rehearse in, earrings, makeup. And I would hide it all and my mother would find it. I told her there was this girl in the show and she didn't want her mother to know what she was doing and I was holding this stuff for her. She believed me. Well, I was finally in show business. It was the asshole of show business—but it was a job . . . Nothing to brag about.

I had friends. But after a while it was so demeaning. Nobody at the Jewel Box had any dignity and most of them were ashamed of themselves and considered themselves freaks. I don't know, I think it was the lack of dignity that got to me, so I left. Oh, I muddled around for a while. I worked as an office boy, a waiter—but without an education, you can't get a good job. So, when the Jewel Box called and asked if I'd come back, I went. We were working the Apollo Theater on a Hundred Twenty-fifth Street. Doing four shows a day with a movie. It was really tacky. The show was going on to Chicago. My parents wanted to say goodbye and they were going to bring my luggage to the theater after the show. Well, we're doing this Oriental number and I looked like Anna May Wong. I had these two great big chrysanthemums on either side of my head, and a huge headdress with gold balls hanging all over it. I was going on for the finale and going down the stairs and who should I see standing by the stage door . . . my parents. They got there too early. I freaked. I didn't know what to do. I thought to myself: "I know, I'll just walk quickly past them like all the others and they'll never recognize me." So I took a deep breath and started down the stairs and just as I passed my mother I heard her say: "Oh, my God." Well . . . I died. But what could I do? I had to go on for the finale, so I just kept going. After the show I went back to my dressing room and after I'd finished dressing and taking my makeup off, I went back downstairs. And there they were, standing in the middle of all these . . . And all they said to me was please write, make sure you eat and take care of yourself. And just before my parents left, my father turned to the producer and he said: "Take care of my son . . ." That was the first time he ever called me that . . . I . . . ah. I . . . ah.

Dante: "Michon and Tony got us all together for the first session. We used a space on Third Avenue and Twenty-eighth Street. It was a Saturday night. Because some of the dancers were in shows the meeting was called for midnight. We talked until noon the next day, straight, nonstop. What people don't know is that dancers are highly verbal. But the first thing we did was dance. Michael had ordered in a round of sandwiches, coffee. We danced, and ate, then went into this other little room, sat in a circle and started to talk. We talked about growing up, six to twelve, twelve to eighteen, then eighteen until you moved to New York, got your first apartment and your first job. There were about twenty-five or so of us, so of course it would have taken twelve hours.

"It was a remarkable evening. Many of us didn't like each other. We were rivals, competitors. But all that feeling left the room. The workshops that came later had a lot of hostility, but at this session— which is where the very soul of *Chorus Line* came from—all the negative stuff just dissipated. It was just that feeling of openness, of friendliness Michael wanted to re-create for audiences because it was an extraordinarily special evening. We all felt very human. We didn't feel alone. You realized that everybody else had the same fears and frustrations. It was just . . . well, all terribly universal.

"At the end of it we held hands to solidify something, we didn't know what, and it was clear we didn't know what was going to come from the session. A show? Anything? But we were all so grateful to have had the twelve hours together. And a lovely thing happened. As we stood there wondering and holding hands in that little room, outside, close by, noon bells rang out.

"And then, of course, Michael's lying and melodrama started."

Having listened to the tapes, Michael Bennett came to harsh, pragmatic decisions. He didn't want to work with Michon Peacock or Tony Stevens. He wasn't even sure he wanted to work with Nicholas Dante, but he saw Dante's monologue as a moment of climactic drama and wondered how he could use it without its author, who happened also to be the monologue's subject. He decided to have another session with the dancers.

Dante: "I'm fuzzy on this, the time sequence, but I think it was after the second session that Michon, Tony and I went to see Michael. It could have been a month or two later, or maybe just a couple of weeks. Anyway, he said—lying through his teeth—he didn't think there was a show in the tapes. He thought, maybe, a book. He wasn't sure. I found out from him that he didn't want Michon and Tony. I figured out later, he didn't even want me. *He wanted my story!* I kept saying to him I was into writing now. I mean, I was an aging dancer, thirty-two. I wasn't going to be a star or anything. I'd dabbled at writing early in my life, and had thought about becoming a writer. But later—after I'd quit high school—I'd put it aside because I felt you couldn't be a writer without an education. I pretty much stopped, became a drag queen and all that. Once in a while I'd scribble something.

"But I knew in my writer's bones—so did Michon and Tony— the tapes were wonderful. We were furious with Michael. Whhhaaattt book? Some book! It was a show! And if he couldn't make a show out of it, he was an idiot! So much material there! What's he craa-azzzeee? So we started meeting with people, having our own work-shop, doing our own thing. The attitude was, fuck him if he didn't want to be involved.

"Then . . . I think about three months later, four, Mr. Bennett called. 'I've been thinking it over and I think there *is* a show here.' Blah-blah-blah. 'How would you like to write it with me?' Blah-blah-blah. 'If we don't get it right, we'll get somebody else and'—blah blah-blah—'keep getting others until we get it right, right?' So we started the process. Later we talked about why he didn't want Michon or Tony up there with him. He wanted total control. He didn't want to share the idea—or the impetus of the idea—with anyone. He wanted my story, not me, but knew he couldn't get it without me. He lucked out because I could write."

Avian: "The fact is that *Chorus Line* began as a . . . Well, here's the history: A couple of dancers, Michon Peacock and Tony Stevens, were organizing an evening with their pals. They just wanted to get everyone together to spend the night dancing and rapping. I think they were Buddhists or something, and wanted to have an experience of their own. Michael heard about it and asked if he could come.

They said, 'We'd love to have you.' He said, 'Mind if we record it?' They said, 'That'll be fine.'

"And what happened was, when Michael got there it was no longer a group thing. He became the figurehead of the evening. And for the dancers, in their own way, it became an audition. Michael knew this. I wasn't there. He'd asked me to go, and I said, 'I don't want to know from that. I hate all that group psychology stuff. I'm not getting up and dancing and running around telling my life story. No way!'

"I really didn't understand why he was going. But he and Donna went, and danced and listened, and he came back with something like nineteen hours of tape. I listened to them, and a lot of it was boring, a lot of it was like more and more vomiting. By the time Michael asked for a second session, he'd set down some rules and everybody really went for it! Then we did some individual tapes, basically from dancers we knew who weren't at either of the sessions. We did them at Michael's apartment, sometimes just a single, sometimes two or three tapes at a time. We wanted their stories. We did Baayork like this, Pam Blair, Mitzi Hamilton."

Bennett was shrewd enough to know the value of the information he had collected. He also knew that without a dramatic context the information might just as well be on file cards. The stories needed focus. Quickly enough, he imagined that focus as perhaps the most ordinary—certainly the most glamourless—activity in show biz, the preliminary audition.

Avian: "So, as he saw it, we had a beginning, a middle and an end. I said, 'Huh? Where beginning? Where middle? What end? Tell me.' He said, 'The beginning is the audition, *and* the end is the elimination, *and* the middle is the Paul story because Nick Dante was incredible that night telling it. He went for the jugular vein with that story and he's very articulate.' Then Michael asked Nick to do a composite of all the tapes as a first draft, the idea being they would collaborate together on a script. I'd hate to say Michael wanted to tell Nick what to do, but . . . well, that's not quite true. Nick's talented.

"And then it got really confused as to who did what."

An initial script was developed with some of the dancers' stories layered on others, with an event from one life slapped across another, so that individual profiles began to blur into composites. Paul's story remained its own—that is, without inserts or imagined details and exactly as Nicholas Dante had experienced it. But Zach, the director who runs the *Chorus Line* audition from the back of the theater, cajoling and bruising egos through a hand-mike, supposedly was pieced together from various personalities. There is a lot of Michael Bennett in Zach, including sexual ambiguity, but it's a fantasized silhouette rather than a mug shot.

When Bennett's former lover Larry Fuller saw *A Chorus Line* he recognized the domestic squabbling between Zach and Cassie as a replay—right down to specific lines of dialogue—of the squabbling that had led to the end of what he had thought was a contented homosexual union.

Fuller: "After I'd seen *Chorus Line* Michael was all excited about my reaction. We were supposed to have lunch, but first we stopped by his office, the office he had in some big building on Park or Madison, not the one he bought later at Eight Ninety Broadway. I remember walking in with him and the place was empty, rows of desks with typewriters, but there was a meeting going on about a television commercial for *Chorus Line*, Carol Burnett head-on doing a direct sell to the audience. Someone asked Michael for his opinion. We watched a couple of takes, he said, 'Yes on that, no on this,' and we walked down a long corridor to his office. He had this huge Cecil B. De Mille chair, a big desk. He sat in the chair, and here was this little kid sitting behind this big desk. He was now the Great Powerful Oz. We started talking and never got out to lunch. His lunch was a joint and two glasses of vodka, and I thought: How can he work after that?

"During our conversation he said, 'What about that scene between Zach and Cassie?'

"I was a little defensive and said, 'What about it?'

" 'Well, darling, didn't you recognize some stuff from our past?'

" 'Oh, well, there were some familiar things wisping through there.'

" 'It's based on a lot of what happened to us.'

" 'Not completely, Michael. Some other tricks in there you got all mixed up.'

" 'What about the line you once said to me that Cassie now says to Zach after he says, 'I came home one night and you were gone,' and Cassie says, 'Why, Zach, you noticed . . . ?'

" 'Well . . .'

" 'Did you notice we named the assistant choreographer after you? Did you notice that? Bob and I both agreed to call him Larry, and we both agreed he had to look beautiful and dance great.'

" 'Well, thanks, Michael. I feel very complimented being im-mortalized in character *and* dialogue.' "

Larry Fuller looks down at his hands clasped in his lap. He clears his throat.

"I didn't see him much after that. We were very close about four and a half years, from 1962 through 1966. We lived together a little over three years. I still remember the apartment. When I met him I was still a dancer, not even thinking about becoming a choreographer. He looked up to me a bit, I was a few years older."

One of the early working structures behind *A Chorus Line* was built on the ages of the dancers, their growing up. The idea was to start out at the age of four or five and track each dancer through his or her career, ending at age thirty-two. Quickly enough, that was found unworkable. From the beginning what seems to have been constant was the idea of using the painful self-revelations on the tapes to make the characters composites.

Avian: "There was a lot of blurring. We'd take a dancer's specific story and have it played by someone else. All through it—and I'm going to get killed for saying this—Michael had everyone believing that they were doing it all! They were writing it! They were singing it! They were moving it! But he really was doing it all. He was just getting them to think they were doing it; it was a collaborative technique of his, but it resulted in the anger that came out later over who wrote what, who said this, who did that, who contributed the most, the least. Michael was the one with the talent to get people to do it. Michael was the one capable of nudging and manipulating and controlling until he got it to be the best possible show it could be. Michael was the one."

"You have to understand," Marvin Hamlisch says, "how Michael got me for *Chorus Line*, how he got Marvin to help Michael, Michael to help Marvin. I had met him in 1966 when I went to see *Joyful Noise* at a preview, in a New York studio somewhere—it wasn't in a theater yet. I was born in 1944, so I'm then twenty-two years old, right? I'm knocked out by the choreography and I gotta meet the man or the woman who choreographed this show.

"*Do I remember!*

"There was this moment in the second act when Alice Playten was dancing and—baaammm!—she's tossed behind, like offstage. What you didn't see were the two guys who were going to catch her. All you saw was this woman being tossed! No catchers! And I'm sitting there amazed, thinking to myself: Marvin you gotta meet this choreographer. And I did. I go backstage and meet this little kid, my age, and I remember him saying, 'One day our paths will cross, just remember me.' That was it, hello and goodbye. I think he was taken by the fact that someone had come backstage to meet him.

"Well, anyway, life goes on, and Marvin likes Michael, Michael likes Marvin. So we do a little work together, a patch up—uncredited—on *Henry, Sweet Henry*, then later some dance arrangements for *Seesaw*. And that was that. Meanwhile, all I wanted to do was write the score for a Broadway show. One of my dreams. And it isn't happening and it isn't happening and, by this time, Marvin's in Hollywood writing music for the movies.

"You have to understand, this particular April or May, I then win three Academy Awards, and there's no doubt back in New York the media attention ignites something in Michael's head. He had wanted to work with me before, but this ignites something new. Before, he may have wanted Sondheim, I don't know, who knows . . .

"The point is, with Marvin, Michael can be in control based on Marvin not having worked before on Broadway. Give a little, lose a little, so let's work.

"What I really know is that anyone Michael was going to get for *Chorus Line* not only had to be eager to work but also had to be in awe of Michael. You have to understand my choice was then to stay in Hollywood and keep getting money to do pictures or . . . ! Or take a shot. It's a shot because you don't get paid anything to do a Broadway show, and when you do, if you do, it will probably take two years. And then I think: But to go with a genius! So I figure I better go with a genius for two years of maybe not getting paid than do six movies not only God knows what's going to happen to.

"By the time I get the call they're already into two or three months with the tapes, and Ed Kleban is the lyricist. From the start I didn't understand why Michael hadn't taken Ed as the composer/lyricist. Maybe he figured the worst that could happen, I could lose Marvin and still stick with Ed. Who knows? So I come in and basically we sit around with Michael listening to everybody. He's very smart. He listens to everybody. He never didn't listen. And from the start, it was suspect whether he'd give you credit for what you added to the show.

"But it really wasn't about Ed or Michael or me saying, 'Hey, wait a minute, that was my idea.' It was a group thing and we were all trying to come up with good ideas. Michael certainly knew a good idea when he heard one and, now and then, he may have portrayed someone else's idea as his own. He could be ruthless if he thought he was right. If I had to say how many decisions Michael made that were right, I'd say he was batting in the eighty percent mark. The twenty percent correction usually came from Michael then correcting himself or from Bobby or occasionally from Ed and myself. It was a working arrangement. But you have to understand that sometimes he was mean and impossible. Sometimes it was like seeing someone you didn't know was carrying a scalpel! All of a sudden you went, 'Oy, wait a minute here, he has a scalpel but I don't!'

"Moments like this you realized you had to be a little more careful."

So the workshops began.

Not yet involved with the Shubert Organization, specifically Bernard Jacobs, who gradually became a father figure he loved and hated with equal passion, Michael Bennett sought out Joseph Papp, who, in 1954, had developed the outline of the New York Shakespeare Festival in a church basement on the Lower East Side, where it was known as the Shakespeare Workshop. In 1967 Papp's base of operations became an abandoned red brick building, south of Astor Place on Lafayette Street, that had once been used by the Hebrew Immigrant Aid Society. Designated a landmark, the big building would eventually house six theaters and become a considerable force in the city's—and the country's—cultural life. Bennett particularly liked the cachet associated with the title New York Shakespeare Festival. The only Shakespeare he had read was *Hamlet* in high school, and he had pursued the author no further. Papp's blue-collar approach to theater, his social-minded plans for developing audiences beyond Broadway's bourgeois limitations, his interest in new, politically relevant material appealed to Bennett. After years of dancing, doctoring and directing, it wouldn't be a bad idea to be tied to something espousing the spirit of Shakespeare. It was good for the image, just as years before, Busby Berkeley, the sissy toy poodle Bob Avian carried everywhere, had been bad for the image. (Busby Berkeley was shipped to Buffalo to live with Bennett's mother.)

As it turned out, the New York Shakespeare Festival would also prove to be a shrewd financial move. It was Papp who suggested that the *Chorus Line* script be developed directly from listening to the tapes. It was Papp who offered workshop space and, later, the Newman Theater, one of the six houses operating under the general term Public Theater.

The first workshop began with a rough script credited to Michael Bennett, Bob Avian and Nicholas Dante. Its shape was very different from what it became. Barry Bostwick played Zach, the director. (James Kirkwood would later say he was the one who contributed the name Zach.) It opened with a dance. There were no songs. The characters all stayed onstage as one or another told his or her story, some of them sitting on chairs and interrupting with snide remarks and marginal stories. As Priscilla Lopez talked out her anecdote about acting class and her calcified emotions (which later became the song "Nothing"), Donna McKechnie and Carole Bishop engaged in bitchy chat: "God, she talks a lot." "Never shuts up." Gradually, the information in the anecdotes and the stories was refined. Gradually, the show's physical shape started to change. As the dancers told their histories and moved closer to the front of the stage, the structure became more like that of a documentary than a play.

The first workshop ran over four hours.

Avian: "It was like *Ben Hur*. Every time someone got up to tell a story they went for the emotion. They were all kids, most of them, and they went for broke, hearts beating, pulses throbbing, tears welling. *Oh, God, just remembering it, gimme a break!* And there weren't any breaks then, just the stories, no music or songs. Ed and Marvin were involved by then, and that was one of the luxuries of the workshop. They could sit and listen to all the stuff, and later write the music.

"We did the first workshop, then Michael and I went off to do *God's Favorite* with Neil. When Michael got to hear some of Ed and Marvin's music, well . . . he wasn't always pleased. He'd sing/scream lyrics right into Marvin's ear, then shout, 'Ya got it? That's what I want! Ya got it?' It was pretty amazing. I hate to say these things, but that's the way it happened, the way the show was put together. He'd scream right in their faces and say, 'Now THIS is what I want!' "

Hamlisch: "When we started we had two songs, a five-hour libretto and two shows. Very early on Ed and I wrote 'At the Ballet,' and Michael cried the first time he heard it. But then we had an argument. It's a little unclear, it was thirteen years ago, but I was fired. Michael told me, 'Don't show up anymore.' And this was after we had given him a song he cried at! He had told me it was one of the greatest songs ever, and now he was going to show off the fact that he was in charge by firing me! I was in shock. You have to understand, this is the thing I wanted to do all my life, theater. He could be unbelievably mean. On the one hand, telling you how great you are; on the other, making the deal so impossible you felt you were working for slave labor. And all the while telling you he loves you a lot.

"I was in shock. It was like, you have an altercation with the director and it comes to this? This is what's done! They fire you! Allan Carr was my manager, and he was a friend of Michael, and he called from California but he had to come to New York to patch things up. So we start again, Marvin and Ed and Michael. Nothing's really changed but we keep going. There are more scalpels."

Dante: "The reason Joe Papp approved a second workshop was because it was working and it was good. Something really hot was happening, even though we couldn't get the Zach and Cassie stuff to work. Marvin Hamlisch kept saying you gotta get a real writer because he considered me just a dancer. That's why after Jimmy Kirkwood was brought in he and Marvin asked for a point. Jimmy gets twice as much money as I do, and all along he's gotten all the credit as 'the' writer. Which he wasn't and isn't. I didn't get anything. I mean, I got a lot, I got a million out of it, but Jimmy has gotten much, much more. It took me nine years to make that million. Jimmy got more faster. And he really didn't do that much. I mean, he added his sensibility but he didn't add a great deal. I'm the author of the show with Michael and Bob, really. I have no ax to grind about it, but ... well, it's just that I've never been able to say that openly to people before. It's taken me thirteen years.

Jimmy doesn't know I feel this way. We've never talked about it. We've been very good friends.

"Michael and I collaborated well after the first workshop. Then we took a break for four or five weeks. Then he announced on the phone, without preamble, that he was calling in another writer, Jimmy Kirkwood, and: 'Be at my house Monday to meet him. Bye.' Click. Like that. There was no discussion. He had never prepared me for it, and that's exactly how he told me on the phone.

"So I prepared myself to meet Jimmy Kirkwood. At the time I was a Buddhist. I mean, I really am still, but I was then actively practicing and very much involved in the organization, Little Goody Two-Shoes, Mr. Into World Peace, all that, and I was very good at Smoothing Things Over. Before I went to meet Kirkwood I chanted. I wanted to be the only writer. Michael wasn't going to get credit as the author. Sure, he contributed, but he wasn't a writer. He had delusions he could write. I think all directors think they can. But I am the one who contributed the two major concepts to *Chorus Line*, Paul's story and the montage of all the dancers' thoughts. When I wrote the montage, Michael and Bob loved it. Bob loved it because he said it was a ballet of words. When I gave it to Michael, I said, 'This is all about lighting; if the lighting doesn't work, this won't.' Thank God Tharon did her usual brilliant work."

"Michael had this extraordinary intuition about people, he was the Ultimate Seducer," James Kirkwood says. "He wasn't an intellectual by any means, and he certainly wasn't well read, but his nose took him right to where he should go. He bore right into you, making you feel that whatever you were about to say, whatever contribution you were about to make, well, it was going to be the most important thing to him in the whole world. He really was like that. Only later you found out he was raping your soul.

"Michael was going to direct my play *P.S. Your Cat Is Dead*. That's how I met him, through Jack Lenny, but then he backed out. We had had rapport, and good meetings, then he just vacillated and withdrew. By the next time I saw him he'd done *Twigs* and *Seesaw*, and we ran into each other at the theater. I was a little angry—thought he was a bastard—but then he said he'd been trying to get in touch with me for ten days because he had this idea for a show about dancers and I might be interested because I'd been a performer. He thought I could write it. He had the tapes by then, but the fact is, I never heard them. I got a transcript eventually, but whoever transcribed them hadn't put in who was speaking or whether it was a man or a woman. You really couldn't read them. I was the last one who came in because, apparently, Michael and Nick Dante were going to write it. Only I knew Michael didn't have the attention span to be a writer. He didn't tell me yet he was linking me with Nick Dante. Michael was a fox.

"And Jesus Christ, guess what? Nick and I got along fine. Never fought except maybe on punctuation. He used dots and dashes and exclamation points, and I just can't read a script without puncutation. It was the easiest show or book I've ever worked on. It was also the most amoral, amorality being Michael's fatal flaw.

"Michael would do anything—*anything!*—to get a show on. The cruelty was extensive. And not just in his professional life. He was amoral. And I don't think he necessarily thought that he was doing some of the terrible things he did. Maybe he did, but I can't imagine living with yourself and doing stuff like that. The whole thing with Donna was messy, the separation, the divorce, then Sabine. The *Chorus Line* kids said they were mistreated by him. He cut people off like baaammm! He lived with Sabine, then suddenly: baaammm! it's all over. You had to think he was out of control, had no sense of morals.

"Most of this behavior was after the success of *Chorus Line*, not before. The power and the money and the ego! The whole trip! I'm God now! I think he was an intuitive genius as far as bringing off things onstage. But a genius who didn't know how to handle that genius. People were always wondering if he was happy, was he enjoying it? Most people said no, but I thought he probably was. I know he was enjoying the power. I think he may have been lonely, but Jesus Christ, he could get almost anyone to do anything! I think he couldn't be alone, I think he panicked and demanded company. He had some deep, innate fear. Which probably explains some of the drugs. I think the drug scene was bad, but I wasn't aware of it much during *Chorus Line*. I'm not sure he was using cocaine much then, but I know he was very manic. One reason Bob meant so much to him, he was always there for him, and levelheaded in comparison."

Dante: "Michael could be very cruel, terribly, terribly cruel. He made me fall in love with him. He makes everybody fall in love with him. He's the best manipulator in the world. What really annoyed me about that—when I realized what he was doing and what he had done playing with my emotions—is that I'd have given him my work without all that. He didn't have to do that to get the work out of me. Which is why he does it: to get the work out of people. This is why I don't think he's a great director. He was very bent, you know that?! He was nuts! A fully rounded monster! A little bit of everything!"

There were numerous other problems. The production didn't progress as smoothly as most of the dealings with Joseph Papp and the New York Shakespeare Festival later suggested.

For all his well-publicized megalomania, his steady, disruptive interference with playwrights, directors and entire productions, Papp left Bennett and Avian alone. But there was a major disagreement on the horizon even before *A Chorus Line* became the talk of the town and the production was scheduled to move to Broadway. Sharpening his scalpel, Bennett was ready to sever his ties with Shakespeare when Papp insisted that the show move to the Vivian Beaumont at Lincoln Center rather than to the Shubert. Papp was then trying to make the ailing Lincoln Center a viable complex. Bennett felt the Beaumont was the wrong house, too big, too open, too public for *A Chorus Line*'s intimacy and personalism. This was, he said, the "ultimate proscenium show and it didn't belong in a barn." He was ready to face down Papp with threats, and carry them out.

Although Michael Bennett was still playing the prodigy in the red baseball cap, sweatshirt, jeans and sneakers, this time the threats were sophisticated in their potential harm. He was no longer a kid ready to holler "Uncle!" when it hurt. He'd learned the tactics of infighting. He was a long way from trying to prove himself. He'd no longer surrender to someone like Harold Prince by countering only with the simple rage of the misunderstood artist. Subsuming both the hurt and the rage, he'd base his logic on what he "knew commercially was right."

Bennett: "Joe kept insisting on the Beaumont for the previews, so Bobby and I go take a look and, of course, it's impossible. I simply said, 'I want the Newman, I'm not playing the Beaumont.' Joe pleads, 'I need you to play there.'

"Now it's time for a little shoot-out, right?

"And, by the way, I've been very happy with Joe up until this point. He's been the best producer I've ever worked with. But I told him no, the Beaumont was out. Maybe he thought I was going to change my mind, but I wasn't. I took Marvin and Ed and Bobby to the Shuberts to run through the score for them and lay out the story. A little audition, right? Marvin plays the piano in the Shubert hallway and the leg keeps falling off, but they like it. Also, by the way, the plan was then to feel out the Nederlanders. By then Joe knew what I'd been doing, knew we were ready to walk, and he said, 'Okay, you play the Newman.' "

As the process went on, Michael Bennett drove himself as hard as he drove anyone. He was popping pills, his own prescription of Valium and Quaaludes—Valium whenever he felt the need to calm down, sound rational and project an image of the stability he didn't feel, Quaaludes to coast him on the high side of his energy. At night, in the dark cave of his apartment on West Fifty-fifth, marijuana hazed him into sleep, roaches accumulating like squashed bugs next to the stubbed Marlboros in black crystal ashtrays. When he was alone, he would coddle an Abyssinian cat named Claire which wandered the terrace and lived part-time with its real owner, Bennett's neighbor Marvin Schulman. (Schulman, who became his friend, confidant and business manager—"close as brothers"—would later sue Bennett's estate shortly after the $14 million sale of the building at Eight Ninety

Broadway, initiating the suit as Bennett was shriveling in death in Tucson.)

Bennett: "I started smoking cigarettes in high school because you couldn't be cool unless you smoked, and besides, my father warned me it was a bad habit. Which right away made it a lot cooler. I've tried quitting. Marijuana's a lot better for you than drinking, and it really relaxes me before I go to bed. Valiums I take during the day. I don't do anything but smoking I'm not proud of."

Nights when the combination of pills failed to bring him serenity, he would make phone calls to the people he had spent the day working with, calls as late as four in the morning and always having to do with the show. Days when he drilled his company through the *Chorus Line* countdown he would appear as rested and energetic as though he had unwound the night before reading Robert Ludlum or Jacqueline Susann. It was after *A Chorus Line* that his "recreational use" of cocaine became an addiction. Then when he showed up for work in the morning or the afternoon there was a viscous glaze in his eyes, a liquefied and penetrating scowl in his look that told the story. Some people deny they ever saw it ("He wouldn't be able to work that way"). Some people discount it ("Everybody was then into social drugs"). Some people feared the worst ("Police are going to bust into Eight Ninety and find him and Bobby dead across the desk, maybe bodies strewn over the carpet, his dog Kila too").

CHAPTER TEN

Metaphors and
Dancing Ghosts

(1975 . . .)

Although Michael Bennett said he "loved" dancers (even as self-image), they sometimes drove him crazy. They had such small minds. There were exceptions, but most of them weren't very smart. Dancers rarely thought about cause and effect. Like the lift into the leap wasn't that important. The leap itself was everything, as though they didn't even think about coming down. None of them knew or even seemed to sense that dancing was a metaphor. For him metaphor was becoming more and more important. What worried him most about *A Chorus Line* was the metaphor. Would people get it? The whole thing wouldn't matter if it was perceived only as a show about gypsies. After months and months of work, was it all "too in, too special"? Marvin kept saying it had to be "empathetic to everyone," and he was right. And then Marvin and Ed had written "At the Ballet," and it was so real and so beautiful it touched him deeply. Even though ballet really wasn't a part of him, the song filled his head with Betty Rogers, Beverly Fletcher, even old Mrs. Dunn, all those dancing ghosts he'd thought he'd forgotten—but, again, the focus was on dancing.

A whole show about an audition?

Seventeen gypsies narrowed down to eight in a chorus line?

And all of them whining, "God, I need this job"?

What if it fucking turned into a metaphor for Marvin's song "Nothing"? Sometimes the only thing he was really sure about was the title, *A Chorus Line*. Not *The Chorus Line*, as someone had suggested. Not even simply *Chorus Line*, although it was likely to be called that. He saw the "*A*" as all-important because it meant the show would head the ABC listing on the *Times*'s theater page—unless someone were to develop *Aardvark Capades* or something like that. He even worried that might happen.

He and Bobby were becoming zombies.

No one was getting any money for all the hard labor, and it was possible that back-to-back four-week (or even six-week) workshops weren't going to be enough. Marvin with three Oscars at a hundred dollars a week? Theoni with an Oscar for *The Way We Were*? Robin, Tharon, with all their credentials?

If the show bombed at the Newman, what would happen next?

There were nagging questions haunting him when he thought about *Chorus Line* flopping: Would Bobby really go back to school, be a schoolteacher?

Where would he be without Bobby? (That question automatically linked to another: Where would we be without Bobby? Wasn't that a Steve lyric from *Company*?)

Why did his thoughts and his musicals circle and recircle show business? Why, he asked himself, why? Because that was his life!

In the taxi slamming him down Fifth Avenue to Lafayette Street, he took a Valium. There was something he had to solve today. If he had to terrify everybody, he'd solve it. He'd worked it out in his head when he couldn't fall asleep, Claire purring in his face. He hadn't even told Bobby.

Near the end of *A Chorus Line*, after Cassie has made her plea to be part of the ensemble, Zach drills the dancers in a routine. It's the penultimate moment before the seventeen aspirants learn their fate. Paul, who has made his wrenching confession and has been comforted by Zach, starts to dance and falls on a turn. An old knee injury has been struck. He lies on the floor in agony. The accident occasions desperation and soul-searching among the rest of the dancers. The moment Paul has reached for throughout his shadowed career, the moment that will give him the respect and credibility his drag queen days have denied him, is about to be lost. The possibility of losing perhaps the only chance you'll have to prove yourself raises the question: What do you do when you can't dance any longer? The fear in that is the fear of the future, everyone's future. The question is stoically passed off by Diana (Priscilla Lopez), who says, "Listen, who knows anything? It's just something you're gonna have to wait and see."

She then sings, "Kiss today goodbye . . . and point me toward tomorrow."

Michael Bennett knew the scene had to have unwavering reality if it was to extend the metaphor. It would have to be played for real, no Shakespearean wounding on the dance floor for him. No writhing. No acting. Reality. Real pain. Which was pretty hard to explain to the cast. It couldn't just be talked out, because then the cause and effect would come out like acting. There had to be immediate impact, then pain.

"I kept wondering how I could get them to a place like this, get them to the truth. It wouldn't be honest—wouldn't come off honest—if I just blocked it out. I couldn't just say, 'Sammy, fall, then Scott, Clive, Donna, Priscilla, run to him, and you others, run away in shock.' I knew that wouldn't work. I also knew it would take me forever. So I worked out in my head, What I'm going to do is: this afternoon, when they're least expecting it, I'm going to take a dive."

Instructing Jeff Hamlin, the production stage manager, to block the doors, and Bob Avian to be ready to rush to the phone, Bennett pretended that he wanted to show the dancers a particular step in the routine leading up to Paul's fall. Mingling among them as Paul, he crossed the white line taped to the floor while Zach (Robert LuPone) signaled the downbeat. He began dancing full out in front to the mirror, his concentration fixed, his movements controlled. The number spiraled around his energy, the presence of the wunderkind taskmaster informing the dancers beside him.

Suddenly Michael Bennett fell to the floor, grabbing his knee, screaming screaming screaming. Doubled up, clutching his knee, he writhed and screamed just off the white tape line. The older dancers rushed to him, knelt down beside him; the younger ones fell back in fear. He kept screaming. When he moved, trying to flex his knee, someone said, "Don't." There was crying now all around him, and someone began screaming with him. As Bob Avian ran to the phone supposedly to call a doctor, Bennett screamed and wrenched through this agony for five minutes.

Then, like harsh sun glaring after thunder, he stood up quickly, wrathful, and said, "Does everybody remember what they just did? Well, *that's* what I want. Exactly *that!*"

Emotions suddenly battered, the dancers became furious. The stage was pandemonium.

Baayork Lee started shrieking at him, then crying. Angrily he said to her, "You remember what you just did?" She wept uncontrollably, unable to answer. Terror was about to be upstaged by tantrum.

"Do you remember?" Bennett shouted.

Baayork Lee said she did, then screamed at him, "How could you do this to us?"

"*Just do it!* Got it? *Just . . . do . . . it,*" Michael Bennett said.

Avian: "He'd always do stuff like that. He'd do anything—anything!—to get what he wanted. The scene was there after that, and when he had Sammy do it they all remembered. He'd buzzed Sense Memory/Acting 101 in all of 'em. And the amazing thing was that he could fool them over and over like that."

The New York Shakespeare Festival Public Theater announced a schedule of six productions and six guest residency programs to begin the first week of October 1974. Last on the list and set to open six months later, after plays by John Ford Noonan, Ronald Tavel, David Rabe, Thomas Babe and Michael Weller, was *A Chorus Line*, which was defined as a "Musical conceived by Michael Bennett; book by James Kirkwood and Nicholas Dante; music by Marvin Hamlisch; lyrics by Edward Kleban." The opening on Wednesday evening, May 21, at the Festival's Newman Theater, was to be preceded by forty-one previews beginning April 15.

Hamlisch: "You have to understand everybody was highly nervous about the opening. So what else is new? We'd all worked and worked. And there still seemed to be some problems. Ed and Marvin's problem was 'Tits and Ass.'

"I'm a good person to know what gets laughs. We're in our first preview, and the song falls on its ass. Totally flat. Over and out. Dead. Zarooommm! Same thing second preview. By third, Michael calls a meeting: 'Okay, guys, if it doesn't get laughs soon you're gonna have to write another song.' I said, 'Michael, there's no other funny song possible for that scene.'

"By the fourth preview, Ed and Marvin think they've done something wrong. I just can't figure it out, then I think: Wait a minute here. Ed and I always came into the theater from backstage. Why not do it the normal way? Walk down the aisle like the audience, get a program. Maybe we're missing something the audience is getting.

"So we do that, walk in from the front, pick up a program, which was then just a mimeoed sheet. We look at the songs, and there's 'Tits and Ass.' Suddenly I knew. There's the mistake, the title. We were giving away the punch line! Next day we changed the title, 'Dance: 10, Looks: 3.' The problem was solved. Everything was fine.

"You have to understand in other areas we were still nervous. Michael and I sat around before we opened at the Newman. For him this was his graduation to being the director/choreographer, all on his own, his own man. This was his baby, his big moment. On the other hand, I think he felt paternal. Like a mother hen, he had brought with him all these people, me, Kleban, Kirkwood, Donna, like he was checking in with everybody.

"I said, 'What happens if it's the biggest bomb ever?' He said,

'Do you think you did your best work?' 'Yes.' 'You think you wasted time?' 'No.' He said, 'That's all anyone can do, Marvin.' "

Yet even through the previews, Bennett had continued to worry about *A Chorus Line*'s message. A show had to offer an audience hope. He was certain the lack of hope in *Follies* defeated it. When Neil Simon and his wife, Marsha Mason, talked to him after the second *Chorus Line* preview at the Newman, Marsha Mason hit upon the problem. In this early version of the show, Cassie's plea for Zach to hire her for the chorus had been brusquely rejected. While admitting Cassie's rejection was "real life," Mason made a plea of her own to Bennett, saying, "She's gotta get the job, she's gotta make a step, you gotta feel hope she and Zach will work it out, otherwise it's a downer." Neil Simon agreed. Bennett argued that giving Cassie the job would be "a lie, not the truth, not the way of the show-biz world, which is bitchy and petty and, as we all know, by the way, cutthroat." Then the old bleakness of *Follies* blew in like a cold wind through his thoughts. Could he risk everything for rigid adherence to reality and truth? A deep cathexis was working within him, the idea of hope. By the third preview Cassie got the job.

While uptown there were plenty of seasonal troubles, the downtown word spread fast. Big musicals were folding. Two had closed on the road, *I Got a Song*, in Buffalo, and *Miss Moffat*, with Bette Davis, in Philadelphia. Jerry Herman's *Mack & Mabel* had opened in October and closed in November. *Man on the Moon*, a musical with a character prophetically named Dr. Bomb, ran five performances. *Sgt. Pepper's Lonely Hearts Club Band on the Road*, adapted from the Beatles album, thrummed for less than two months. *The Lieutenant*, a rock opera about My Lai, lasted a week. *Doctor Jazz* ran five performances; *The Rocky Horror Show* thirty-two. *Goodtime Charley*, a musical with Joel Grey, was gasping. *Shenandoah* and *The Wiz* were the 1974–75 season's only real hits.

Off-Broadway the musical situation wasn't much better.

But there was this "show about dancers" being performed in a black box with mirrors at the Newman Theater. The canyonlike, slightly derelict streets around Astor Place and Cooper Union were suddenly lined with limousines. Broadway and Hollywood celebrities and moguls were mingling with Papp's 7,217 regular subscribers, some waiting in line for tickets. Among them: Al Pacino, Angela Lansbury, Burt Lancaster, Lauren Bacall, Gower Champion, Tony Perkins, Barry Diller, Adolph Green, Dom DeLuise, Gerald Schoenfeld, Kermit Bloomgarden, Cyril Ritchard, Dore Schary, Edward Albee, Raquel Welch, Elia Kazan, Sam Cohn, Joseph Kipness, Juliet Prowse, Mary Martin, Kurt Vonnegut, Bobby Short, Kirk Douglas, Lucille Ball, Edward Villella and Groucho Marx.

Avian: "It was amazing. Diana Ross sat on the steps in the theater. I remember she was pregnant, and there were no seats. Everybody was down there. Katharine Hepburn, Joshua Logan, Henry Fonda, Richard Rodgers, Jacqueline Onassis, Baryshnikov; limos coming and going. The first day the word was out the box office went SRO. The same thing happened when we moved uptown. And we were nervous about the move, despite everything. How was it going to work in a bigger house? It was very different when you knew the actors could see Zach at the back of the Newman, but what was going to happen when—all of a sudden—he's farther away in a bigger theater?

"The first uptown run-through we had for an invited audience at the Shubert was very bumpy. But the opening night went great, we didn't lose any emotion.

"And then there we were eight years later playing hockey rinks before six thousand people! I went to see the show at the Fox in Atlanta. It's like Radio City Music Hall; holds four thousand, and it was standing room only. From the back of the theater you couldn't see the actors. I only knew who the characters were by the colors they were wearing."

Even Off-Broadway, however, the show's success didn't suit everybody. "The funniest remark made in 1975," Michael Bennett said, "came from Steve Sondheim, who saw *Chorus Line* and said, 'How can you care about *those people?*'" Harold Prince was equally contemptuous. "They were both real shitty," Avian says. Prince has now changed his opinion, although the show he first saw was close enough to its final refinement as to be almost interchangeable.

"*Chorus Line* is a major work," Prince says.

"Major," he repeats, the repetition a forced gift, generosity fueled by envy and driven by guilt. "But, again, Michael got trapped in its metaphor. Show business as the microcosm. And he was trapped by a combination of success and competitiveness. I don't think the money had much effect on him. He had an acute sense about money, acute and funny. He once said to me, 'Do you know how much money I made this week?' I think it was $70,000. I said, 'Gee! Wow! Gee!' Then he said, 'And how much did you make?' And, y'know, fine, I think that's all fun. But I don't think he was trapped by money because I don't think he got much fun out of it."

According to Prince, Michael Bennett restricted his life to theater, and that was "the real trap." With the exception of *Company*, all the shows were "almost exclusively about show biz, which means . . . you don't have to research the Jewish *shtetl*, the German cabaret in the 1930s, Sweeney Todd in London in the nineteenth century, women in Ibsen's day." Pondering his own importance, Prince adds, "What I meant when I gave Michael the dictionary was: Here's a book, explore it. He had a very inquisitive mind but—my guess is—not a very long attention span."

When *A Chorus Line* began performances at the Shubert on July 2, 1975, the longest-running musical on Broadway was *Fiddler on the Roof*, which had opened at the Imperial September 22, 1963, and run 3,242 consecutive performances. The next two longest runs were plays, *Life with Father* and *Tobacco Road*; then three musicals, *Hello, Dolly!, My Fair Lady, Man of La Mancha* and—spaced by *Abie's Irish Rose*—*Oklahoma!* and *South Pacific*. Spaced by *Harvey*, next came *Grease*, at 1,763 performances.

Fifteen hundred performances—a three-and-a-half-year run— was considered phenomenal. Anything reaching beyond 2,000 was super-phenomenal. No one associated with *A Chorus Line* had any idea that words like "innovative," "original," "breathtaking," "break-through" and "beacon" would wrap themselves into the simple term "classic." No one had any idea that *A Chorus Line* would become a moneymaking machine speeding by every other show on Broadway (except *Cats**)—no one, not even Bernard Jacobs and Gerald Schoenfeld in their wildest maven zeal.

Jacobs and Schoenfeld are formally known as the Shubert Organization, and familiarly as the Shuberts, although with no blood ties to the real Shubert brothers, Sam, Lee and J. J. Shubert. Sam died early, 1905, at twenty-nine; Lee and J. J. in the 1960s. The real Shuberts were outwardly nasty and vindictive in protecting their empire. The new Shuberts are friendly, tough, capricious. Inwardly they have the same goals as their imperious namesakes: real estate management and the control of Broadway. They own and operate sixteen theaters in New York (with a half interest in a seventeenth) and own or lease five more across the country.

When Bernard Jacobs met Michael Bennett, he realized that the Italian-Jewish kid standing in front of him, slightly below his eye level, wanted to control Broadway in another way. A lawyer and business-man, Jacobs was in awe of creative talent, although not always. Sometimes he knew the range of the talent; sometimes not. In Bennett, he sensed a no-nonsense kind of artistry, and his awe became a volatile mixture of idolatry and rivalry. In a shifting shadow play of identity, Jacobs perhaps saw himself as both Michael Bennett's father and what he himself might have become had he had Michael Bennett's gifts, his artistic genius of will. Jacobs has two children, a son and a daughter. In his eagerness to claim a third, they were seemingly swept aside. In Michael Bennett he found a worthy surrogate for his son, who, through Shubert influence, is a show-business merchant. As one observer has it, Jacobs' son "sells T-shirts for *Cats* and *Les Miz*, all the touristy

---

*As of 1989, *Cats*, Andrew Lloyd Webber's dance musical set to poems by T. S. Eliot, had earned $44 million, approximately $10 million more than *A Chorus Line*.

souvenir crap." (Crap it is, but it accounts for considerable revenue, specifically when a show is a long run.)

Mrs. DiFiglia identifies "Bernie Jacobs as the father Michael never had. Michael treated him that way, and he treated Michael like a son."

Avian refers to the "symbiosis" between Bennett and Jacobs: "It was an intense relationship, they fed into each other's needs. Bernie loved Michael deeply but it was a manipulative kind of love."

Sabine Cassel says that Bennett was always trying to prove himself to his real family but that once he had, the proof was often slighted by his father. The proof of his accomplishment meant far more when offered to Bernard Jacobs.

Even those less intimately involved were aware of the father/son pattern. Some thought it was contentious and sick. Some saw Jacobs as the villain, Bennett as the victim.

According to one observer: "Bernie had this shrine in his house at Shelter Island—I don't know if he still has it—a room with nothing but Michael pictures, Michael awards, Michael memorabilia. No photographs of his own kids, whom he almost never mentions. It might have been just, you know, 'admiration' for Michael. But it was all pretty peculiar."

One of the things Bernard Jacobs admired most about Michael Bennett was his seemingly unrivaled ability to design a product that would sell Shubert seats, his ability to make money and, year after year, lots of it. When *A Chorus Line* first opened at the Shubert the top ticket price in the orchestra was $15, with balcony seats going for $8.00 and $6.00. The orchestra now commands $50 a seat, the balcony $40. The show's highest gross for a single week was $395,627 for the eight performances ending December 30, 1984.

Downtown at the Public, with everyone working above scale, *A Chorus Line* cost $549,526 to produce. The move uptown cost $595,921. The total for the entire project thus came to slightly over $1 million. As of 1988, *A Chorus Line*'s gross earnings were $260,422,157. Profits earned by the New York Shakespeare Festival, the show's sole producer, have totaled $30,698,134. At one point *Variety* tabulated Michael

Bennett's weekly take as $90,000, a disclosure which angered him while simultaneously appalling the show's original cast members, none of whom could temper his or her shock with the comfort of stardom. The only star to emerge from *A Chorus Line* was Michael Bennett. The rest—with the occasionally flitting exception of Donna McKechnie—have been trapped in the chorus, frozen figures circling an endless strut beneath the pendulum of an endless clock.

Now in its fifteenth year, *A Chorus Line* has employed approximately 475 actors during its Broadway run and on varied tours. There have been national and international companies, with a string of return engagements. There was a movie version deliberately delayed so as not to interfere with the show's "live popularity." A Broadway company has continued at the Shubert long after the movie's release and critical dismissal. There was an extravaganza on September 29, 1983, when *A Chorus Line* hit 3,389 performances at the Shubert and surpassed the run of *Grease*, which, by this time, had surpassed *Fiddler on the Roof*. Michael Bennett crammed the stage with 332 members of as many *Chorus Line* companies as he could find, with nineteen additional performers chosen at random from various stock and amateur productions. On August 10, 1987, two days after reaching its 5,000th performance, there was another celebration, this one saddened by Michael Bennett's death forty days earlier. Mournful as the evening was, it ended in a name-calling brawl between James Kirkwood and Joseph Papp that made the newspapers. *A Chorus Line*, the musical about love and understanding, made rivals out of collaborators, enemies out of friends.

Liz Smith: "Michael was hurt by a lot of the stuff Hal and Steve said about *Chorus Line*. They were very snide at first—snide doesn't even do it! They were just plain fuckin' awful! Jealous. Envious, Spiteful.

"Hal and Steve are these hopelessly elitist Anglophile guys, and they love to shut people out. They shut Michael out. When Steve sang and was overcome at Michael's memorial service, that was nothing but pure, unadulterated *guilt*! I thought Hal and Steve were terrible to him. Michael came along as this tough little kid who was a gypsy, then all of a sudden he's this force to be reckoned with. A lot of people on Broadway had a real hard time with that."

Bennett: "After *Chorus Line* I was put in a bizarre situation. It was a huge smash, what Bobby and I always dreamed of, our own *Hello, Dolly!*, a real hit. And then I became known as 'Michael the *Chorus Line* Millionaire Bennett.' Day in, day out, Liz Smith, Earl Wilson, Jack O'Brian wrote about me. Everyone kept talking about how rich I was. *Variety* had me earning $90,000 a week. I became the symbol of someone who got rich off everyone else's life. I ruthlessly put the lives of all those chorus kids on the stage, and I was vicious, driven, pitiless, uncaring. No one ever said, by the way, that my life was up there on the stage too, and just as complicated and as unflattering as some of the others. That was all conveniently forgotten.

"The truth is, I gave a half percent of the show's profits to the *Chorus Line* kids, something I didn't have to do. And that half percent is like a royalty for them, for the twenty-six original members of the company.* They'll go on getting it as long as there are first-class companies performing. It doesn't amount to a fortune, but it's like $5,000 a month divided among them all. It's my own way of paying them back for the rap sessions we had, all the preparatory stuff that went into the show.

"And what happens? All I hear is how manipulative I was! What a monster!

"The $90,000 *Variety* figure seemed to turn people against me, make me unclean in some way I haven't figured out yet, as though I were a thief or something. The $90,000 really amounts to something like $12,000 a week. That's not bad. I'm not complaining. But the point is: it's not $90,000.

---

*Actually, the half percent comes to a full percentage point. In addition to .05 percentage from Bennett's royalties on the weekly box office take, the original cast members receive an additional .05 from subsidiary rights.

"*Variety* didn't say I was $300,000 in debt before *Chorus Line* opened. I had people forced to work in hallways because we didn't have money for space. I'd put money into *Seesaw* so Joe Kipness wouldn't close it, and I never got royalties back. If someone had pointed out to me that I'd have to earn something like one and a half million to pay back the $300,000, I probably would never have done *Chorus Line*, never have taken the risk. I'd have done TV spectaculars instead."

Yet the image of Bennett's wealth and power increased, an image he tried to counteract by continuing to dress like a gypsy who was hurrying off to an audition in a darkened theater whereas his real destination was a meeting among moguls in rooms shining with money. He would drink at the upstairs bar in Sardi's rather than the first-floor bar just off the street in an effort to publicly distance himself from the celebrity tone of the latter. He pretended to scoff at his fame as though he recognized celebrity, in Shakespeare's words, as "the bubble reputation." Upstairs at Sardi's, he'd sip straight-up vodka and stare at the customers from under the visor of his red baseball cap. Playing the gypsy sometimes neutralized the envy and resentment he sensed from some of his colleagues. At Ted Hook's Backstage and Joe Allen's he'd play the same role, only here he was more apt to find himself among tap-dancing hoofers who knew the pretense for what it was, patronization, a kind of "I'm just like you guys" pandering.

Some of his friends were fooled, others weren't. Thommie Walsh, *A Chorus Line*'s original Bobby, who provoked some of the original cast members into writing a book about their experiences with the show, says, "After all the sweat we all felt a little cheated and it was pretty hard watching Michael and Bob Avian in a white Rolls-Royce riding through Times Square, then hearing how generous Michael'd been." Walsh refers to the profits Bennett turned back to the cast as "that fabled half percent," then says, "The tops that came out of it— for any of us—was about $9,000, which figures out to something like one twenty-seventh of a hundred percent."

In another attempt to minimize the outer trappings of his importance, Bennett took a second look at his white Rolls-Royce and saw it for what it was, "a little showy." He wondered what he could do about it. "I liked the image of a white Rolls," he said, "then I had it painted brown." The duller color would perhaps make it less noticeable. He also began telling a story about the day the Rolls broke down in Times Square.* He and Bob Avian sat in the back seat while the chauffeur checked "under the bonnet, you know, the hood." Then with the chauffeur pushing from the driver's side, his hand guiding the wheel, Bennett and Avian, their shoulders against the brown trunk, cushioned the Rolls against the curb. "So much for image," Bennett said.

To some any attempt by Bennett to humanize himself, to undercut the glamour was just another act of manipulation.

Kirkwood: "He was a master of manipulation, and Jesus Christ, sometimes it was so humiliating and damned sick.

"I had a hard time dealing with him after *Chorus Line*. I felt betrayed by him. And I had a hard time understanding how the best working relationship in my life had turned into such a cesspool. It was as though I'd been dismissed, and I was very angry, hurt.

"We were supposed to work together again. I brought him the script of a murder musical, *Murder at the Vanities*, which he said he loved and wanted to do. These two guys, new to the business, Don Oliver and David Spencer, had come to me with the idea. We did a first draft, went to Michael and in effect auditioned for him at Eight Ninety with eight singers and me telling the story. He called and had me come into the office a couple of days later, and said he wanted to option it for the spring. This was in December; it made the guys' Christmas.

"Then, over some phone calls, I began to hear the demands, and they were *outrageous*! The percentages were just awful! And the whole thing was very insulting to me. We had brought the show to him— this wasn't Michael's concept—yet the contract specified that anytime he wanted he could be named co-author. I mean, even if I were willing

---

*Robert Avian states that the Rolls-Royce broke down in a Central Park tunnel and that the car was pushed to West 57th street.

to accept the percentages—CO-AUTHOR??? Don and David didn't want to lose the deal, but the whole outline was just outrageous, even down to legal entanglements in case he decided to drop the show altogether.

"I told him we thought it was terrible, unacceptable. He said, 'Ya, well that's what I want and I'm producing it and it's my money and I'm Michael Bennett.'

"So we decided, no concessions, and it just dribbled off. Actually, at one point, I think he said Bob didn't like the score, and I said, 'But you did,' and he said, 'I know.' It was as though he was a spoiled kid saying, 'I won't let you set the terms and I don't want to do it anyhow.'

"By then the dew was off the rose, and I didn't see him very much. And then I ran into him at a supper party after the theater, I think at Frank and Barbara Perry's. Frank did *David and Lisa* and that Joan Didion movie, *Play It As It Lays*. He's now married to Barbara Goldsmith. I was there with my analyst, Mildred Newman, and she certainly knew my feelings about Michael. A group of us were sitting in the den and Michael came in. This was one of the times he was arguing with Bernie Jacobs, and they were sniping at each other in another room. I remember Michael said to him, 'I'll keep *Chorus Line* running when you're dead and buried!' Bernie walked out, and people were looking at Michael like that!

"He came into the den, and there was still this tension. Michael was very high. I think he was on something. He sat down next to me, put his arm around me and said, 'Now, a lot of people think I'm this, think I'm that, but Jimmy knows what a good friend I am, don't you?'

"I said, 'Not exactly, Michael.'

" 'Yes you do, come on!'

"Then he said, 'People keep saying terrible things about Donna and me, and that's all wrong, isn't it, Jimmy? I've always been a wonderful lover.' This was in front of a lot of people, some he didn't even know. He turned to me. 'Tell them what a good lover I am, Jimmy. Tell them. I'm a marvelous lover, aren't I, Jimmy?'

"And he kept it up. Mildred was aghast. I never went to bed with Michael.

"He said, 'I've never had an affair with anybody who didn't end up loving me.'

"I said, 'I don't think that's exactly true.'

"He was so self-important by this point, so sucked into his own sense of power, he came to the party that night to bury the Shuberts and everyone else . . ."

Diane Judge, Bennett's favorite press agent, says, "Michael was all about sex and show biz. He never thought about anything else. Love never entered the picture. He was really like this machine you couldn't get close to because he was working, almost as though he had a sign up: YOU CANNOT COME IN HERE.

"Once in a while Liz Smith and I would have dinner with him and Bob. We'd gossip, tell stories, and Michael would become human—human in his need to talk and share. The housekeeper, Claudine, would serve dinner, but by then we'd all be pissed. We'd let down our hair, tell everything. It was very cathartic. Michael would confess and tell fabulous things where he made mistakes. Nothing would ever leave the room because we were all too drunk for anything to leave the room. But what I remember about those evenings is feeling that, no matter what, Michael *was* a human being and wonderful."

CHAPTER ELEVEN

Living the Script

(1975–1977)

Bernard and Betty Jacobs sit in the red leather and deeply lacquered chinoiserie splendor of the Shubert offices above Shubert Alley, he in a high-backed wing chair, she facing him from a plush sofa in this conference/living room. Two floors below them the computer-run Artkraft/Strauss marquee soundlessly corners Michael Bennett's name across the Forty-fourth Street side of the building. The marquee has been in operation ever since *A Chorus Line* opened fifteen years ago, on July 25, 1975.

"Michael was always living a script," Bernard Jacobs says, "he was never living a real life. Michael did *Chorus Line*, and it was natural that the director should marry the star of the show. So he married Donna, not because he loved Donna; he married Donna because it was the normal thing to do."

Mrs. Jacobs: "It was the right thing to do, it followed the script."

Jacobs: "We were driving him home one night. At that point I was kind of naïve in my relationship with the gay community. I made some comment which, in retrospect, was kind of stupid. I said, 'Why don't you straighten out and marry Donna?' "

Mrs. Jacobs giggles.

Jacobs: "Not realizing at the time how absurd the whole thing was, 'cause it wasn't in Michael's nature to straighten out. No matter which way Michael went it wouldn't be straight. I don't know . . . subsequently he blamed me for marrying Donna—"

Mrs. Jacobs: "Not really—"

Jacobs: "Michael would always remember anything you said. Throw it up to you, usually in a three, four, five o'clock in the morning phone call."

Mrs. Jacobs: "They were very much alike in many ways, those two, Mr. Bennett and Mr. Jacobs."

Jacobs: "Well that's what she says."

Mrs. Jacobs laughs.

After 101 performances at the Newman Theater, the show opened on Broadway in July and it was a pearl. Delayed by the musicians' strike, the press opening wasn't until October 19. When the reviews appeared, they were unanimous. The critics were moved as much as the general audiences. It was a perfect bare-bones musical, an astute summation of all that was show business yet offering an easy, identifiable exchange with other professions, other endeavors. As Michael Bennett said, it was about "everybody who ever stood on a line anywhere, anytime, for whatever reason." It was about striving and rejection, success and failure. It touched people. It explained complex relationships in direct, everyday terms. Its psychological histories were steadily revealing, and universal. Its small anecdotal stories of growing up and being confused by parents who sometimes cared too much, and sometimes cared not at all, were real and poignant. It suggested that early experiences of ambivalent affection offered a kind of brutal education and little protection for life's later ambiguities, which, more and more, seemed a wide open embrace followed by a knock on the head. Its in-focus/off-focus homosexuality had something profound to say about human identity and courage in meeting hostility and prejudice. Although there were some complaints about vulgarity, specifically the "Tits and Ass" lyrics and Bennett's own dissatisfaction with a number called "Sing," which he felt was never right, the show reached across class and discrimination and seemed to beguile just about everybody.

Avian: "So suddenly there's all this money, and I'm not worried about a stove anymore or going back to school or anything. The gamble's paid off. Michael was never about money, really. And now *Chorus Line* is off and running, and the phone never stops ringing. He becomes the Millionaire Director, and hates it, and the reason he hates it is that people can't seem to see beyond the numbers. Every dancer out of work reads that Michael's making a lot of money, and the calls start coming, people asking for loans, down payments on houses, down payments on old debts, and Michael could never say no. I think he gave out something like $300,000—I'm not sure exactly how much but *a lot!* The estate is still handling that stuff. He helped an awful lot of people.

"There was a point that second and third year he was almost making $90,000 a week with the national company, all those road companies, and business SRO in New York. He made about $80,000 a week, but that was cut, like, 10 percent to an agent, 5 percent to a manager, 50 percent to taxes, so he'd really come down to, maybe, $30,000 a week. Then he'd sink it right back into the business."

Whatever praise *A Chorus Line* had earned downtown now ricocheted above the squeal of Times Square. It was certainly the show of the season. It revived everyone's spirits, particularly those involved in the business, particularly the moneymen. It reclaimed Broadway. The American musical wasn't moribund after all. It might stumble and fall from time to time, but it could be rejuvenated.

And how could you fault someone who could rejuvenate it with an inexpensive, nonstar cast, with virtually no scenery, scant props, very little spent on costumes? It had cost only $46,000 *more* to move the package uptown than it had cost to wrap it! You had to welcome someone as savvy *businesswise* as he was *show-bizzy*. Had to hand it to him. The little kid peering out from under the red baseball cap was a homegrown maven, a little flaky maybe, a *faigeleh* sure, so who's looking? Theater's full of them. Besides, there were stories around about women. Women loved him. Wives loved him. Daughters, sisters, mothers, grannies, aunts. Some kind of mysterious chemistry, with those little black pencil holes all over his face, those milk-muddy eyes, thin wiry hair, bat wing mustache, scraggly beard. Times he didn't seem to be one thing or the other, but he sure as hell had an impact on people.

The impact steadily gained force as Michael Bennett and the box office hummed.

As he became more and more powerful, he became more and more tense, attempting to cover his more than occasional inattentive lapses by humming to himself. He would make a rapid point in conversation and then, while seeming to wait for the point to be absorbed, or simply losing his own concentration, he would hum, sometimes a nameless melody, sometimes "Me and My Shadow," sometimes "One" or a strain from *Ballroom* or *Dreamgirls* or whatever he happened to be working on. The humming became as reactive as his increasing perplexity about where he found himself in his career, the King of Broadway yet still forced to deal with uncrowned heads ruling dominions of greater power with greater wealth. He would plot his way into areas where supposedly he had no expertise. Tap-shoe baby, chorus boy, choreographer, director, producer, there didn't have to be limits either to his vision or to what he could achieve.

Where next? Hollywood and a deal to make a movie before making the *Chorus Line* movie?

What about superseding the musical with the circus? A circus performed as a musical by five hundred or a thousand kids in ice arenas or in a space like Madison Square Garden? Before developing "the circus idea," he had contemplated becoming the Czar of Broadway choreography, as Balanchine—and now Jerry Robbins—were in terms of ballet. According to Tommy Tune, it wasn't just an idle notion.

"Way before *Chorus Line* I remember him sayin', 'I'm going to get an office high to the sky and we're going to control all the choreography on Broadway, and if they want choreography they're going to have to come to us to get it,' " Tune says. "That's a Mafia mentality applied to the theater, and I thought to myself: This is a young man talkin' here and, *wow*, this is pretty amazing! He's gonna control all the choreography in the world! I mean, I was *amazed*!

"I went to Buffalo with him once and it was all a language I didn't understand. And I don't mean Italian. He became . . . like Mickey DiFiglia rather than Michael Bennett. And with his father, it was Dad and Mickey, a tinge of that. I think that's what the Shubert appeal was. He wanted to become the godfather over them all but in the meantime he would settle for the godson-in-law . . . until it was his time.

"Adulthood never would have become Michael. He was trying so hard to become the businessman, and all he did was get mean. His whole life was really about playing and dancing and the mirror."

Night after night on Broadway, Donna McKechnie was spinning inside a costume made from Bennett's favorite color, red, spinning in front of the *Chorus Line* mirror, blurring her own image in the dance patterns he had devised. Night after night as Bennett watched her, his feeling of pride in McKechnie's accomplishment turned sentimental. He saw her as his own creation, the female extension of his scrambled sexuality. She had first become his friend, then something like a sister. Why not now his lover and his wife? McKechnie suggests she was also part of his inspiration.

"I gave Michael an Art Deco figure, a Lalique dancer lifting her skirts. Lovely crystal. He was living on West Fifty-fifth Street, that dark weird apartment with all the mirrors, and he put it in a corner, in front of a mirror, and cast a spotlight on it. The statue gave him the germ of the idea for Cassie and 'The Music and the Mirror' number. Those little things are so wonderful, where ideas came from."

Avian remembers the crystal dancer in the apartment, "underlit in a mirrored corner," but adds that Bennett never mentioned it to him as "an inspiration in any way, although it might have been." Avian is clear about one specific inspiration. The success of *A Chorus*

Line—with its attendant recognition of Bennett as a "name director" and McKechnie as a "star"—inspired "the fantasy of their marriage."

In Room 210 of the Bureau des Mariages in Paris, on December 4, 1976, Michael Bennett married Donna McKechnie, their witnesses being Jean-Pierre Cassel and his wife, Sabine. The Cassels hosted a wedding reception at their home in Montmartre. Best man Jean-Pierre Cassel, who had played Zach in the London production of *A Chorus Line*, had become Michael Bennett's newest best friend. Bennett adored the Cassels, including their two sons, Mathias, then nine, Vincente, six. They were his "European family" within the family of the theater. Donna McKechnie was charmed by Sabine Cassel; Sabine Cassel was skeptical about Donna McKechnie.

In her flawed English, Sabine Cassel explains that she first met Michael Bennett in 1972 at a party for *Company* in London. According to her, on the night before his wedding, Bennett told her he loved her. "He told me he was getting married to Donna because I was already married; I try avoid what he is saying, not think about it, because then I'm really in trouble."

Within three months of married life the blissful Prince and Princess of the Great White Way were emotionally bruised and battered, as Michael Bennett said, by trying "to live up to the image." Within three months, they were thinking divorce.

Describing Bennett as a "complicated sensual man," Betty Jacobs says, "There are a lot of stories from people who were bitter about Michael because he was tough. When he decided that was the end of somebody, that was the end. I think with Donna it truly was a fantasy. I think they lived together before *Chorus Line*. I remember they called from San Francisco. 'Marriage is wonderful, sex is terrific.' What they had to tell us that on the telephone for, I don't know! It lasted about six months, long enough for Michael to play out that script. They went around in a white Rolls-Royce, and they were acting. It was great! A fairy tale. Except it wasn't."

Whatever was happening behind closed doors in their marriage, before becoming husband and wife Bennett and McKechnie were the *Chorus Line* celebrities, he the kid from Buffalo whose name was soon to be above the title, she the chorine from Detroit on the cover of *Newsweek*. They had both crossed the line. If her "stardom"—which he pushed with his newfound power—would eventually seem questionable, his was always a certainty and would soar. Although their life was tied to dance bags, leotards and sweats, they dressed up to lead the parade, he in expensive *Gentleman's Quarterly* "work" clothes and Armani suits, she in an elegance that included a full-length sable coat. She danced Cassie for a year after the Broadway opening and, taking time off, was replaced by Ann Reinking. After four months free to be Mrs. Michael Bennett, she returned to the company for another Broadway stint. During a similar hiatus before the marriage, she had flown to London, where he was in the midst of a fierce squabble with British Equity over the West End *Chorus Line*.

The squabble had them headlined in the Fleet Street tabloids. It also deepened Michael Bennett's paranoia, blackened his Mafia fears.

At issue was the casting of elfin (then forty-one years old) Elizabeth Seal, whom Bennett found unacceptable as Cassie. Elizabeth Seal had been a hit in London in 1958 as the only female in the cast of *Irma la Douce*, a hit she duplicated on Broadway two years later. But she was not up to Bennett's standard. She didn't have the grace or stamina for the "Music and the Mirror" number. She was nothing like Donna McKechnie, his "favorite instrument."

Michael Bennett fired Elizabeth Seal, who suddenly emerged as both the darling of the London theater scene *and* an endangered species. He hired a Lithuanian dancer named Petra Siniawski. Backstage tattle rumbled into war talk. America was yet again striking back at England. This time on the symbolic—and long since sacred —stages built by Shakespeare. With Vanessa Redgrave supplying the political gunpowder, British Equity loaded the muskets.

There were death threats.

Fear—more than love—was now motivating *A Chorus Line*.

McKechnie: "Michael asked me to come to help out the situation, basically to train this new girl. Because I'd worked in London, and had credibility there as a star, British Equity allowed it, saying I was the only one who could come over. I wasn't a replacement for anybody. The idea was: I'd do five previews to keep the show going but not open it. In that time the Lithuanian girl could be trained, we could get her on, and there'd be a real London company.

"The London papers got word of it, got it mixed up and blew it out of proportion. They said Michael was bringing his wife over! We weren't even married then! I walked into this whole political thing and it was really shocking. Vanessa Redgrave was paying actors a pound a day to march against us, and all the unemployed actors in the West End were out in force marching! Vanessa Redgrave organized the whole thing. I don't know that it was her alone, but her name was used.

"Michael and Bob were holed up in this hotel. They were, like, living this old movie. You'd look under the door and see the shadows of feet going by! It sounds funny now but it wasn't then. They had a driver who was a bodyguard type. I'd gone with such excitement because Michael was giving me the chance to help him. Once I got there . . . !

"We were prisoners in the hotel, didn't go anywhere—I mean, I went out to the theater, and that was it. I became furious that no one had forewarned me. One night Michael, Bob and I were coming out of the theater and suddenly we're faced with this wall of photographers—twenty-five of them, thirty!—coming at us. I'd been used to photographers, but not the kind that rush against you and push. Somehow I got separated from Michael and Bob, who were ducking behind cars parked in the street. I was suddenly alone! And I panicked! I didn't know if I was facing cameras or guns! I was really scared. It was all coming at me.

"By the time Michael and Bob got me out of there, I was crying, I couldn't focus, I was babbling.

"And . . . and, well, Michael became enraged *at me*! Enraged that I would lose my demeanor.

"In his head, I guess, it was like I had given up and wasn't fighting back. It created a lot of personal problems for us; I mean, it was a very upsetting thing. He was concerned for me, but the one thing I needed him to say he couldn't say. Instead of handling me himself he called Elaine Stritch—she was in London—and asked her to come to the hotel and take care of me when he was at the theater. She did. She helped. But what I needed was for Michael to say, 'I'm sorry.'

"There were death threats.

"While all the furor was going on, I was sneaking into the basement of the theater rehearsing this Lithuanian girl who spoke very little English.

"We got her on and, finally, Michael said we're going home. We came back bloody!"

Avian: "He always adored Donna. They always loved each other, and it went back to the old days when they were on *Hullabaloo*. Michael and Donna did Milliken Shows together, those big industrial promotional jobs that were put together like Broadway productions. And they did *Promises*. They were just great pals, really liked each other. We all got caught up in the success of *Chorus Line*, the rush was so overwhelming. We all went through our nervous breakdowns on that one! It was tough. Harder than failure. It changed your life so tremendously. And it was all a whirl-wind blur. I didn't know what was happening.

"All of a sudden the *amount* of power, the *income* coming in, the dream show everybody in the world ever dreams of having and . . . and suddenly we had it all! And there was constant publicity, and talk and plans and projects and movie offers! It left you breathless. Our heads were spinning! Overnight, life changed drastically! Every-body's off buying homes, apartments, cars. And suddenly people who were your friends are your enemies, enemies friends. You didn't really know what was going on, and you found yourself clinging to the show, to the same experience. It's your whole world now, and this atom bomb has gone off beside you, a good one but the impact is devastating.

"And Michael and Donna get caught up in the life-imitates-art metaphor, and around and around they go. It's like a payoff for them to share it now emotionally. The Director Marries the Star. It *was* the fantasy of it all. I'm sure Michael knew this, he was always going to his analyst about it. But he really loved Donna. Ultimately it would be hard for anyone to be married to Michael, to try to be part of him, because he was so controlling, so intelligent, so hyper. The marriage happened because it was the show going on in another way.

"And it didn't work out partly because of all the tension. Michael and Donna were under a microscope. They might have seen what the fantasy was, that it was exhilarating but not real. Donna had a rough time because—I'm guessing at all this—because now the balance had changed, they had both made it. Now, in a sense, she was his equal, and she might—in a way—compete with him. She really tried that. She began dressing like him, had her hair cut short like his and started going out there trying to be him.

"And that, of course, is not what he wanted from her. She might have *thought* that's what he wanted. What he truly wanted was a wife who was a Broadway star. When they got married, Donna stopped doing that. She wanted to be where she was as opposed to being on the stage. By the time they went to Hollywood, which was kind of a glamorous honeymoon, the marriage had really started to fall apart."

While Broadway had always been the goal, both Bennett and Avian had had childhood movie-time dreams of being dancers in the steps of Fred Astaire, a fantasy overtaken by their success in the theater. A different Hollywood dream surfaced in 1973 when Bennett—with some envy—measured the acclaim that his Broadway rival, Bob Fosse, was duplicating in movies.

If Jerry Robbins had been his idol, Michael Bennett was open to other influences as well, and Bob Fosse was a heady influence. In 1973, two years before *A Chorus Line*, Fosse not only won his sixth

Tony Award for choreography, for *Pippin*, but also won a seventh for his direction of the musical. He'd gone into the Tonys having won—two months before—an Oscar for his screen direction of *Cabaret*, with Liza Minnelli, and later that season had won an Emmy for *Liza with a Z*. He is the only director to win the so-called Triple Crown in the same year. Fosse could rightfully claim Broadway his monarchy (which he never did), then justifiably include Hollywood in his musical fiefdom.

A hoofer as a kid, Bob Fosse was hounded into show business by his father, Cyril, a salesman who had a vaudeville act with his brother. By the time he was fifteen, Fosse was a Chicago emcee, then, throughout the 1940s, a dancing comic in New York nightclubs. By the early 1950s he was dancing in movies (*Give a Girl a Break*, *Kiss Me, Kate*). After winning the Oscar for *Cabaret*, he earned a 1974 Oscar nomination for his direction of *Lenny*, the movie bio about comedian Lenny Bruce. His skill was not strictly musical. And unlike Robbins, who had veered into ballet, Bob Fosse was single-mindedly fixed on the world of stage, film and video.

Michael Bennett admired Fosse's versatility. By the time *A Chorus Line* proclaimed his own "backstage genius," he was willing to test his versatility on the back lots of Hollywood. There was nothing he couldn't do. When Universal Studios optioned film rights to *A Chorus Line*, Bennett decided it was time to learn moviemaking, a subject he had been absorbing "by Buffalo osmosis" from all the musicals his mother and father had taken him to when he was a kid. When you came right down to it, he and Bob Avian "saw life as a movie." In terms of technique, their post-*Chorus Line* career was an attempt to make "what happens onstage as rapid and seamless as what happens in a movie."

In Hollywood, with his bride, Bennett was chauffeured around in his Rolls-Royce. Secure in the success rippling across the country from *A Chorus Line*, his ego was at its peak. He had made it. He would never be a co-anything again. He wouldn't have to compromise, or kowtow to anyone. He would be a star director, as important as anyone in his field. He would widen his range and increase his latent power. So, in Hollywood, he was surprised—and increasingly annoyed—to find himself applauded yet treated like a second-class citizen. He was welcomed, then ignored. If he thought of himself as a suzerain, he was finally treated like a squatter. The soon to be crowned Broadway King was, at best, a talented but troublesome flea in a blank office on the Universal lot.

Bennett had gone to Hollywood with what Avian describes as "a fabulous three-picture deal." Supposedly, Universal was to allow him to produce and direct anything he wanted. The first thing planned was an adaptation of one of the stories from Tom Tryon's *Crowned Heads* called "Bobbitt." Well before he left New York, he had persuaded Tryon to dramatize the story, which, ultimately, Bennett came to think wasn't "movie material." As good as he felt "Bobbitt" was, he found it didn't transfer to a scenario. Bennett was determined, however, to complete at least one more movie project before he took on *A Chorus Line*.

Avian: "We get to Hollywood ready to work—only all anyone seems interested in is: 'How do you want your office decorated?' We're in this three-office complex, right next to Verna Fields and Steven Spielberg. The office has a desk and a couple of chairs, very adequate. We try to work and all we hear is: 'What kind of decor?' We said, 'Just bring a bottle of vodka, we don't want any decor.' But every day the same hassle. We'd pull in in the morning—the hardest thing of all was getting a parking space, which, at the studios, is a status symbol. We'd walk in, and the first thing'd be: 'What do you want for lunch?' 'Don't want lunch, just the vodka, please.' 'But you have to order now so it will be ready when you want it.' 'Don't bother.' 'But you must order . . .' Every day like that, back and forth, a ritual."

Bennett had arrived in Hollywood having read a script sent to him by a screenwriter named Jerome Kass, a story about a girl from the Ozarks who heads to California with her husband with the idea of becoming Sonny and Cher. The husband dies on the way in an automobile accident; the wife survives, arrives in L.A. and winds up a taxi dancer in a place called Danceland, which was the title of the script. Bennett thought it would make a good movie. All Jerry Kass knew about Michael Bennett was his work on *A Chorus Line*.

"He was renting a house in the Valley," Jerry Kass says, "and he asked me to come see him. Donna was with him, and Bob. I went and it was instant! He wanted to do *Danceland* at Universal as one of the movies he'd make before *Chorus Line*. Then he went back to New York and said he couldn't do anything he wasn't involved in from the ground up. That sounded valid to me. I mean, he was this creative artist who wanted—perhaps *needed*—to be there at the start.

"Then he said he had something in mind he couldn't tell me about. He was still trying to make a deal and soon as it happened I was to be the writer."

What Bennett had in mind was, again, a show-business script, this one taking off from William Gibson's play *Two for the Seesaw*. Within three weeks of his tantalizing promise to Kass, Bennett had secured the rights to the play. In a series of meetings with Kass, they roughed out the idea, which was to center on a touring production of *Two for the Seesaw*. Firing ideas one to the other, they came up with the perfect title, *Roadshow*, and even the leads, Bette Midler and Robert Redford.

Kass: "We go ahead. David Merrick gets script rights, and it's budgeted at $15 million, which was high. Universal didn't want Bette Midler, said she was too ugly. Merrick agreed and wanted Streisand. I told him, first, Streisand was too old for the part and, second, you just don't make a movie with Barbra Streisand: *she makes a movie with Barbra Streisand*! All through this Michael kept insisting on Bette Midler. He pointed out that his contract said if they didn't approve of his casting, he could walk away *with* the project. Universal made out the contract didn't say that, gave him some cockamamie excuse."

Avian: "At first *Roadshow* goes great; working with Jerry's a lot of fun; then we find the studio resisting Bette Midler. They didn't like her, didn't want her. She hadn't done a movie yet. We keep hearing Streisand's name rumbling around, and Michael finally said, 'I don't want to make a picture with Streisand, I want Midler.'

"Then Michael discovers he has to do all this studio politicking, has to go to all these dinner parties with the Ned Tanens and the Sid Sheinbergs. He'd go to these parties and they'd show him off. There were signs all over town: Universal Has Bought *A Chorus Line*, and Michael would become the dinner star for foreign promoters and distributors. Sid Sheinberg didn't take to Michael at all—some competition in there somewhere—and Michael couldn't care less. He was down on everybody's ass because they were giving us such a hard time, because they hated Bette Midler."

Bennett's stubbornness was beginning to bug Universal. At a commissary lunch one day with George Roy Hill, with whom he'd done *Henry, Sweet Henry*, Hill told Bennett there was a lot of talk about him. "Your image is: you're a kid out here walking through a minefield."

Avian: "We kept working, kept having our lessons every day about making a movie. The studio would let us watch the rushes of all the movies being made, *MacArthur*, *The Car*, *Smokey and the Bandit*. Verna would explain the clips to us in detail, focus and style, stuff like that, and about texture. She'd show us different pictures because we were trying to decide on a cinematographer, everything from *Breakfast at Tiffany's* to *Harry and Walter Go to New York*.

"Then we'd go and deal with the studio's music deartment, with scenery, with costumes. Then we'd watch big scenes being shot, *Airport '77* one afternoon, and the plane being crashed, then flooded, and thousands and thousands of gallons of water all over the sound stage, and I'm wondering why everyone isn't electrocuted on the spot and, well, 'because the current is DC.' Then Verna would take us to George Lucas' studio somewhere in the Valley, where we'd watch these guys making the first little models for *Star Wars*, stuff that you'd see later on the screen and would go *zzzooommm*!"

When it came time for the studio to budget *Roadshow*, Bennett and Avian took a $6 million guess, a below-the-line cost without the stars. The Kass script was complete and ready to be sent to the various technical departments (music, costumes, set design), but it took the studio seven weeks to work up the budget, which finally figured out at $5.9 million.

Avian: "Here we were not knowing anything about Hollywood budgets and we came up with it fast. It took Universal *seven weeks*. And we waited. And we waited. Michael was getting unhappier and unhappier. We were being treated like nobodies, not what we were used to. We were hanging out doing nothing. We got through the seven weeks by putting our fingers up our noses a lot and seeing movies, movies, movies. And we waited, waited, waited."

During the waiting Bennett spelled out to Avian some of the ideas he had for the *Chorus Line* movie. Although Universal had been planning on a straightforward adaptation of Bennett's original concept, he had another idea: *Chorus Line II*, which would entail the radical restructuring of the musical's audition. He saw the movie version as a documentary. The gypsies who once angled for a Broadway job were now out in Hollywood hoping to be cast in the *Chorus Line* movie. Instead of seventeen of them, their numbers comprised anyone who had ever played the role on the stage. There would be four aspirants, say, for the role of Cassie, the role of Paul, the role of Mike, and the movie would detail a scene, a song or a dance in four interpretations. What Bennett wanted to achieve in the screen version was the kind of reality he had found on the stage. None of this was known to Universal.

As trustful as he was of Bennett's instincts, Avian was perplexed. "I kept saying, 'Michael, they've spent $5 million on the show and now you're giving them a different show.' He was trying to keep the material true to the movie medium as he had kept it true to the theater."

Plans for *Chorus Line II* occupied some of the time they spent waiting for word on *Roadshow*.

"While we were waiting the question still was: 'How do you want your office decorated?' "

Finally, fed up with Universal's treatment, Bennett walked away from the studio and, as it turned out, from any future in Hollywood. He called his lawyer, John Breglio, who had made the picture deal at Universal, to get him out of the contract.

"Before Universal I hadn't handled Michael directly," Breglio says, "but through the firm I did a lot of work for him. I'd been involved with his idea to do a murder-mystery musical, *Pin-Ups*, before he took on *Seesaw*, the musical. I'd met him through John Wharton, one of the founders of the firm, whom Michael had come to see for help on saving *Seesaw*. Michael wasn't a rich man then but he kept *Seesaw* running out of his own pocket, paying the actors' salaries for a week to keep it going.

"After I'd made the Universal deal, and he got out there, he discovered the rhythms and traditions of Hollywood had nothing to do with Michael Bennett. He just had to find out what it was all about. Stayed about a year, maybe less. Then one day he just disappeared. No one knew where he was. He called me from some island somewhere, or maybe it was from San Francisco, and said, 'Get me out, I don't want to do films ever again.' I flew out, met with Ned Tanen, at that point the head of production at Universal. Ned said, 'He doesn't want us but we love him. Anytime he wants to come back . . .'

"So I got him out of the deal and Michael parted ways with Hollywood."

Avian: "Universal let him out of the contract, which really meant Sid Sheinberg was happy not to have him around the studio. Goodbye to Hollywood! We felt bad. We'd both grown up with movies and we could have made them well. Sad we never got the chance. I know, with Michael, it would have been one long technical rehearsal, but they'd have been great. He was such a visual artist. I think once he understood the medium, he'd have run with it."

Bennett's defection left a scramble for the rights to *Roadshow* in its wake. Bette Midler wanted the property, so did Robert Evans, so did Larry Kasha. David Merrick, who owned the movie *Semi-Tough*, which Universal wanted for a television series, tried to barter *Semi-Tough* for *Roadshow*. Kass found a director for Merrick, Fred Schepsi, and there was talk of having Tommy Tune choreograph it but nothing came of it.* Universal was also left with the headache of turning *A Chorus Line* into a movie. After Bennett pulled out of the project he was approached by one director after another who considered taking it on, principal among them Sidney Lumet and Mike Nichols. ("Lumet finally threw up his hands and said it couldn't be done," Avian says. "Nichols wanted to know what the Cassie story was about. We saw it bounce from person to person.")

Meanwhile, back in New York, *A Chorus Line* was still packing the Shubert Theater.

Avian: "We had no idea about the life expectancy of the show on Broadway. The picture deal had been designed to be released five years after the opening night. At the time, we thought that was great. Then the movie finally appeared eleven years later! And it made no dent at all on the show. The movie's now on HBO in the afternoons, and it doesn't seem to make any difference in terms of the Broadway run. We can keep it going a long time more. The break-even is very low, $150,000. Then we have a profit-sharing thing and everybody takes salary cuts, goes on waivers. When there's a good week's profit, the split is different. It's a new formula, and it does well for everybody. Our business this year is better than last, although I don't think there's a person in the audience who speaks English! Mondays are our best nights because everything else is dark, and Saturday nights are next. We've now run twelve years, why not twenty?! It's all pretty staggering to me."

Although Hollywood had been a humiliating standoff with a whore, Bennett returned to New York like a husband eager to waltz with his abandoned wife.

Breglio: "When Michael eventually came back to New York, if anything he was infused with more power and energy to get going about theater. 'This is who I am, I'm going to do eight shows a year,

---

Roadshow has not been filmed.

produce five, direct three, choreograph two.' This was Michael at his height, with more energy and electricity than anybody. After *Chorus Line* he was probably *the* most important entertainment figure in the country. He represented the kind of artist who generated all other artists into creating great works. He was an incredibly exciting man to be around. I'd been with the firm about five or six years then, and no one was more inspiring."

During the Hollywood hiatus, there was backbiting excitement about a musical called *The Act*, which was trying out in San Francisco. Financed by the Shubert Organization, it starred Liza Minnelli. Written by George Furth, the book told the confessional story of a singing star, Michelle Craig (Minnelli), who, during a Las Vegas booking, recalls her ignominious struggle to reach the big time. Insiders said *The Act* itself was unintentionally mirroring its own story. Furth's book struggled, so did the John Kander/Fred Ebb score. Added to that was the confused and flaccid direction of movie director Martin Scorsese, who'd never done a play or a musical before. Gossip had it that Scorsese, then romantically linked with Minnelli, was so far gone on drugs that "he was walking around with a Kleenex box," and his actions were as erratic on stage as off.

The Act needed help, and fast. Bernard Jacobs called Michael Bennett. Would he take a look? Scorsese didn't seem to know what he was doing; Ron Lewis' choreography wasn't very good either. Jacobs later called Gower Champion, who, in addition to some restaging, eventually played the Barry Nelson part opposite Minnelli during the Broadway run. When Michael Bennett got Jacobs' call he was in Los Angeles and at a low point with Universal. He walked into his still-bare office, sat down at the empty desk, wrote "Gone fishin' " across a piece of studio stationery and leisurely drove up the coast.

Tharon Musser had done the lighting on *The Act* and was with the show in San Francisco. "One day there was a note in my box from Michael saying he was here and call him. I called and said, 'What are you doing here?' He said, 'Hiding. I'm not going to do that movie. I can't stand the look of fear in everybody's eyes in Hollywood.' He was going to hide in San Francisco for a while. The very next morning

Cy Feuer and Ernest Martin, who were producing *The Act* with the Shuberts, saw him roaring down the street to the theater wearing red and on a motorcycle. I called him later and said, 'Michael that's a helluva way to hide!' "

                  In Hollywood the fantasy image of Michael Bennett's marriage to Donna McKechnie had begun to fade. He was beginning to think she was locked in artistic competition with him, a thought he'd later dwell upon when, after they were divorced and her career failed to develop, McKechnie tried to direct, choreograph and star in her own club act. In his changing view over the three months they were together, she was losing her individuality and trying to become him, a transference he could not understand. At the same time Bennett thought this was happening, McKechnie began to think that the complexities unwittingly created when they united their personal and professional lives were stifling them both.

McKechnie: "Before we got married, when my friends asked, 'Is he husband material?' I'd say, 'Call me naïve, but when people love each other'—and I really believed this—'love will prevail.' I'm not sure I do anymore. And at the time I felt I could not *not* marry Michael. I knew there'd be problems, but marriage wasn't about just having a nice safe little thing going and having a kid. His father told me to have children. He told me it was the only way I was going to hold him. I think Michael would have liked children or, at least, a child, but we were really more responsible than that. We didn't get married to have children. We got married to have a relationship."

Avian: "I don't know about the sexual side of the marriage, but I do know that Michael had always been bisexual. I've always thought of sexuality in terms of an applause meter, a scale from zero to one hundred. Everybody tilts in there somewhere. Whether you're a hundred or below, well, it's usually a little in here, a little in there. And Michael just wavered. It was boys and girls. He had so many girlfriends over the years I knew him, and I always felt that was part of his Italian nature."

"I really tried in my marriage," Bennett said. "I really, truly tried. We were chorus kids together. We grew up the same way, dancing-school darlings, lessons in tap, Spanish dance, the schmear. We did shows together, and she was my Cassie. I loved Donna. And I needed someone, and I thought we could work out whatever problems we might have. I was wrong. I couldn't. She couldn't. We lasted—what? Three months?

"It was very painful for me, for her, for our friends. We tried to live up to the image. We got a Central Park penthouse. I kept it after the divorce, but I was never very happy there. And we began riding around in the Rolls. Then the image began to suffocate me, and I knew I couldn't play the game. I didn't belong in the back of a Rolls waving out at Times Square like some little king. I sold it and bought a Ford van and set it up in back with a conference table, stereo, TV, phone, so I could get some work done riding around New York or while waiting to get somewhere in traffic."

McKechnie: "I knew people would think I was nuts to marry him, but after *Chorus Line* we both felt that there was an inevitable step that couldn't be overlooked. And there was some other element going on too. We were caught in *Chorus Line* fever, and instead of being two grown-ups we kinda thought that if we merged we could be a fortress for each other.

"I was engaged to Ken Howard, and Michael said he wouldn't let me marry him. I remember telling him it was none of his business, and he said, 'I want to tell you I have been going to therapy for a year and a half to make myself good enough for you.' I was totally stunned. It just came from out of the blue like that. Then he said, 'I can't let you marry him.'

"Michael had kept Ken away from me during *Chorus Line* rehearsals. Ken had looked up to Michael, and it was all so much a part of the business he didn't want to interfere anyway, so he had just stayed away. I didn't want to argue about all that. But here Michael was telling me *what to do in my personal life*! I was in shock because part of me was celebrating that I was so important to him that he would try to run my life. And besides, I loved him so much.

"I figured out later that Michael really cared for me in a way, but he wasn't able to meet my emotional needs—*or anyone's.* I think he knew he was someone who wasn't capable of something, I think he knew he was missing—lacking—something. I didn't grasp all this when we were married. I had to work it out for myself later.

"I remember saying to him, 'I'll do whatever you want, whatever you say, just tell me. Tell me. Talk to me, Michael!'

"And he said, 'The one cardinal sin—'

" 'Michael, I'll do anything!'

" 'The one cardinal sin,' he said, 'is that you made me feel. And your flaw is—'

" 'My flaw? What? Tell me! I'll change! I'll change! I know I'm not perfect, I know I'm not patient, I know I'm not understanding, I know I'm insecure, I know—'

" 'Your flaw is . . . that you love me, you really love me. I think that's a great flaw in your character. *I RESENT YOU!*' "

Donna McKechnie exchanges this dialogue as though she is Cassie battling Zach. Bravery has been beaten out of time as a hard glinting shield.

"You could take things Michael said one day with a grain of salt, and forget them. He'd just say things. You had to let it roll off. But there was something in what he said that night I've never forgotten because it was so truthful—as shocking as that may sound.

"I had to start believing him because he kept saying it. He kept saying, 'Get her away from me! GET . . . HER . . . AWAY . . . FROM . . . ME!' "

Avian: "When he left Donna, he moved into my apartment on Eighth Street. 'How long are you moving in for, darling?' 'Oh, a week or two.' Four months later, six months later, I said, 'You gotta get out, I hate this.' Meanwhile, he's having this on/off—but hot and heavy—affair with this dancer, a boy, Richard Christopher, who did die of AIDS a year or two later."

During this time there were long, romantic telephone calls to

Sabine Cassel in France. Within a few weeks of Bennett's move from Avian's apartment back to 40 Central Park South, Sabine Cassel had moved into the duplex tower on the twenty-second floor, one story above the penthouse. Her intention was to marry the former groom she had toasted with champagne in her Montmartre living room. Leaving Jean-Pierre Cassel, to whom she had been married fourteen years, she lost custody of her sons during a searing courtroom confrontation when Michael Bennett's best man/best friend accused him of being both an adulterer and a notorious homosexual.

Sabine Cassel says she "fell in love with Michael little by little." She talks of their relationship without complaining, with a quizzically worried look in her dark eyes, and a smile that seems like a wry scar.

"I knew he admired Jean-Pierre very much, and us as a couple. He want—wanted!—very much to be a couple like we were. It was all very nice. I had kids, a beautiful house, everything I want, but it was like . . . ufff, sometimes you get bored. That was my life a very long time, bored. I was very young when I married Jean-Pierre. I loved my children and my husband very much, and I never had any extra affair. The only one who came into my life was Michael, and we were friends a long time before anything happen. So, little by little, I fall in love with Michael, little by little, *peut-être* without knowing it. Michael was, like, for six years my best friend.

"When he decide to marry Donna, he call and Jean-Pierre answers the phone. I hear them talking, some of what is being said, and I'm thinking: I'm not so happy. It's bizarre, like losing a friend. Then he call—called!—me back later and said he want to get married in Paris because he want to be with us. So I arrange everything. It's difficult for American people to get married right away in France, so I went to City Hall and because of Jean-Pierre it was easy for me. Michael got married in the *same room* in City Hall where I was getting married, like, fourteen years before!

"The night before he marry Donna, he said, 'Oh, I want to marry you and you are not free.'

"And I said, 'Ahh, *oui*, well, another life.'

"Then when I come to New York to be with him, absolutely

marriage is what he wants. But I thought I was losing my children by getting divorced, and didn't want to get divorced right away. I wanted to take time. But Michael push me to get divorced. My children would be taken away from me because I would not be living in France, and the court didn't want them to come to America—especially to meet with this gay person, because this is the description Jean-Pierre is giving the judge. That was the whole idea behind Jean-Pierre.

"I knew Michael was gay, of course. I knew. I knew that. It was no problem."

"When I first knew Michael and he came to Paris, I thought he was married, he had this girlfriend. I didn't know him very well. Later when he went to ski with us he had a boyfriend come. I found that extremely confusing. Michael was always telling me these romantic stories. For a long time my life was only Jean-Pierre, and I didn't have any romantic stories to share. Each time Michael was tired, or sad, or bored, he was coming to Paris to spend time with us. We were always spending it together, Michael, Jean-Pierre, I. Always together. He was coming for dinner to our house or we were going out to dinner or to a play with him. He was friend to both of us, *oui*.

"I have lunch sometimes alone with Michael. Once in London at Joe Allen's—I remember because Jean-Pierre was having trouble about *Chorus Line*. Michael had promised him the rights, and some guy who was like a close friend of Michael's was doing Zach. Jean-Pierre thought the guy should be dropped. I told Jean-Pierre he was not handling it right and I would talk to Michael, tell Michael not to give the guy the rights. And I did, *oui*.

"I told him, 'You know, we are very good friends, and I love you very much.' I guess at that time my English was not as good as now—and now not so good—and probably he misunderstand me . . . or something I said I felt and didn't mean the same way. He understood that I was very much in love with him, and he says, 'But me too!' Then it was like . . . !

"We came to love each other more than friendship. Ahh, *oui*, this was during his honeymoon with Donna. But nothing ever happen,

I didn't want anything to happen then. That was the only time like
that.

"Jean-Pierre never knew.

"My psychic, Yagel Didia, knew. A long time ago she find Michael in my thoughts, finds he is gay, finds he is taking drugs, everything! I didn't know her so well then, so I didn't believe too much.

"Michael later went to her twice. She predicted *Dreamgirls* and
Scandal, and all the trouble with Treva. She said, 'You are going to
do a show with black people.' He looked at her cuckoo, and she said,
'You are going to have trouble with the leading lady and take her
back,' and she said, 'I can see the finale with three women in white.'
She knew he would work on a show about sex. When it was true,
Michael told me how good Yagel Didia is. When she came to New
York he went to see her. It was absolutely clear what she predicted,
so good I could not believe it.

"The last time I saw Yagel Didia she told me he was dying . . .
and this was before he was dying—before anyone knew anything . . ."

Sabine Cassel looks in her teacup.

"And . . . Yagel Didia tells me the *way* he is dying, *oui*? . . .
For a while, what Michael and I have is true love."

She looks up, staring blankly, giving silent testimony to La
Rouchefoucauld: "True love is like ghosts, which everybody talks
about but few have seen."

CHAPTER TWELVE

Waltzing Through the Plague

(1977)

In 1977 in San Francisco, Michael Bennett met someone new, James Georgedes, whose friend Robert Herr later became chief secretary at Eight Ninety Broadway when Bennett suddenly fired his staff of female secretaries, principal among them Marilyn Mury, who frequently accompanied him to Broadway openings as his "date." Georgedes introduced Bennett to Robert Herr's friend Gene Pruit. At this time the steam was off the Herr/Pruit relationship; former lovers—with an interest in bodybuilding—they'd settled into being "lifelong friends." In a manner similar to the waltzing exchange of sexual partners in Arthur Schnitzler's *La Ronde*, Pruit became Michael Bennett's last lover and, with Herr, a major inheritor in his will. Pruit and Herr, who together nursed Bennett after he was diagnosed with AIDS and were with him when he died in Tucson, now share a house in Hollywood. Among their possessions is an urn containing Bennett's ashes, which they intend one day to scatter on the sea surrounding his favorite island, St. Barthélemy in the French West Indies.

Robert Herr: "Michael and I were friends in New York for a while in the late 1960s, long before San Francisco, when I was a student at NYU. I was pre-med, or so I thought. Then I went to graduate school thinking I was some kind of Renaissance man and would end up a teacher, or in publishing. This was in the 1960s when it didn't matter if you had money as long as you could pay the rent. I moved to San Francisco to work with Bank of America, in 1979 or 1980, after Michael had had his *Chorus Line* success. He had been coming out to see Jimmy Georgedes, with whom he was having an affair. Jimmy worked for Wilkes-Bashford, the men's clothing store. Michael met Gene through Jimmy.

"Gene and I were together then, and it was Michael and Jimmy Georgedes. I haven't spoken to Georgedes in a long time. I remember he was worried about AIDS, but who isn't? He had some gland problems.

"Gene and I had a very close relationship—still do—but in those days of sexual activity we were like the closest, closest brothers, and it has stayed that way. Because of my connection with Gene, Michael may have felt I'd be jealous or something because there was an instant physical attraction between them—Michael always had an eye for beauty and Gene is a beauty!—and, sure, those things crept into my head. Beyond physical attraction to each other there was this mind pull. Gene is extremely smart; Michael was too. And they had this incredibly playful intellectual good time.

"When Michael asked me to work for him, and I moved to New York, Gene moved with me, we set up household, and he and Michael continued knowing each other. But he never lived with him except after Michael was diagnosed. Gene always lived in his own apartment, or with me. It's a lovely, strange relationship.

"I've heard that Michael's mother thinks Gene led him down the homosexual path! Well, Gene didn't! Helen can't blame herself is what that is, and I suppose that's true in any parent-child relationship, especially in Helen's relationship with Michael. But the problem is, Michael did it to himself. He decided he was gay and followed that road. She happened to give him some genes and, maybe, set his early direction, but from all accounts Michael took control of his own life very early, and from his own say-so. He knew he was gay when he was a kid, and he pursued it. That must have hurt Helen. Plus her husband was a philanderer, and that's documented."

As his surrogate parents, Bernard and Betty Jacobs were often concerned about Michael Bennett's erratic life. They were well aware of the divisions in his nature. They knew, for example, that his homosexual affairs in San Francisco kept company with his liaisons with women in New York. Smiling grimly, Betty Jacobs says, "I never knew where they came from but there was always another guy somewhere. I just think Michael couldn't make up his mind whether he was homosexual or heterosexual. He told me once that his dog was his best friend."

Bernard Jacobs says, "Who the hell knows about Michael anyway?"

Mrs. Jacobs: "There were private sides to him I don't think anybody will ever know. When he bought Sabine that house on Sixty-fourth Street, and they started fixing it up, they seemed very happy. As time went on, Michael was less and less happy. They weren't really meant for each other. Sabine loved entertaining, jet-setting, partying. Michael was very private, didn't like entertaining or a lot of strangers. He didn't speak French and there was always a lot of French around."

The purchase of the town house at 174 East Sixty-fourth Street was not made in the name of Sabine Cassel, nor was it made as a gesture of their shared love. According to Cassel, Bennett was "drugged a lot" when they were living together in 1978 in the duplex tower at Central Park South. Cassel says, "People who are doing drugs don't do it in front of you, and he didn't do it too much in front of me." But, increasingly, she became aware of violent shifts in his mood.* He told her he felt trapped in their relationship. She saw him "paranoiac—really like crazy." To lessen the trap (and perhaps to escape Sabine Cassel's wifely surveillance), he suggested buying a town

---

*Marvin Schulman recounts an incident when Bennett "flew into rage" when he and Sabine Cassel suggested he enroll in a detoxification center for his increasing dependence on drugs.

house where she might live. That way they might separate their problems and eventually work something out.

The marriage Sabine Cassel had envisioned seemed more and more a dangerous miasma, yet she still hoped it might happen. At the climax of a furious argument, Cassel screamed she was leaving him. "And he said I could not leave him anymore because now I am divorced, now I have nowhere to go." She tells this mimicking Bennett's speech, putting her hand on her hip, ending her sentence hissing like a cat: "*Hiss hiss hiss!* If anyone was going to leave, he would! *Hiss hiss hiss!*"

Caterwauling through these fights on cocaine, Bennett bought the town house. Although it was only partially furnished, Cassel moved in with a housekeeper whose presence was to allay Cassel's fears of living alone. One afternoon the two women were confronted in the kitchen by a threatening "young Puerto Rican" who tied them to kitchen chairs, ran through the rooms, stole what he could and fled as nimbly as he had arrived. After the housekeeper, who was more loosely bound, freed Cassel, Cassel ran to the building next door. The neighbor called 911. Cassel then called Bennett at Eight Ninety Broadway. Whatever relief she may have felt when she reached him was undercut by the immediate terror in Bennett's voice. He was convinced the break-in was part of a Mafia contract. *They* were after him; *they'd* always been after him; *they* were going to get him! While Cassel thought these accusations were only further examples of paranoia, she too became frightened. By the time Bennett reached 174 East Sixty-fourth Street, the police were on the scene and Cassel was nervously explaining what had happened. Bennett kept his fears to himself, then refused to set foot in the house again. Cassel moved back to 40 Central Park South, where the Mafia now seemed almost as menacing as the dark paths she could see stringing through the park twenty-two floors below the duplex-tower windows.

It was a brief reunion.

At the end of yet another scathing argument, Cassel, feeling as trapped as Bennett, said, "Listen, do whatever you like, nobody keeps anyone. If I want to leave, I leave; if I stay, I stay. If you want to leave, the door is open—just go." And he left. "He went to San Francisco to his boyfriend."

Jacobs: "Everything came to a head when the house was robbed, all of Michael's madness about the Mafia. He moved out overnight. He called us at one in the morning, and what do you do? 'There are people outside the house watching.' He thought they might have been cocaine dealers. And he owed them money? Who the hell knows? There are myriad things related to that phone call. After that night everything seemed to change with Sabine. There are things Sabine doesn't even know. At one point she had Michael ready to go to Connecticut to marry her."

Jacobs nods to his wife.

Jacobs: "Remember that?"

Mrs. Jacobs: "Uh-huh."

Jacobs: "He came up here with Bobby and we had lunch. When he finished lunch he had made up his mind he was not going to marry her. But he had been ready to because she had convinced him he'd ruined her life. He owed her."

Mrs. Jacobs: "And she would put up with anything! Boyfriends—"

Jacobs: "He had a boyfriend in San Francisco during this period."

Mrs. Jacobs: "Sabine suspected it."

Jacobs: "Sabine said this: 'He came back from San Francisco with gay clothes.' "

Mrs. Jacobs: "Whatever that means!"

Jacobs: "What? Gay clothes? Sabine said, 'If he thinks I don't know what's going on, he's crazy.' She put up with it because she was in love with him, really in love with him. I'm sure San Francisco's where Michael got AIDS. I don't know that for sure, but there was a time, just before he broke up with some boy out there, when the boy had the AIDS syndrome. Michael was not one to be sleeping around. He stayed pretty much within his group. I can't perceive any other place it could have happened to him. He broke up with Sabine at that point. Paid her off."

Mrs. Jacobs: "Didn't he buy her that apartment?"

Jacobs: "No, he didn't buy her the apartment. He bought the apartment for Donna. Sabine he gave something like seventy-five, a hundred thousand. Wasn't that it?"

Mrs. Jacobs: "I don't remember."

Jacobs: "Donna got a settlement—"

Mrs. Jacobs: "All his women cost him money, and his men gave him aggravation."

Jacobs: "I can check on it. My recollection is that Donna got a quarter of a million, and he bought her an apartment in the same building we have an apartment in—Seventieth Street and Park Avenue. Jerry Minskoff owned it. I got Jerry to find an apartment for her, similar to ours, cost like seventy-two, seventy-four thousand. She eventually sold it for $160,000."

In San Francisco, after the bruising treatment in Hollywood, Bennett found himself celebrated in a particular gay circle. When he returned there on an audition tour for *Dreamgirls* in 1982, he staged a Ralph Lauren fashion show for Wilkes-Bashford as a gesture to his friend Georgedes. A colleague who observed him closely says he had "a lot of lovers" between 1977 and 1983, the precise time when AIDS was beginning to surface. One of these lovers "died almost immediately from AIDS," apparently one of the earliest cases. In addition to his promiscuity, Bennett was "absolutely drunk all the time, chemically out of his head." There were "outrageous get-togethers" in Bennett's hotel rooms: "all-male and down-and-dirty." Although the women traveling with him would most often be excluded from these encounters, on occasion he would invite a particularly close female friend. The drug supply was unlimited. So were the blond-and-blue-eyed hustlers.

Diane Judge, whom Bennett eventually hired away from Merle

Debuskey, a long established New York agent, first worked with him on *Dreamgirls*. Judge says, "Michael tried out his sexual magnetism constantly. Flirted all the time. Men, women, young, old, it just never stopped, *if*, that is, he was interested in whatever it was the other person had to offer. I'm sure he started with Donna the same way. I wonder what the challenge was there. To conquer the heterosexual world? Or to please his mother, his father? To show he too could have a wife? The moment Donna and all that happened he was showing off a lot. He had the money, the white Rolls, the house. For Donna it must have been a challenge. All women have it: they're the one woman who can change the homosexual man."

Marvin Krauss, who managed *Dreamgirls*, says, "I'd known Michael since *Joyful Noise* in Cleveland. And during the time we were working together, he became very, very close to my wife, Elaine. In San Francisco Wilkes-Bashford was opening a new store, and Michael's very close friend at the time, Jimmy Georgedes, was a partner in the store and Michael was backing him financially. Jimmy asked him if he'd put on a fashion show that ultimately turned into a mini-musical, *you know Michael*! At his own expense he brought in writing people, sound people, designers, choreographers, and he asked me to go out with him, help a little, just be around. That's when he really first got to know Elaine. Later he asked me if I'd let her go with him on a six-week casting tour for *Dreamgirls*, L.A., Houston, Atlanta, and I didn't see my wife for seven weeks!"

Elaine Krauss: "That was a turning point for Michael and I. I went on the tour with him, Bobby, Michael Peters, who was doing the choreography, and Cleavant Derricks and Yolanda Segovia, who were working on the music, and Michael and I became close friends. Michael loved women! Michael adored women! He chose carefully who'd be his friends. What I had to offer—he loved Marvin, our family, the stability of our marriage—"

Krauss: "Thirty-five years married! She looks like a child, doesn't she? Two when I met her!"

The Krausses lap each other as though each is a different-flavor ice-cream cone.

Mrs. Krauss: "Michael loved our children. He got an insight into a different part of life he said he always loved but didn't have. I saw a part of his life many people didn't, personal things he couldn't share with others. He was comfortable with my being with him and Jimmy, then with Gene and him during the last years of his life.

"Early on, when we didn't know much about the disease, one of Michael's friends thought he had it. He called Michael and said he was coming to New York for a week and wanted to stay with him. They'd broken up at that point. The friend just needed the support, and Michael said of course. He was nervous about it, and I said, 'How could you let him?' I mean, none of us knew what kind of disease it was, and it was almost like you can catch it by being in a room with someone who had it. You loved people and you weren't going to turn them away, but you were frightened, you really were! Michael was incredible, wonderful, a genius, but at a point he was very promiscuous."

"Michael had an incredible unholy attitude about sex, totally different from normal constraints and ideas," his friend and East Hampton neighbor Kenneth Lipper says. Lipper, his wife, Dr. Evelyn Gruss Lipper, and their four children shared a common ten-acre "mall-like lawn" with Bennett's house on 40 James Lane.

"He'd talk to me all the time about this stuff, his relationship with boys, girls, wives, girlfriends, boyfriends! I was overwhelmed just listening. I just can't explain it. I had the feeling that this was a—I just never!—I mean, it was divorced from all the two thousand years of Judeo-Christian civilization, out of any kind of normal situation, not just one deviation or another, it was everything!

"The only thing I could observe from watching him was: like the world couldn't contain him! Try it all! See it all!"

Frank DiFilia remembers his brother was "a racehorse that wanted to run the race the whole time." Mrs. DiFiglia's memories of Mickey as an infant suggest a baby rocking his own cradle and gnashing on a brass ring. "He never walked, he bounced . . . He was born driven, something he couldn't control. Pathetic. And he had this way of knowing about people. I never learned where that came from. From the time he was little, there was this purpose, this drive. It never stopped haunting him."

DiFilia: "He balked at everything Mom tried to do, except for the dance lessons. For years he accused her of holding him back. Agents wanted to take him to New York when he was ten. Maybe Mom nurtured him too much. He lacked control in his personal habits. He was pretty indulgent—almost as if he had no self-control. His philosophy was: you want to do it, do it!

"What made my brother homosexual or bisexual, here's the answer: the man was born that way! Perhaps we're all born bisexual and make choices, choices based on certain emotional dynamics.

"Neither Mom nor I knew about his AIDS, and the way it was kept from us was pretty cruel. She just had no suspicion. I had some. She knew about his sexuality way back, fifteen or twenty years ago, and I can't remember how it all finally came out. I don't think Dad was there; I don't think Dad ever knew or, at least, it was never spoken about with Dad. Mom and I now occasionally ask each other, 'Do you think Dad knew?' And we'll go, 'Yah, he had to.' He wasn't *that* unobservant, that insensitive. It just wasn't something he wished to discuss. There was nothing for him to say about it."

Mrs. DiFiglia: "This is what has got me so confused: Michael was always so in control of everybody but himself. Why wasn't he shrewd enough to know he was in danger? Why did he want to shorten his life—if that's what he did? Maybe he felt he had given all that he could give. Maybe there wasn't anything more in him to give. He'd worked all his life since a baby. He'd been dancing, performing. Everything was stage to him. Maybe he was just tired of it and didn't know how to get out of it . . . But then again, don't you think you have to look at it this way? This is what God had planned for him. This is the way it was meant to be. I've often said to myself, 'Maybe if I hadn't let him go into show business he'd still be alive today . . .'"

Mrs. DiFiglia looks brightly hopeful—for a moment. Reshaping the years, she changes her part in the scenario. Someone else had culpability for her son's relentless career. She might have directed him elsewhere. But her attempt to characterize Destiny as the Stage Mother of Us All quickly shades to uncertainty. She seems to know her explanation is desperate, an argument to free her of possible blame.

DiFilia: "We were brought up Catholics, but Mom would say to you, 'I'm a Jewish person.' She goes to temple sometimes. We went to Sunday school—not with her, she never practiced Catholicism. We went to Mass pretty regularly, had the sacraments, First Communion. She signed a paper in order for them to be married anywhere in the church. It turned out they were married in the vestibule, not at the altar, but for them to be married even there she had to sign a paper saying she'd raise the children Catholic. Which she did. And she never had any problem with that.

"Dad would go to church Sundays, and also say, 'I'm a Catholic.' He believed that system but he wasn't really an active participant, a religious person. They had no problems with religion. They had other life issues. Mom told me they had almost agreed not to argue about religion or politics. I think at one point Dad started to become a little Republican, and Mom stayed Democrat.

"I was raised a little more Catholic than Michael because I went to Catholic school. Michael never did. Michael wasn't actively religious. He never doubted the existence of God, or certain moral codes, but it was casual. I think he believed in an afterlife as much as anyone. The difference between us was that I was always fascinated by religion. I'd come home from Catholic school and say to my mother, 'They taught me that Mary was Jesus' mother and she was a virgin,' and, y'know, 'What is this, Mom?' And she'd say, 'Well, Frank, anything is possible, and Jesus was a very wise man, but maybe she wasn't a virgin, still he was a wise man.' And then she'd tell me her more liberal viewpoint. So I grew up with a comparative religious understanding. Michael was more interested in worldly emotional things."

Yet Bob Avian recalls a night when Bennett, stricken with the flu in his apartment, waiting for a doctor summoned by their "doctor expert," Marvin Hamlisch, had a dramatic vision of death. Avian tried to humor him. In a whispery voice Bennett asked him to straighten up the apartment, particularly to rearrange a cluttered drawer.

"Smirking, I go, 'Is this the death drawer, darling? Anything else?'

"He said, 'Don't laugh at me now. I just want everything cleared up before . . . I go.'

" 'What else, darling?'

"He said, 'I probably should do my last act of contrition.'

"I said, 'You're still a Catholic, Michael, when it comes to death.' "

It's Frank DiFilia's impression that his brother "never had doubts or confusions," all very different from the sibling confusion DiFilia himself felt, all very different from his own bewildering role as family go-between, which he offers as proof of his importance to his mother and father. Resentfully, DiFilia watched his brother climb as he stood in the dust.

"But as his success grew, as he extended his ability to become more and more individual, his ability to become a simple human being became less and less. He was always preoccupied with the tune in *his* head, with *his* dance, with *his* rhythm.

"When he was young Michael used to harbor emotional energy. The situation between Mom and Dad was pretty explosive. Michael thought there'd be an eruption one day. Suddenly—no family! The security would be gone. When I came along I was basically at the mercy of the three of them. Mom and Dad were well-intentioned, loving people, but they couldn't achieve harmony in their lives. I remember thinking: Why are these people so unhappy? How can I make them happier? I'd try to be pleasant to all of them. Michael would control my insecurities. He was very good with 'Relax, it's okay, I'll take you out of this.' He would control everything, save us, save the family.

"When he was dying and finally let Mom and me see him in

Tucson, he still had to pretend he was in control, still had to present this image of strength. Here was this shriveled E.T. in a wheelchair, a hairless, alien creature, brownish in color, less than ninety pounds, a shriveled horrible sight, and he was still playing control. It had been maybe ten or fifteen years since I needed that from him."

Mrs. DiFiglia: "Oh, he changed, my Michael changed . . . Oh, he danced so beautiful, my Michael . . ."

CHAPTER THIRTEEN

Mind Games and the Universe Cue

(1978)

Two days before the first run-through of *Ballroom*—after sixteen weeks in workshop at Eight Ninety Broadway—Michael Bennett had dinner at Wally's on Forty-ninth Street with Bob Avian and Susan MacNair. MacNair had worked on *A Chorus Line* as Bennett and Avian's personal assistant/chief secretary, had become a trusted associate and had joined Bennett, Avian and John Breglio—under the name Quadrille Productions—to produce *Ballroom*. MacNair's enthusiasm, intelligence and dedication appealed to Bennett, whereas Bernard Jacobs, who was now manipulating some of the strings, wondered why "a secretary" was being pushed as a producer.

Susan MacNair loved and admired Michael Bennett as much as anyone. And like some of the women who would get close to him, she was finally treated with casual brutality. Unlike most of the others, she would never forgive him: "I left the job at Eight Ninety, walked out because I didn't want to have any bad feelings about him." She later worked for Mike Nichols, and witnessed Bennett's "outrageous meanness and financial demands" after Nichols and Tommy Tune secured his help on *My One and Only*. MacNair remains silent: "Everyone is not entitled to the truth."

At Wally's restaurant on September 25, 1978, Michael Bennett coddled fear like a cat ready to claw anything in its path.

"Paranoia? Wanna hear about my paranoia? The exhaustion after *Chorus Line*; the trouble I had with Universal over movies I wanted to make; the trouble *I imagine* having with Universal over the *Chorus Line* movie, which now, by the way, I plan never to have anything to do with; the trouble about the *Chorus Line* royalty I gave to the kids when I didn't have to; the gossip about the Rolls, with no one saying, by the way, that I had never owned a car before, had never owned anything in my life, not a house, a boat, anything, and no one saying I didn't drive and had to hire a driver; my failure with Donna, and our failure with each other; the Equity hassles over workshop—wanna hear more?

"Yes, by the way, I'm paranoid. You wanna hear about my paranoia? I'll tell you about my paranoia."

The nasal tone of Michael Bennett's words suggested drowning.

"Look, I had a nervous breakdown in November. I got this crazy idea that somehow, unknown to me, I was a protégé of the Mafia, that they owned me, had owned me from birth in Buffalo, that my parents were in on it, even my dancing-school teacher, and that I owed everything—even critics' reviews!—to the Mafia. I've gotten over some of that, worked it out with my analyst. I'm a lot less manic.

"Now, wanna know why I'm doing *Ballroom*? I mean, beyond the fact that I happen to like it as a property. Wanna know why I'm doing *Ballroom*? It's about two vulnerable middle-age people and how they fall in love. As uncomplicated and sweet as that! Wanna know something else? Everything I have—*everything*—is riding on *Ballroom*. My career, all my money. I'm the sole producer. I own it through Quadrille Productions. At one point, and this is a whole other story, Joe Papp was going to produce it with me. He backed out, came back in, backed out, and this went on and on. Finally, I couldn't take it anymore and I gave him until the last week of our tryout in Stratford to buy in twenty-four percent. Then I just set about raising $1.5 million to produce it.

"I'm thirty-five years old now, and I'm Michael Bennett. I didn't want to have to go to a roomful of investors and then have to put up with their suggestions. I don't want to do that anymore. I don't want to hassle over budget. I'm not extravagant but I am indulgent of talent, and talent costs money. The only shows I worked on that failed, failed because some producer, like a David Merrick, cut costs here and there. I just made up my mind I wasn't going to tap-dance for investors.

"So, with the help of Bernie Jacobs and the Shubert Organization, I sat down and figured out how I could own *Ballroom*. I got $1.5 million from Morgan Guaranty by signing over to them everything I had, the building I owned on Broadway and East Nineteenth, my workshop, my van. What it comes down to is: a bank is backing a Broadway show.

"What it also comes down to is my feeling that this is 'Get Michael time.' "

A Chorus Line was a tough act to follow. It took four years to follow it. The true extent of the show's success was still unknown (no one yet knew it was a theatrical phenomenon) when Michael Bennett decided to do *Ballroom*, an adaptation from Jerome Kass's 1975 teleplay about his mother called *Queen of the Stardust Ballroom*.

In outline, it seemed an odd choice, a menopausal musical about a lonely widow who has a ballroom romance with an unhappy man burdened with a complaining wife. But Bennett saw the story as a continuation of—almost a sequel to—*A Chorus Line*. Neither the major nor the minor characters in Kass's script were allied to show business, but dancing was an important part of their lives. In *A Chorus Line*, the act of dancing was an avocation and a livelihood; in *Ballroom*, it became a hobby, a pastime, a weekly escape, a Saturday evening spent in a Bronx dance hall where weak streaks of light from a spinning crystal ball hid the truth, where the closeness of the tango and the acceleration of the waltz were an escape from life's indifference and dreariness.

Ballroom became Michael Bennett's answer to *A Chorus Line*'s nagging question about what you do when you can't dance anymore. You dance as best you can, dream often, barter old hopes for new ones and, always, you go on. It was also a testimony to his parents, particularly to his mother, and to Bernard and Betty Jacobs. If Jerome Robbins had dedicated *Fiddler on the Roof* to the Jews in Russian pogroms, *Ballroom* was a reminder of far less global suffering, smaller disturbances of heartache in a world apart from international calamity. Although *Ballroom* wasn't about performing, it was still about dance, and its fifty-year-old characters could be interpreted as the *Chorus Line* hopefuls grown older and, perhaps, wiser. In a sense the difference between *Fiddler* and *Ballroom* was Michael Bennett's limitations. There was never a political frame around his musicals. They stayed within the family, whether that family was the generic family or the symbolic family of show business.

"*Ballroom* was about real human beings, from the Bronx, for heaven's sake!" Jerry Kass says. "And it turned out that Michael didn't know from the Bronx *despite* his upbringing. My feeling was the show should have been done small, and in a small house like the Booth Theater, like *Sunday in the Park with George*. And for one-third the cost. It wound up a $2 million show, and it had only cost $800,000 for the TV movie! Michael once told me a story that turned out to be prophetic. He told me he had put on a show in high school and the budget was the highest in the history of the school, $2,000. He borrowed the sets from the local television network, and I remember him saying, 'It could have gone to Broadway.' The fact that he was living in Buffalo had nothing to do with it; he was living on Central Park South even then!

"I knew *Ballroom* was strange for him, but he did it with love. But it was really Bob Avian who wanted to do it. When we were working on *Roadshow*, Bob had a collection of television tapes. He told me he usually only taped musicals, yet he had taped *Queen of the Stardust Ballroom*. We watched it, and I sensed then that Michael was attracted to it for reasons that had less to do with what it really was."

Having met John Breglio and felt bonded by "smart little Italian guy closeness," Bennett wanted Breglio to be one of *Ballroom*'s active producers. When he presented the idea to Bernard Jacobs, the response was fury. By this time Jacobs had become the serious surrogate Jewish father offsetting the Sicilian wild-card instincts of Michael Bennett's irresponsible sire, and he was simply unable to tolerate Bennett's intimacy with Breglio. He was deeply resentful of the developing closeness he felt between them. It was as though his Jewish-Italian "son" were turning his back on Tel Aviv to live in Calabria. Jacobs, the lawyer turned Shubert expert, also resented the notion that just anybody could become a successful producer. According to Avian, Jacobs "pressured Michael into getting rid of John; they're good friends now, but it *was* open warfare."

Jacobs: "Breglio was the typical little Italian boy making good, and Michael had a soft spot for poor little Italian boys—like Breglio and Matty Serino. Michael wouldn't have anybody else do the advertising but Matty, and he always stood up for him.

"Understand, Michael was always about games. Long before he tried to break away from me and buy the Hellinger Theater, he had the idea in his head and he brought John Breglio into it. I had lunch one day with Bobby, Breglio and Michael, a hamburg joint, Charley's at Forty-fifth. After I came back to my office, there was a message from Michael. 'You and I shouldn't be so friendly. I want to be an independent producer. And people out there cannot perceive that I am your pigeon. I have to have my own independent life, so we really should break it off.'

"This was Michael's game, and he promoted Breglio to sell that bill of goods. And John really didn't know he was being promoted. Michael came up here later that day to see what would happen, to play out the game. Ultimately what happened was that John got fired. That broke up the whole arrangement, and Breglio went back to his law firm. Before any of this even happened Michael was involved in another of his games. Bernie Gersten wanted to be one of the producers on *Ballroom*, so Michael had all that conflict going on between Bernie and Breglio. Michael enjoyed all this, particularly provoking all kinds of arguments between John and me.

"One evolved over John's law firm and their handling of the divorce from Donna. The firm was getting deeper and deeper into legal complications. Donna had signed an affidavit—it hadn't yet been filed—alleging Michael was a heavy user of cocaine, homosexual, a whole host of disclosures. The affidavit had been served to Michael, and he and Sue presented it to me. Donna was suing for alimony, separation—God knows what. I talked to her, arranged a meeting with Breglio's firm and settled it. Michael and Sue were exuberant. Everything was settled. Michael was happy. But happiness with Michael never lasted more than twenty-four hours. It was something you won."

"Bernie and I have had an electric relationship," John Breglio says, "but, ultimately, a very good one. Sparks flew between us for a long time. I don't know if it was resentment, or a sense of competition from a young kid suddenly close to Michael and trying to run his business. I came into it with good intentions, planning to work with everyone, including Bernie Jacobs. I was a thirty-year-old kid mesmerized by Michael Bennett. I wanted to produce, wanted to be involved, and, naturally, leaving the firm put me in that circle. I did come right up against Bernie and his love and affection and loyalty for Michael.

"I think, at first, he may have . . . resented . . . or . . . or . . . or . . . or . . . distrusted my intentions. People are—rightfully, I think—cynical and suspicious when anyone gets close to a powerful, rich entertainer. There was just no way I could prove to anyone I was trying to do something good for Michael other than to just do it. Michael and I believed in each other strongly.

"Bernie made it clear I had to get out. Finally, one day at Eight Ninety, Michael came into my office, closed the door and said, 'It's not working, is it?' 'No, it's a disaster.' We agreed it was best to stop."

Mrs. Jacobs: "*Ballroom* was a very tough time. Just before it, Michael and Sue asked me to read musical scripts for them at Eight Ninety. They wanted to liberate me, put me to work so I'd be independent. They both said my taste was pretty much the same as theirs, so I became a reader. In the seven years I never found a thing. Michael's dream was to be the Musical Joe Papp, to have Eight Ninety a beehive of shows going on, with him running in and out of each room teaching them how to direct. He'd become Joe Papp, and eventually I'd have a staff of readers. I knew it would never happen, but I enjoyed being there. After I'd read for a couple of years, the situation was just *un*believable! Not a germ of an idea in any script.

"Sue MacNair and Bernie Gersten became the *Ballroom* producers after John Breglio left. Sue didn't know anything about producing, and Bernie Gersten had only produced nonprofit theater. It was a tough time. Sue's very bitter. When Michael gets angry he gets good and angry. I guess he must have made it uncomfortable enough for Sue to quit. I like Sue. She was really crazy about Michael. She did everything and anything for Michael."

Jacobs: "The point is, there was a different development in their relationship, and Susan came to think her position was not what it should have been. When Michael makes up his mind somebody is going to go, he doesn't tell the person to go. He just makes life so impossible for them that they make up their own minds to go. This whole thing goes through a whole host of things. When Michael made Sue the producer of the show, he didn't do it because he wanted her to produce the show. *He wanted to prove to Susan that she could not produce the show!* You gotta remember that Michael was always a little bit crazy! Everything Michael did was half sane, half crazy. And if it worked out right, he knew it all along and that's why he did it!"

Exasperation scrapes irony in Bernard Jacobs' words.

Jacobs: "He'd always be able to figure out fifty different reasons why he was right all along."

It has been suggested by Avian that Bernard Jacobs felt his place was being usurped by John Breglio. Jacobs was being pushed out in the cold. And Jacobs' wife, now the established reader at Eight Ninety as well as a maternal presence in Bennett's life, was caught in the middle. In near-hysteria Mrs. Jacobs would confront Bennett and Avian day after day, saying, "You can't do this to Bernie, it's making him crazy!"

In the meantime Breglio had cut his ties with his law firm and was playing Jacobs' role as Bennett's producer/lawyer, but the role was doomed to a short run. As Mrs. Jacobs' cried in her Eight Ninety office, a few rooms away Bennett and Breglio were being castigated on the phone by her husband. Finally, Bennett gave in. He told Breglio he couldn't fight it anymore. Jacobs had won. Shelving his plan to become a producer, Breglio went back to his law firm.

Breglio had been with Paul, Weiss, Rifkind, Wharton & Garrison only six years when he left to form Quadrille Productions with Avian, MacNair and Bennett. "No one could deny the power of Michael Bennett," Breglio says. "There was no way I could resist the power at that time. So I took the chance." Bennett was well liked as a Paul, Weiss client, and the capper to Breglio's decision was the firm's offer to rehire him if the producing deal didn't work out. *Ballroom* was not yet on the Quadrille schedule, but there were three other projects: a revival of *Peter Pan*, a Western musical and the Jerry Kass *Roadshow* script. Bennett eventually decided to go ahead with *Ballroom* because, at that point, it seemed the simplest and the most practical. It had had a tryout of sorts on television, Kass was available, so was Billy Goldenberg, who was going to write the score, so were Alan and Marilyn Bergman, who were to do the lyrics.

At this time, with Breglio's legal help, Michael Bennett was blueprinting the standard structure for workshop productions with Actors Equity. Although *A Chorus Line* had been done in workshop, the process hadn't been formalized. There had been after-the-fact grumbling from Equity that actors had been—and were still being—exploited.* They were being worked hard and paid little, and their

---

*Priscilla Lopez became the Actors Equity representative for the *Chorus Line* cast.

efforts inevitably far exceeded any potential reward. Actors submitted to the process because they believed in dreams: discovery and possible stardom meant more than an equitable hourly wage.

The *Chorus Line* workshops taught Michael Bennett many lessons. It was imperative to keep costs down during the period of refinement. He had seen shows swallow profits during standard rehearsals, as well as during costly out-of-town tryouts. Musicals, particularly, needed time. Too often he'd been involved with productions so rigidly scheduled that there was simply no way of gaining time. You were straitjacketed at center stage. He wanted the ultimate creative freedom of being able to say to a Bernie Jacobs, "No, we're not going in yet; we're not ready to open."

Usually a production had to go forward no matter what. Opening nights were mostly immovable. Theaters had been booked months in advance; tickets sold; theater parties lined up. Overeager for the applause of dollars, investors cared only that the work was good enough, not whether it was the very best it could be. *A Chorus Line* became what it became because of Michael Bennett's painstaking dedication. To maintain the unhurried atmosphere he needed, he knew he'd have to pay more than he had for the *Chorus Line* workshops. He couldn't afford normal rehearsal rates. All that had to be discussed and agreed upon with Actors Equity and that, in itself, took a lot of time. Retroactively, without prior agreement, he had given the *Chorus Line* dancers a piece of the show. He hadn't had to do that. But he thought it showed good faith, as well as belief in the workshop process.

Breglio: "During this period Michael was also looking for space, a building. Eventually I started negotiations with the owner of a building on lower Broadway, Eight Ninety. The owner found out it was Michael Bennett, then didn't want to rent, he wanted to sell. Michael bought it for $600,000, which wasn't insignificant in 1977. I mean, the area was known as up-and-coming but no one was buying buildings down there at that point. Marvin Schulman, Michael's business manager at the time, wasn't very happy about it. But like anything else, when Michael made a decision—"

Smiling, Breglio hears Michael Bennett in his head and starts to mimic one of his frequent little-boy question-and-answer speech patterns.

Breglio: "Michael would say, 'I've never been a landlord, why can't I be a landlord? Sure I'll buy a building, why can't I buy a building? Let's buy a building.' He did the same thing about East Hampton. 'I've never owned a house, why can't I own a house? Let's buy a house.' It didn't matter the house cost $3 million."

Good ideas gone awry, Eight Ninety Broadway and *Ballroom* would pace each other in decline, both ending in recrimination and antagonism. Both would show promise, then pass quickly into history—quickly, not quietly.

Eight Ninety is a stolid brick building on the corner of Broadway and East Nineteenth, an eight-floor structure with the bulwark ambience of a forgotten era. (The neighborhood used to be a department-store area; it was later developed for light industry.) When Bennett bought Eight Ninety the ground floor was leased to an indoor tennis club; taking advantage of the first floor's double-high ceiling, he turned the club into a 299-seat theater. He tried to turn the rest of Eight Ninety into an arts complex of sorts, refurbishing a whole floor for Plum and Quadrille, then seeking support for his own "creative space" by leasing quarters to members of his technical team, designers Robin Wagner and Theoni Aldredge. (Needing "a certain sense of independence," Tharon Musser, who often does her lighting plans "at odd hours of the morning" in her house in the Village, refused to move into the building.) Eight Ninety became a series of vast, interlocking rehearsal halls for incoming shows, even some on-location movies, and it later housed a restaurant.

But as a landlord Michael Bennett was no more successful than as a husband. His developmental plans for the building ("a major workshop/meeting place for theater artists") floundered. Just before his death, with his tenants howling foul, Eight Ninety was sold for $14 million. After the sale there was an inimical financial scramble by his former friend and business manager Marvin Schulman, who claimed that he had been, in part, responsible for Michael Bennett's stardom.

Ballroom, the first musical to be developed within the walls of Eight Ninety, was a prophecy of what would later happen to the building itself. Like the howl set up by Eight Ninety's tenants, *Ballroom* would end with virulence and irony: with its associates cutting each other dead (and a once admiring member of its creative personnel deriding Michael Bennett as "that little faggot"); with the production rumored to have been internally sabotaged after it opened at the Majestic to basically hostile reviews; with the cast feeling "not only screwed [but] abandoned" when—at the crux of its post-opening trouble—Bennett left for a Columbia University trip to China in the company of fifty arts-related people, including Bernard and Betty Jacobs.

Dorothy Loudon: *"Nowhere to Go But Up* was my first Broadway show—1962—and that's when I met Michael. He was nineteen and assisting Ron Field. He was given the job of teaching me all the routines because Ronnie had the job of teaching Marty Balsam and Tom Bosley. Michael was so sweet to me. He could tap-dance, and I'd studied tap for fourteen years. I could tap better than I could do anything else, but I gave up dancing because I thought it was so disciplined. Little did I know that dancers are *the* most undisciplined people in the world, and have more fun than anybody.

"When he was working on *Ballroom* at Eight Ninety there were rumors all the time about who was going to get it, Sada Thompson, Dolores Gray, Beverly Sills. He really wanted Beverly Sills but she was still singing opera and her schedule was booked way ahead. I only got it by default, and I'm sure Michael didn't think I could do it until he came to see *Annie*. He was worried about the parallels. Bea in *Ballroom* has recently been widowed, and my husband, Norman, had just died. Michael thought it might prove too emotional for me. Like just about everybody, I think he thought I could only do comedy. But he was so perceptive. I played Miss Hannigan in *Annie* from the inside out, not as a comedic person. There was tragicness about her, great strength, survival. People loved her, crazy as she was. And Michael saw that.

"When he came to see me in *Annie*, Dolores Gray was rehearsing Bea for him. I went to the Bob Fosse party for *Dancin'* at Tavern on the Green, and Dolores was there, and I was so envious. I wanted so much to be involved. And there she was complaining bitterly about how hard it all was, and I was so furious because I thought: You son of a bitch, you cunt, oh God how can you? She hated everything, all of it. The first thing I said to her was congratulations, and she just started! I was with my friends the Hallorans and I said, 'Get me outta here, get me away from this woman or I'll kill her!' "

Bennett: "When I was considering Dolores Gray—who didn't know from subtext!—I'd been thinking of Dorothy. But Mike Nichols told me she was signed for *Annie* through November. I knew we were going into workshop in April, and there was no way I could wait. Dorothy's agent called and said she couldn't be available for the workshop but could for the Broadway production. And that was just not understanding what it is I do, thank-you-very-much! Then I found out: yes, she is signed until November, but there is an out in her contract—beginning August 6—specifically for a lead in a Broadway show. I was in the process of hiring Allyn Ann McLerie. Dorothy came in, sang, danced, read, then began sending me messages through people about how much she wanted to do it.

"Same time, by the way, I was very interested in Beverly Sills because she was beautiful and from the Bronx or Brooklyn, and I'd heard she didn't want to sing opera anymore. I called her agent and found she was booked two years in advance: 'So if you're talking about 1981 we're interested and please send the score.' I wanted to pair Beverly Sills and Dick Van Dyke. It was a hell of a lot easier getting chorus kids together who had nothing to do, no Broadway shows on the horizon, no bookings beyond the weekend.

"Surround this little scenario with the fact that I was under the microscope. It was my first show since *Chorus Line*. From the moment

I started to move on *Ballroom* I was under the magnifying glass, whereas with *Chorus Line* no one paid any attention for months and months."

If the casting was complicated (Dorothy Loudon and Vincent Gardenia were to be the musical stand-ins for Maureen Stapleton and Charles Durning in the teleplay), it turned out to be one of *Ballroom's* easier two-steps. The infighting between Bernard Jacobs and Michael Bennett's Quadrille allies flamed, then flickered out, only to flame again. And the heat was reflected in creative fire storms among Bennett, playwright Jerry Kass, lyricists Alan and Marilyn Bergman and, to a lesser extent, the Wagner/Musser/Aldredge team. Some of it was typical tryout frenzy; some of it was more serious. And, sadly, like *A Chorus Line*, *Ballroom* would end with its ensemble looking back in frustration and anger.

Bennett: "During the workshop, and later in Stratford, every time I got negative about the show—negative about my feelings in fixing it—I'd think about how I rescued all these old dancers. I'd look at the stage and remember what they were all like before they met me, what they were doing . . ."

While many of his colleagues talk about his pitiless drive toward perfection, some were happy to be his passengers. He could be abruptly, stingingly cruel. Yet it's probable that art—any kind of art, serious, commercial or for its own sake—needs demand and pressure to work its way to completion. Ruminating in contemplative quiet before the last line of a quatrain, poets are likely to be as inwardly exercised by turmoil as any director ragging his cast before opening night. Obligation is the pressure. Those who understood Bennett's drive, his self-willed obligation to show business, overlook—or temper—his cruelty, sometimes saying it mirrored their own similar compulsions. Yet the stories of "ruthless behavior" are the ones most frequently told. A gentler anecdote, such as Vincent Gardenia's about *Ballroom*, is easily upstaged by more dramatic backstage tattle.

A well-known actor, Gardenia started in the theater in Italy at the age of five with his father's troupe, the Gennaro Gardenia Company. Since then he had made his way to Broadway and Hollywood, winning awards (a Tony for his performance in *The Prisoner of Second Avenue*, an Oscar nomination for *Bang the Drum Slowly*) and a reputation as a reliable "character man" (specifically for impersonating Italians and Jews, notably Joe Benjamin in *God's Favorite*). Although he had once played *Fiorello!* in stock, Gardenia had never done a musical on Broadway or played "a leading man," the description given him when he auditioned for the role of Alfred Rossi in *Ballroom*. Bulky and balding, everybody's uncle, Gardenia was surprised to learn the role was not just that of a leading man "but a *romantic* leading man who sings and dances!"

Bennett hired Gardenia for his reality: he looked the part and he could act. But Vincent Gardenia was about as musical as an ocarina and his dancing had the same sweet-potato shape. "In all my life I never danced onstage! *Mai!* I was a little kid in Italian theater with my father—used to joke a little, sing a little, sell programs a little, never danced!"

Bennett was patient with Gardenia's lack of musical skills. But midway through the workshop, Gardenia, feeling he "really didn't have it," was ready to quit. "Tried like hell, just couldn't dance."

Listening in his comforting way, Bennett asked Gardenia to drop by Eight Ninety the next afternoon. He had something in mind he'd like to try. In the meantime, Bennett called Robin Wagner and asked him to dress the studio like a nightclub, "the Brown Derby, the Mocambo, the Latin Quarter, whatever." Then he arranged for a band and a bartender. When Gardenia arrived, half expecting he had been fired from *Ballroom*, Bennett ushered him onto the nightclub set— dimly lighted, with an extra-soft glow from a neon Stardust sign— and ordered him a scotch.

"We kibitzed a little," Gardenia says, "then Michael said, 'Drink a little, dance a little, have a good time.' I turn and see two good-lookin' girls. I like to drink, I like good-lookin' *signorine*, so I drank. And I danced."

Every afternoon for a week Gardenia went back to the makeshift

Stardust, got drunk and danced. And his fears took flight: *"Bellissima,* outta nuthin' I start to dance!"

Watching him waltz with Dorothy Loudon during a Stratford preview, Bennett said, "Vinnie's getting better. He's very good on the floor. He's not Fred Astaire. He's the spirit of Fred Astaire. And I'll settle for that . . ."

At Stratford, at the ill-conceived American Shakespeare Festival, which since 1955 had been trying to prove itself one way or another (in 1978 as a tryout house), *Ballroom* began the inevitable shakedown process after the Eight Ninety workshops. If, as Harold Prince suggests, Bennett thrived on "crises and drama," both were now reaching a dangerous climax. The danger, however, was not readily apparent to everyone. Increasingly Bennett was turning to drugs.

"It was simply one of the best working experiences in my life," Dorothy Loudon says of *Ballroom.* "Michael was so sweet and patient and understanding, and always so perceptive. He hated the way I bowed. 'You bow like Helen Hayes.' I'd been bowing in what I thought was this classy, hands-down-to-the-floor, ballet bow. He said, 'Bea wouldn't bow like that. Pretend you have a ten-carat diamond on both hands.' And from then on I went walking around with my hands up. He'd say things like that, and they'd never leave you.

"I honestly believed everything he told me was right. I'm just sorry he didn't fight more to keep the show running, but I wasn't mad at him for that. People criticized him because they felt screwed and abandoned after the opening. I didn't become bitter about it. I felt—and still feel—Michael was mortally wounded by what happened."

Kass: "I guess he was spaced out so much of the time you have to forgive him.

"At the beginning of the *Ballroom* rehearsal process I was going through a divorce. Michael said to me, in all seriousness, 'I don't allow divorces during production.' I said, 'Michael, there are *certain* things you don't have control of.' This was in Stratford. He thought the show was in serious trouble. It wasn't getting the reviews he wanted, nor the audience response, so he prepared me early on that he might bring someone in—some other writer—to add some jokes. The story was that Neil Simon had written ten jokes for *Chorus Line*. One day I saw Norman Lear at a performance, then at another performance and another. I was asked to meet with him. Norman Lear is a great friend of Alan and Marilyn Bergman. It turned out the Bergmans thought the show's problem was the book. I had the meeting, and Lear explained what he was going to do, all on tape. Every time I talked he shut the tape off. And I was hurt.

"It was Thanksgiving weekend. The divorce was happening back in L.A., and I told Michael I had to go back. I'll never forget this! He said, 'You see why theater is mostly gay? The straights always have to worry about their families!'

"I went to L.A., got a call from Michael. At this point we're still buddies. He got on the phone. 'Honey, I think we have to bring in someone else. Larry Gelbart is sitting here with me, and he's willing to rewrite the show.' *Rewrite my television script, my play, my show!* Of course I was upset, not only because he was bringing in someone else but also because I didn't think Gelbart was the right person. I said, 'Michael, am I out of the show?' He said, 'No, no, no, I'm just going to ask him to write some jokes.'

"When I got back and went to a rehearsal, I couldn't take it. It was full of awful jokes about old ladies buying dog food to save money for their dresses at the Stardust Ballroom. I found out later that part of the deal with Gelbart was that they would have to stage every word he wrote. That was it. I couldn't possibly go back to another rehearsal; Gelbart didn't want me there in the first place."

After the first *Ballroom* preview in Stratford, Michael Bennett had a small party in his suite at the Stratford Motor Inn. The show had gone well. The mood was ebullient. Nearly everyone seemed satisfied with the production, including Alan and

Marilyn Bergman, who later would wind up not speaking to anyone. Primarily "movie people" who wrote songs for Hollywood films, the Bergmans had done only one other Broadway show, a 1964 flop called *Something More*. At first Marilyn Bergman thought Michael Bennett was a genius. A big woman given to voluminous caftans and weighty perfume, Mrs. Bergman appeared at all meetings and rehearsals carrying a single long-stem rose. She was used to thorns and had some of her own. By the end of the Stratford run, her hostility toward Michael Bennett included scabrous name-calling.

What few of the creative people knew that night in Bennett's suite was that, within thirty-six hours, he would pull *Ballroom* apart and do it in a substantially altered version. The praise for the first preview, he thought, was flattery. Later still, as he sought to give the show "muscle and toughness," he changed it further—and was accused of playing mind games with the material. That night, after Dorothy Loudon, the Bergmans, Bernard Jacobs and Bernard Gersten had left Bennett's suite, he tracked his friend Ron Field through a moment-by-moment, scene-by-scene description of what Field thought was wrong with the production. Field, who was having troubles of his own with *King of Hearts*, which had opened two nights before, talked with surgical precision, *Ballroom* being his desperate patient in need of a triple bypass.

Bennett, in fact, had persuaded Ron Field to return to Broadway, which he had more or less abandoned in the 1970s for Hollywood. Bennett had long admired him, although Field qualifies the admiration.

"Our relationship only worked after he had jumped over me. While I was winning the Tonys and he wasn't, he couldn't relate to me, too jealous. Once I acknowledged that he'd done the most fabulous show ever! Y'know! I went down to the Newman for *Chorus Line's* first performance. When the lights went down and it started— 'Five . . . six . . . seven . . . eight'—I didn't laugh, breathe, applaud. I couldn't fuckin' move! Afterwards I couldn't see going backstage. I had to be by myself. I just walked around a drizzly Greenwich Village for hours. Next day I sent a telegram to the cast. For years afterward Michael said he knew he'd done it when he got that telegram. And that's when we became intimate and close. He was my best friend after that because he knew I could never equal what he had done."

Bennett listened intently as Field skewered *Ballroom*. Nothing missed Field's attention. He criticized everything from "the too costumey dresses" worn by the dancers to the opulence of the set to the Ballroom hostess, whom he pitilessly characterized ("Miss Arkansas on the runway"). He was as ruthless as only a caring professional could be. He pinpointed specific details and a general pattern, giving Bennett the critical stimulus he needed. As dawn came up, Bennett had a flash of inspiration. Referring to a metaphoric moment when the spin of the crystal ball was meant to suggest something more than raking the darkness of the Stardust, he said, "It's like life. If I can solve the beginning, middle and end, I'll be just fine. Maybe I'm late with the Universe Cue. The Universe Cue is the repetition of life's circle, and the circle is the metaphor, and the whole thing is a circle, and it's Bea's life and Al Rossi's life, and yours and mine, and none of us can be late with the Universe Cue because . . . where are we then?' "

Seemingly simple as *Ballroom* was, Michael Bennett gave it an interesting and innovative complexity. Sweeping away the Talmudic righteousness of Kass's teleplay, which had Bea Asher paying for her "sin" of carrying on with a married man by dying (as Kass's mother had done), the script allowed Bea and Al Rossi to waltz into an unknown—if perhaps bittersweet—future. Michael Bennett didn't believe in moral penalties. He believed in widening the straight and narrow. Here, just like the middle-age couples in *Follies*, Bea and Al are at the summing-up part of their lives. They've already proven themselves, and been tricked by the turns in the road, Bea in the sudden death of her husband, with whom she has lived thirty-eight years, Al in the unexplained loneliness of his marriage, as well as in the gradual diminution of his goals (only a mailman, he's a sensitive soul who reads and recites Shakespeare).

What Bennett was saying through *Ballroom* was that life is a continual sorting out. Problems don't significantly change as we grow older, only the energy invested in their solution does. To get at this subtext he had Billy Goldenberg and the Bergmans compose a score that occasionally had one character's thoughts echoed by another. In the cast of twenty-seven (plus an ensemble of thirteen), the show's eleven songs were sung only by Dorothy Loudon, Vincent Gardenia and the two Stardust Ballroom bandstand singers, played by Lynn Roberts and Bernie Knee.

But for all the steady refinement, finally, the musical didn't make it.

Kass: "What I really think is: Michael was shallow. That's why he could never make *Ballroom* work. When I said to Sue MacNair that I felt it was a betrayal for him to take my show away from me, she said, 'Jerry, you know Michael has no emotional scope.' Oh, sure, he had something else, energy, glitz, all the external stuff. If a show of his was in trouble, he knew how to pull out the lighting, knew how to change the costumes, or how to get somebody to do those things. But to get to the heart of the problem, to get to the human pain involved? No no no! He didn't know how. He couldn't. I think he was insensitive to other people because he was so self-involved, so narcissistic. I trusted his deep friendship. Then you learn—when the chips are down—you're the last person he's concerned about. He's mostly concerned about Michael; then he's concerned about something . . . called . . . the Show! That comes first, and he doesn't care how many bodies he leaves behind.

"Okay, on a certain level, I understand that. It may not be my way of dealing, but it's his. It's his value system. If having *Chorus Line* run for a hundred and twenty years is more important than having a person in your life for fifteen, well, then, that's who you are.

"When opening night came I decided I didn't want to go. My sister-in-law, Nora Ephron, said, 'You can't stay away from your own show.' I didn't want the credit for having written it unless Gelbart shared it and, for some reason, he didn't want credit at all. I told Michael I didn't want it either, and he pleaded with me. 'You can't put on a show without a writer's name; that says something to an audience.' So I accepted credit, then I got a Tony nomination, which was absurd. I went to the Tonys with mixed feelings, then to a party Michael had. That was the last time I saw him.

"See, I'm pretty naïve about coke and that stuff. During the *Roadshow* collaboration in Hollywood he used a lot of drugs, but he was always there! By *Ballroom* he was over the edge. It wasn't just the cocaine, it was cocaine after vodka. He did everything. During the last days of rehearsal, and at the opening, there was a glazed look in his eyes. I wasn't going to go to the opening. My excuse was, I didn't have a tux. When Sue MacNair heard that, she got a limo, took me to Saks, bought me a tux and said, 'Now you have to come to the theater and reconcile with Michael.' I wasn't sure I could do that, but I went to the theater. He was having a final rehearsal. I watched a little, then he and I went to Sardi's. *And at Sardi's I was sitting with somebody I didn't know, somebody who didn't see me!*

"That's who Michael was at the end. It wasn't that he was mean. It was that he wasn't there!"

In 1978 after *Ballroom* opened and through 1980, Michael Bennett's paranoia became more severe than at any point in his life. While his Mafia dreams had had the occasional goombah to quiet his fears, the terror behind the dreams now had diurnal insistence. He thought the Mafia was everywhere, behind the stage scenery and around every street corner. He thought there was a contract on his life.

Avian: "Michael was always truthful and I believed what he told me, that when he was a kid his father wanted to sell him to the Mafia.* The idea was they'd make him a star. They'd make money from him

*Discounting Salvatore DiFiglia's relationship with organized crime, Frank DiFilia says the Mafia story has been "overdramatized" by his brother. DiFilia's version is that their father may have approached the Mafia "for three, four, five hundred dollars, because Michael needed dental work." In return for the money, the Mafia would get "half of Michael's earnings" for life. "They turned him down."

and control his life. And he thought everyone was involved in a plot, that he was really being watched, that the Jacobses were part of it. Betty gave him a book and he thought it was all hidden messages within the story. He had a driver then, Paul Flannery, who had a motorcycle, and he swore that when he rode around town on the back of the motorcycle he was being watched, that they were out to get him. This was major psychosis! He'd been going to a psychiatrist forever, ever since I knew him.

"I believe the Mafia story's true because I'd heard it when I first met him. And his father did have Mob connections.

"After *Ballroom* in 1978 he thought everybody was going to kill him. There were guns pointed out windows. He once thought Paul saved his life when they were on the motorcycle. Michael saw guns in a window, and they zipped through and got saved. Paul took care of him. They got an apartment down in the Village, and Paul sort of like sequestered him for a while, kept him out of the public eye."

Jacobs: "We're in St. Thomas. Sue calls and says Michael wants to come down for the weekend. It'd be kind of crazy, you understand, this is Thursday, and he wants to come down Saturday, go back Sunday."

Mrs. Jacobs: "And we had to have him put up on a couch in somebody else's house."

Jacobs: "Yeah, and he stayed two nights. We picked him up at the airport and he was fine. We go out to dinner. After dinner Michael wants to go downtown. Nine o'clock at night! And he wants to go out! Instead, we brought him back to our house. He starts to talk to me about his youth, and how eleven or twelve years old he was in the Mafia—"

Mrs. Jacobs: "No he wasn't—"

Jacobs: "Brought into the Mafia by his father. Who knows, Betty, if this is true? Understand, I'm just telling the story. He was sworn into the Mafia. He starts telling me how he was riding around with Paul Flannery—as a matter of fact, he was a boyfriend during *Ballroom*. That was a peculiar relationship. Riding around with Paul

Flannery, they almost had several accidents and each time it was because the Mafia was looking to kill him—"

Mrs. Jacobs: "To shoot him."

Jacobs: "And he winds up this whole thing by telling me, 'I know you're my Mafia godfather! So just tell me!' "

Mrs. Jacobs titters.

Jacobs: "What do I do? I look at him and laugh. 'Michael, I'm just a middle-aged Jewish man, and I don't know what the fuck you're talking about!' He said, 'Don't tell me that! You're my Mafia godfather and you have to tell me what to do!' "

Mrs. Jacobs: "That was all coke. It had to be coke."

Jacobs: "The Mafia was going to get him because he wasn't turning all his earnings over to them, wasn't paying their taxes. When I got back to New York I called Sue and got the number of Michael's psychiatrist, the guy on Ninety-sixth Street, whatever the hell his name is. The psychiatrist apparently realized from what I said that Michael needed more surveillance. But I don't know about that psychiatrist either! He was having Michael come to see him four times a week! *Double sessions!*"

Mrs. Jacobs: "Sometimes five times a week."

Jacobs: "Double sessions. Back to back. He never got any better. Michael only got better when things got better."

Mrs. Jacobs: "When he got off the coke he was fine. He was clean regularly, I think."

Ballroom was a $2.2 million disaster. It was said to be overproduced and overdanced. The favorable reviews came too late to help. Michael Bennett's head was whirling with old grievances: his father telling him on opening night that the show was good but not another *Chorus Line*, and the loathing he felt for his father when he said it; his giving in to Hal Prince on *Follies*, and his insane attempt to throw Hal out the hotel window during the Boston tryout; his inability to put *Chorus Line* behind him, and to stop feeling like an abused father at the hands of ungrateful children; his rankling business relationship with Bernie Jacobs, never mind the loneliness he felt in his emotional life and his basic unwillingness to connect; his compulsive need to work and, ironically, how relaxation in the Caribbean had turned against him, with the sun's rays poisoning his system and giving him an immediate rash; his ceaseless longing for drugs, even though now the escape drugs offered required cutting longer lines and gulping more Quaaludes.

Having listened to Bernard Jacobs' doom about *Ballroom*'s fate, Bennett left for China. Just as *Chorus Line*'s original cast had felt betrayed when he distanced himself from them as the show carrying their dramatized lives spiraled to success, *Ballroom*'s waltzing hoofers (average age forty-five) felt betrayed as he left the country, their hopes for an extended career dwindling with his departure. The show gradually failed, running only 116 performances.

Backstage gossip has suggested that some person or organization sabotaged *Ballroom* and deliberately made the show fail. Bennett himself? The Shuberts? Why?

Bennett had had heated disagreements with his inexperienced producers, particularly with Sue MacNair and Bernard Gersten, Breglio's replacement. MacNair once implied that Bennett was so warped by his own sense of power that he came to resent not only her and Gersten but Avian as well. Although the three of them had been chosen by Bennett, he was determined to keep them in their place, especially MacNair, who had a way of being more independent—and threatening—than Avian or Gersten. While the three worked together successfully, *Ballroom* itself wasn't doing it. Early in the Stratford tryout Bennett had come to the conclusion that the show was going to be a lost cause. He needed to spread blame, if for no other reason than that his name was slapped all over the production. He also needed to prove to Avian, MacNair and Gersten that they couldn't produce without him. Despite his $2.2 million investment, he would scuttle the show by turning his back on it. If, indeed, this is what happened, it was an expensive way for Bennett to define his ego.

Or was Bernard Jacobs the person who made *Ballroom* fail?

During the falling out over John Breglio, Jacobs observed a less filial side to his surrogate son. Not only was Bennett pushing him aside; he was also trying to rival him on money matters. Bennett had to place himself at considerable risk to finance the show alone. Jacobs was glad to offer his expertise on the financing, but the gamble was that if *Ballroom* made it, he might lose his protégé, Bennett might come to think he was a Broadway entity unto himself. If *Ballroom* didn't make it, Jacobs would be able to prove that Michael Bennett's "own money" wasn't enough, that he was still a kid who needed the business and legal acuity of others, meaning himself, of course, and the Shubert Organization.

Or was it, as the lore had it, sabotage by the box-office personnel?

The ticket sellers at the Majestic knew *Ballroom* had not won the reviews it needed to run. The good reviews were few, the majority were either mixed or negative. Lacking both the support of the critics and an aggressive ad campaign, *Ballroom* was bound to be short-lived. To the box-office personnel an abbreviated run meant an interruption of their employment. Meanwhile, word of mouth was highly favorable on a new incoming musical starring Liv Ullmann, *I Remember Mama*, which was looking for a Broadway house. Rumored to be a likely hit, it might run two years or more. And here the perfect musical house, the Majestic, was stuck with a sure loser. In order to make *Ballroom* fail more quickly (it was attracting some attention because of the Bennett name), was the Majestic box office engaged in dirty tricks? There are stories about people calling for information on the availability of seats and being told *Ballroom* was sold out for weeks on end. Did the box office hasten *Ballroom*'s dismissal by telling callers it was SRO, thereby hoping to bring in more quickly a show with long-run potential? If that was the case, in this now legendary backstage mystery, the sabotage had an ironic sting. On May 31, 1979, sixty-eight days after *Ballroom*'s last performance, *I Remember Mama* opened at the Majestic. It closed the same night.

Loudon: "Michael was heartbroken at the reaction, heartbroken! The fact that some people thought *Ballroom* was insulting to older people, to middle-age people filled with false hope, well, that just bewildered him. Then a lot in the show felt he just gave up on it. There were the usual speeches from the Shuberts about how we were going to run, all that. Meantime—and you can't hide these things—people are calling the box office and are being told, 'Sorry, sold out.' That stuff got back to us. Something funny *was* going on. I'm not sure what, and I'm sure everybody would deny it."

In Bennett's mind, in the midst of *Ballroom*'s problems, there was a paramount image, the disturbing figure of a man with a crippled leg, a powerful New York drama critic. If not actually in the Mafia's employ, to Bennett he was a symbol, a strange warning from which there was no recourse. He disliked *Ballroom*, and the hard wallop of his review was in no way softened by a later Sunday piece by Walter Kerr in the *New York Times* praising the show. Bennett, who had a far more level respect for critics than, say, Harold Prince had, saw himself up against something he could neither manipulate nor control. Tangled in his own psychological web, he saw his work warped in the critic's dark psychology. Years later Bennett said, "He wrote about the show's graceless movement. Graceless movement! He was accusing me of *his own* affliction! How can anyone deal with that?"

To escape the *Ballroom* brouhaha, Bennett accepted an invitation from Columbia University to visit China. The trip was one of the first cultural tours before the United States had an ambassador in Beijing. Approximately fifty guests were invited, among them architects, sculptors, museum directors and theater people. Bennett's group included Bernard and Betty Jacobs; Philip Smith (of the Shubert Organization) and his wife, Phyliss; Anna Sokolow, the choreographer; and Robin Wagner.

"Michael wasn't a tourist," Robin Wagner says. "I mean, he wouldn't get up at seven in the morning to go sightseeing, and he hated all the restrictions by the Chinese government. We had to scrounge around at night to find vodka and a place to drink. One of the happiest memories I have of him is the Peking Ballet. We went to a ballet class and he just took it over, the way Michael would. The big movie when we left New York was *Saturday Night Fever*, which had Travolta doing the Hustle. Someone had a tape of the music, and Michael decided to teach the Hustle to the Peking Ballet. These were the regular members of the company, twenty years old or so, not kids—and they just went wild! They'd never experienced anything like it. They were full of pride because they knew they were the only ones in the whole vast sweep of China who could now do the Hustle!

"The next day we were leaving Beijing for Nanking, then down to Shanghai, and the whole ballet school came to the train to see him off. One of the dancers came up to him, hesitant, very deferential. She was afraid he was going to teach the Hustle along the tour. She said, very shyly, 'Mr. Bennett, please don't dance in Shanghai.' "

Recalling Bennett in "his Mao uniform," Mrs. Jacobs says that he told her husband, " 'Bernie, if you and I were in this society we'd be commissars.' "

On one occasion, visiting a historic grave site in the company of thousands of Chinese tourists all dressed alike in olive drab or navy, Bennett said, "There really aren't a billion people in China. There are only about twenty-five thousand, and the government just keeps moving them from city to city."

He hated China for the opposite reason he hated London, servility opposed to snobbishness.

"No matter where he went Michael was just never able to relax," Bob Avian says. "He couldn't find the answer for that, although maybe later he did, in East Hampton. He had this fixation—and it happened whether he was stoned or not. If he was working on something and was interrupted, or an unknown element developed, his brain waves would, like, be disrupted. He'd have to regear, and maybe at that moment he wasn't ready because his thoughts were fixed with such intensity on one subject, one project. He couldn't just turn himself away to something else.

"I was always looking to get away from the pressure, and I found the answer in hundreds of ways. He was very upset with me on that score. He found the house in East Hampton but, of course, it had to be a big splashy estate. Bing! He gets there and he's on the phone!

"The only way he knew how to function was in the show-business world. It was very sad. I'd go, 'Baby, let's go antiquing, shopping, do crosswords.' He couldn't, wouldn't. He just never stopped working. Work burned in his brain like a drill. He would tell me about sleeping. He never slept on any deep level. His mind was always close to the top, and everything was always, always cookin'."

The patterns Michael Bennett had developed to get him through *Ballroom* had become habit. He was hooked. In addition to Marlboros, marijuana and vodka, he was pacifying demons with three Quaaludes a day—"gorilla pills," as one of his friends calls them. Within a short time the daily combination included cocaine and five Quaaludes. One Quaalude is thought to be enough to purr the most jangled system. For all the sought-for quiescence, Bennett's behavior became more fevered. The physical intensity relaxed only to spring from his mouth in furious words. When the words weren't erratic, his actions were.

CHAPTER FOURTEEN

Steppin' to the Bad Side

(1981)

If *Ballroom* was a mistake, Michael Bennett considered he had paid his dues, $2.2 million worth. He had given the street the flop it expected. And earlier, down off a high horse, he had altered his image by shifting from the Rolls-Royce to the Ford Econoline van. Was all that enough to make him appear humble? Was the real mistake that he had done a musical outside his territory, a musical that wasn't about what he knew best, show business? Was his affection for the middle-age dancers as remote as his affection for his parents? Did audiences, somehow, sense the distance?

What would he do next?

What about the project he and Bobby had in mind of musicalizing *Love Me or Leave Me*, the old movie with Doris Day as Ruth Etting? That was real backstage stuff. They had already talked to Ann-Margret.

What about this "black opera" Bobby had heard about at Joe Papp's? Could a black opera be backstage enough to keep him interested?

Avian: "A lot of *Dreamgirls* came about because of me. I'm not tooting my own horn. For some reason Tom Eyen thought I was

Michael Bennett. We ran into each other one day on the street, and he told me about this show, *One Night Only*, he and Henry Krieger had been working on down at the Public. Eyen had written it, and he was directing it, but he worked so slow he couldn't seem to get anything on long enough to judge it. So they'd let it go. He wanted to audition it for us at Eight Ninety. By this time he had gotten over the confusion of who I was. I said, 'Sure.'

"He came in with Henry, who'd done the music, and three black girls. Henry narrates Tom's story. The girls get up and do all these routines. And I love it! Who can resist three black girls singing those kind of numbers?"

Bennett wasn't as sure about the material as Avian. They had had an opportunity to base a show on the Motown Catalogue of 1960s hit songs and Bennett had turned it down. Wasn't this much the same kind of music, and, strictly speaking, only a kind of facsimile, not 100 percent original? During this discussion, Avian mentioned the possibility of letting Eyen and Krieger proceed alone, with him and Bennett as producers. And that became the first arrangement. Bennett and Avian suggested to Eyen that Michael Peters would be the perfect choreographer. Peters had done the dances for *Comin' Uptown*, a black musical based on *A Christmas Carol*. Although the show had run only forty-five performances, they thought Peters' work was superior. He was bright, very talented and black, all of which would be an asset.

Bennett put up the money for a *One Night Only* workshop at Eight Ninety. While still searching for something that would involve them creatively rather than just as producers, Bennett and Avian occasionally looked in on Eyen and Krieger, who were hammering out their ideas in a studio next to Bennett's office. Avian recalls that the "book was awful, nothing like what it became." In the second act, Effie, the central character, left the singing group and "became a nurse taking care of an old woman, Estelle Getty, who had lines like: 'It's not the race I hate, it's the radios!' "

By the end of the first workshop, Bennett was beginning to lose faith in the overall project. He felt the only thing Eyen and Krieger had going for them was one song, "And I Am Telling You I'm Not

Going," an astounding masochistic ballad about hanging on to love even though your lover has shown you the door. He and Avian told Eyen what they thought the show should be about. Halting the workshop, Eyen and Krieger started rewrites based on some of the new ideas. But by the end of a second workshop, Bennett was ready to drop the project. Then Avian came up with the plan of Bennett replacing Eyen as the director, which, to their surprise, Eyen and Krieger accepted.

A third workshop began, with Bennett directing, as well as choreographing with Michael Peters and Avian. Because they had no cast, for a week or so the three of them mimicked the lead singers, the so-called Three Dreams—Bennett as Deena, Avian as Lorell, Peters as Michelle. Eventually real singers were hired and plot and characters were refined, but again Bennett became dissatisfied. By now each workshop had absorbed six weeks, with breaks in between. The time had mounted close to eighteen months, and there was very little to show for it. Various singers had come and gone, come and gone, including Jennifer Holliday. Bennett wanted out, but Loretta Devine, who'd been involved in the musical from its inception with Eyen and Krieger, persuaded him to give *One Night Only* one more try.

"During six weeks of the fourth workshop," Avian says, "we just sit around a table and do it as a radio show. Which, possibly, is why it turned out so cinematic. Jennifer was back with us. What we were doing was just getting it *written*, inch by inch, note by note, working up to the big day at the end to present it to the moneymen. We're about to have the Shuberts and a few others see it, right? And Michael and Jennifer have this big fight, and she walks out—like two days from the backers' audition . . ."

Beyond Loretta Devine's persuasion, what had kept Bennett interested in the project was "And I Am Telling You I'm Not Going," specifically as sung by Jennifer Holliday, a big, innocent, twenty-year-old black girl who was creating a lot of attention in *Your Arms Too Short to Box with God*—a gospel musical based on the Book of Matthew—at the Lyceum Theater. He knew Holliday's Abyssinian Baptist Church coloratura stomp-and-holler was the real thing and not easily duplicated. He thought he could make her a star. What he hadn't counted on was a confrontation with an ego as big as his own, in this case the "God-directed" ego of a two-hundred-pound Texas Baptist who, as Jennifer Holliday herself says, "didn't really give a hoot about no Broad Way!"

Holliday: "I left the first workshop because it was then more like a real corny Supremes story. I was doin' *God* at night on Broad Way, the workshop during the day, and gettin' myself real tired, somethin' like seventy-five hours a week. When I came back for the second workshop it became more like it was bein' a story, y'know, but my character was not to have appeared at all until the second act, and they kept comin' at me, y'know, with how Effie was supposed to be on drruuggss and, like, she couldn't get her life together, and this whole kinda thing. I said this is ridiculous, I'm not playing puppet to this here girl. Effie to me was, like, oh, sickening! So I left the second workshop too and went back to Texas.

"When I came back again I told Michael, yah, I'll do the backers' audition but I'm not goin' to Broad Way. Which is when he fired me or I quit, I don't remember . . ."

Bennett remembered.

Working night and day, unable to sleep, calling friends and colleagues in the early-morning hours, allaying tensions with coke and pills, he was plagued by a series of illnesses, including what was thought to be an allergy to cats, as well as a virus labeled CMV, which eventually caused hepatitis. Exactly at this point he had a knock-down-drag-out shouting match with his presumed star.

Bennett: "Here I was . . . this . . . this—what? Producer, director, choreographer—with Broadway behind me, right? And here I am thirty-eight years old and this kid, this plump twenty-year-old, is sitting in my office, looking at me and saying, 'So what?' about being a star. And it blew my mind. Physically upset me. Made me dizzy. I remember I had to get up from my chair and stare out the window to collect myself.

"I fired her because she wasn't doing the part, she wasn't acting it. I've always believed that with talented people the talent is tied to the reality of their existence. And Jennifer was tied in to this attitude that it all just didn't matter! It didn't matter if she was in a big Broadway show. It didn't matter if she was front and center with a tear-your-heart-out, once-in-a-lifetime ballad she would be originating! It didn't matter if she became a star. I had a hard time with that—you know what I mean!?

"But Jennifer had this quality, and the quality seemed to be made up of opposites, like independence and vulnerability, and I wanted them in the show, wanted them as part of Effie's character. But she didn't always trust me. She backed off. Got independent. Then I backed off! We didn't communicate onstage or off. It was an awful situation, a dead end. But when Jennifer first sang 'And I Am Telling You I'm Not Going,' it haunted me. All the time and ever after. I went around humming it, like I couldn't escape the heartache.

"After I got mad and fired her, I knew no one else could sing the song that way, with that fire, with that pain. I knew I had to resolve our differences, but—in my own way—I'm as stubborn as she is."

Holliday: "Like when I said I'd do the backers' audition and nothin' else, he said, 'I don't want you to do that. I don't want you to do anything for me.' I said, 'Fine then, we won't do anything.' "

Now, with the backers' audition forty-eight hours away, everyone connected with the production tried to find another Effie, if only, as a workshop joke had it, "for one night only." There was no way the role could be talked, no way "And I Am Telling You I'm Not Going" could make its impact without being sung. Michael Peters brought in Alaina Reed, who, although physically not right for Effie, was a fast learner. Since Eight Ninety was under renovation, the audition was to be simply staged around a big U-shaped table on the seventh floor, with chairs on casters rolling one member of the cast or another up and away from the strategically placed microphones. Avian recalls the place "was a shambles, like a set for postwar Berlin, half-torn-down walls, naked light bulbs, cables and wire, a *shambles!*"

Decor and refinement could not have meant less to the Shuberts or to the record producer David Geffen, who were interested in investing. What they heard and saw in the gutted rehearsal space, they liked. Bernard Jacobs imagined it refulgent in the ambience of one of Bennett's favorite "musical houses," the Imperial, a Shubert property. Geffen imagined some of the songs throbbing their way up the record charts. Thus the Shubert Organization and Geffen Records became backers. The fresh excitement stimulated a creative esprit de corps the work had lacked. Rehearsals were scheduled, then Michael Bennett fell ill with hepatitis. During the three-month delay Eyen and Krieger continued to write and rewrite. A number called "Steppin' to the Bad Side" was imagined on a hydraulic bridge in front of a wall of colored headlights, like a *West Side Story* rumble up from beneath a rubbled back lot, and was subsequently given a dazzling scenic design by Wagner and Musser. When Bennett recovered from his illness, the first thing he did was to try to win Jennifer Holliday back where he thought "she belonged."

Holliday: "Like a month went by before he called me. 'How'd ya like to be a star?' I just laughed at him and said, 'I'm goin' to be a star, probably not a Broad Way star, but I'm goin' to be a star on records, and, like, you can't have anything to do with that!' He said, 'Why don't you come in and talk about it, okay?'

"So I'm in New York and it's about three days before he saw me. He was in meetings, didn't have much time and was always just about to get to me. So I wait—you know what I'm sayin'? Then we have this date, a Friday night, and we talked for about four hours. We realized we had never talked before. He was always the director and I was always the act, and there'd been no communication. That weekend he took me to see Lena Horne at the matinee and *Amadeus* at night, and we went to Brooklyn for dinner. And, like, we were all over the place after that. I went back to Houston, got my things together, and we went into rehearsal. It was during those eight weeks that 'And I Am Telling You I'm Not Going' was really put together, when he took it, staged it and made it, y'know, into a piece of art."

In perfecting the art, Bennett was molding the artist, who was now in the palm of his hand. He was also shaping her emotional response specifically toward him—and affecting her deeply.

"Jennifer fell madly in love with him," Bob Avian says. "Totally. To the point she used to tell people they were lovers. He would buy her gifts because she was his leading lady. We were dealing with a girl who was a nineteen-, twenty-year-old virgin falling in love with Michael, who was not only her director but a white man!

"I don't think he led her on, but she interpreted it her own way when he bought her something, held her hand, had her out to the country. She was as great a manipulator and control freak as he was. She'd been dealt a wicked hand of cards, this great voice, then the physicalness, her size. Her father had been a preacher and had run off, something like that. And she had illusions about the relationship with Michael."

Did Michael Bennett love Jennifer Holliday or was he still playing dangerous games, fanning emotions he had no intention of protecting as an eternal flame? "If Michael romanced his leading ladies to get them to put out the best they had, so what?" says Henry Krieger. "Given the fantasy world of the players involved, that factor has its own fantasy life. What's so heinous?"

Sabine Cassel's thoughts about Bennett's emotional manipulation are more incisive, perhaps closer to the cruel truth. "I told Michael once, 'It's easy for you to have an affair with people you work with because they don't have the choice to say no. They need to survive and make a living. Maybe you'll find somebody next time at your level, then it will be okay, and perhaps you'll learn something.'

"With me he was testing all the time. And it didn't work between us because he thought I was too strong and . . . I don't know. He wanted and he didn't want children. He wants but he is scared, scared because . . . they might not be perfect, perhaps because of the drug problem. He was always scared the creativity is going to disappear, like you were going to take something from him. He was unable to live with someone too long. I mean, bang!—just like that it is over between us when the town house was broken into."

Everyone in and around *Dreamgirls* knew Jennifer Holliday "had a crush on him," Diane Judge says. There were jokes all the time about their "love life," some crude, some gentle. Those who knew

Bennett at a certain objective distance felt he encouraged the gossip as a way to control her, keep her in the show, Svengali again scattering spoor to keep his prey on track. Stardom wasn't that important to her. And bright as Jennifer Holliday was, she suddenly realized that *Dreamgirls* needed her more than she needed it. She was a star in spite of her disinterest in being a star, and that gave her a security that—at times—overshadowed Bennett's power, which was always a little uncertain.

Dreamgirls chronicles the career of three young black singers from Chicago who begin as the Dreamettes, become the Dreams, make it to the top of the charts and lose each other and misplace their values along the way. It's close enough to the saga of the Supremes and Diana Ross to qualify as a musical à clef, although, from the beginning, there were fierce denials about the similarity. Despite Michael Bennett's various explanations, the very sound of the names Supremes and Dreams made both the protest and the rationalization disingenuous.

Repeatedly, on the possible snarl of libel, it was said that Eyen's script was not about the Supremes. And there *was* a major difference. In the mid-1960s Florence Ballard, one of the original Supremes, had been replaced by Cindy Birdsong. Ballard dropped from sight, went on welfare and died in Detroit in 1976 at the age of thirty-two. In Eyen's shifting plot, when Deena Jones replaces Effie Melody White, Effie staggers down a path similar to Ballard's (she has an illegitimate child, gets hooked on drugs), but rights herself, marries and returns to conquer the dream that once disowned her. For all the pain, Bennett finally offered, as he did in all his shows, hope and optimism. In *Dreamgirls'* closing moment, the Dreams are reunited in a farewell concert.

Aside from any legal threat, the show was a logistic nightmare. The plot covered ten years, 1962–72 and traveled through twenty locations (among them Harlem, St. Louis, Miami, Cleveland, San Francisco, Las Vegas, New York, Chicago, Los Angeles, Chicago again and back to New York; with episodes in nightclubs, television studios, a photo session at *Vogue* magazine and a national Democratic fundraiser). Against the Krieger/Eyen parodied Motown music, Bennett wanted the story to travel as quickly and dramatically as a movie. Feeding ideas to Robin Wagner and Tharon Musser, he watched as they designed and developed a workable plan. He was about to get a scheme that would later be called Meyerholdian, although, until then, Michael Bennett had never heard of Meyerhold.

Wagner: "Michael was always like a little kid—he *was* a little kid!—when we would start the design process. I mean, the stage really was his toy. Tharon and I came up with a floor and lighting plan. The first one involved four hydraulic bridges and six towers, Plexi towers wired with lights. Michael came and sat and looked, and was mesmerized by the possibilities, which were kinetic, dynamic, not specific, and allowed him all the cinematic transitions he wanted. At that point the towers were set in place. They didn't move. I remember he tapped one of the scale models with a finger and said, 'They turn,' said it just like a kid playing with a Tonka truck. 'Could they turn 180 degrees?' 'Sure, Michael, why not.' We did 180 degrees. He looked and looked, then tapped again with his finger. 'How about 360 degrees?' 'Why not, Michael.'"

Thus, the Imperial stage was kept spacious and undefined. At one moment it was a limitless limbo, then the towers would glide into place and turn and, with Musser's light patterns raking and focusing, the space would become as specific as a scene needed. Bennett thought that together he and Wagner and Musser had solved the staging problem for anything that could ever be imagined in the future of the musical theater. The validity of this grandiose claim is, of course, open to question.

"When Michael started bragging all the time about the *Dreamgirls* sets," Diane Judge says, "I told him that there was something on Broadway even more advanced. At the Metropolitan Opera House! Five stages that could do anything! I made him go to see David Hockney's set for *The Bluebird*. I had a friend get him a seat in a box dead center of the opera house so he could go in and leave whenever he wanted and no one would notice. I begged him to go to *Tales of Hoffmann* just to see the production, to see the one-act opera ballets. And he did. Sat through all three. By himself. In the box. When he got bored he'd go have a drink, then come back. He lasted all the way through, and no one knew he was there.

"I ran into him and Robin at Philip Glass's *Einstein on the Beach* at the Brooklyn Academy, and there was Michael, bored, stoned out of his mind. He had lived through the first half, but he said, 'I think it's like the emperor's clothes. Nothing there.' He said he was trying to talk Robin into letting him go home the next act. Michael's work was wonderful, but it was limited."

Produced by Bennett, Avian, Geffen Records and the Shubert Organization, *Dreamgirls* opened December 20, 1981, at the Imperial, received strongly favorable reviews (including one from London equating Michael Bennett's staging with the abstract theatrical art of Vsevolod Meyerhold) and ran 1,522 performances, closing August 11, 1985. It cost $3.6 million and paid off its initial investment in the record time of thirty-four weeks. Jennifer Holliday lasted a year on Broadway and was replaced by Vanessa Townsell.

As *Dreamgirls* continued on Broadway, there was considerable backstage bickering among its principal women, some of it occasioned by the star treatment (cum romance) Bennett accorded Jennifer Holliday. Holliday blames others for the bickering and—while loving Bennett's coddling yet suspicious of his control—gives it a dizzying anti-Bennett spin. "I didn't cause trouble with the other Dreams. Those stories weren't true. It wasn't like that. I didn't do it to them. It was the other people that did it, Bennett, Peters, Avian. You know what I'm sayin'? They got the other five women upset with me because they feared I was young, and figured I didn't know what I was doing shooting off my mouth, y'know, and tellin' Bennett what he could do with himself, and all this other kinda stuff, like I was going to mess it up for the rest of us. With me, it was, like, oh, hey, I can do better than that, I can just leave! I won't cause trouble for anybody. At this point I was just twenty and, like, well, I was going back to school or something.

"Then they came up with this Favored Nations contract.* And I was goin', like, to the other girls, 'I can't believe you-all are goin' sign this!' It was, like, for no money, fifteen hundred a week or something, and I was making that doin' *God*! I left *Dreamgirls* after the first year on Broad Way. Fifteen hundred a week! I was the only one who left. I don't know what they got after I left, but I don't think that much more.

"When Michael got me back and I went to L.A. in March '83, I was gettin' twenty thousand a week. I stayed less than nine months. When I was on Broad Way they had that ridiculous contract for performers, that so-called Favored Nations thing, and I was, like, makin' no money. Michael took care of me with money on account of I wouldn't have been able to make it, y'know, otherwise, because my name preceded the salary and I needed certain things: a nice place to stay, nice clothes, different things for interviews, and he just took care of me, is all.

"We got close, very close, and maybe I'd have been better off if I'd taken the route of not being close to him and letting my managers and my agent beat him up. But my people were only being paid their fifteen percent, and they didn't interfere, and Michael had something to say about everything. You know what I'm sayin'?"

Avian: "Everything had to go Jennifer's way or she gave you a lot of headaches, and big, big trouble. The way a song was arranged, the way a scene was played, the way she was treated. She could be very troublesome, and as far as the show went, it was life imitates art all over again.

"She hated all the girls who played opposite her as Deena—all of them, always!—and it was hard making that relationship work

---

*The term Favored Nations comes from international trade agreements and refers to standard regulations set up so that one nation does not have an advantage over another. In the theater— where the term has been in use for about twenty years—the Favored Nations contract refers to various matters (billing, salary, treatment) relating to specific actors or groups (featured actors). In the case of *Dreamgirls*, the agreement was that the principals were to be paid the same salary.

onstage when they were supposed to begin and end friends. It was open warfare all the time with Sheryl Lee Ralph, all created by Jennifer. She was in love with Michael by the time rehearsals started, then over the edge about him by the tryout in Boston. And that probably all started when he got her back into the workshop, talked to her about what the theater was all about, took her to *Amadeus*, explained the art form, made her understand. Jennifer's a very smart girl.

"But the illusions! I would see it in her eyes. Then I heard it from one of the girls in the show, Debbie Burrell, who was her best friend. Debbie'd go, 'Bobby, I gotta talk to you. Jennifer says that Michael has asked her to marry him.' I'm going, 'Debbie, never, never, never, never!' 'But Jennifer has never lied to me.' I go, 'I've known Michael a long, long time and he would never say that, never.'

"Jennifer never brought up marriage when I was with them. It was enough for her just to be in his environment, in his home, out with him. She'd let that speak for itself."

While this romantic interracial standoff was going on backstage, *Dreamgirls* was creating a different kind of racial chaos out front. During the Boston tryout, when the title *Dream Girls* was elided into a single word (it had previously been changed from *One Night Only* to the working title *Project #9*, then to *Big Dreams*), the Serino, Coyne & Nappi advertising agency had designed the show's stylish logo: three pairs of long lustrous legs, feet arched on heels, knees akimbo through slit skirts, with three hands holding separate microphones at hip level, and the *Dreamgirls* title running beneath the legs like a platform. The three Dreams were, of course, black. The logo legs, it turned out, were white.

When a poster went up above the Imperial marquee, the legs were a discreet light tan—"definitely they weren't black," according to one source. Light tan wasn't good enough for one of the show's producers, who was trying to kill the impression that *Dreamgirls* was neither a mulatto nor a black show. The tan was lightened to white, and an observant reporter made the discovery. The poster's skin tone became a hot item, an embarrassing column item. It appeared that the Shubert Organization was afraid of identifying the show for what it was, a black musical.

Michael Bennett found all of this inexplicable but funny, a perfect example of meddlesome interference. And then there was a sequel to the logo legs story. When a television spot was being prepared after *Dreamgirls* had opened, "some very powerful people" insisted the spot feature more white people. In *Dreamgirls* cast of thirty-five, which included fifteen principals, there were three whites. Again, Bennett was laughing.

What wasn't so funny, according to a source closely involved with the production, was "the way Bernie Jacobs persecuted" Michael Bennett throughout most of the *Dreamgirls* workshops and rehearsals. "He would make Michael pay for his mistakes, or try to, and it was just something that welled up out of Bernie's personality. He stepped in a lot when he didn't have to. It's a convenient sentimentality to say Bernie Jacobs was Michael's surrogate father. If Bernie wanted to be someone's father he should have started at home. I remember the day his son came in to show Michael some *Dreamgirls* towels, tourist stuff. Poor guy. Son of the mogul. And straining. A young man without any background in life, given a job by the big Shubert boss."

Showing the usual care he lavished on all his work, Bennett spent close to $300,000 revising the original *Dreamgirls* production for L.A. With Jennifer Holliday as Effie, the show opened March 20, 1983, and quickly developed a bad reputation. Holliday frequently didn't show up and eventually had to be replaced. When word got out that the temperamental star was steadily missing performances, business fell off. "If that happens in New York," Diane Judge says, "you take your rain check and go to a show next door. But in California *they have driven, they have eaten, and there is no show right next door!* There's no place to go if your star ain't there! *Dreamgirls* never made big money, it wasn't that big a hit. The $300,000 spent on revisions went down the toilet. And Jennifer bled it dry on the West Coast, ten thousand a week, plus a percentage of the gross, plus a dressing room, a limo, and on and on.

"When the show made it back to Broadway in 1987, it won a Tony for best revival."

In California, on December 14, 1983, Michael Bennett learned of his father's death in Buffalo.

As remote as he had been from his parents, he had talked over a period of years with Louis La Russo about writing a script based on his father's life. During the 1975–76 season, when *A Chorus Line* was the talk of the town, La Russo's *Lamppost Reunion* had stirred conversation on its own. A three-act play "about a kid from Hoboken" who becomes a singing superstar, it was said to be about Frank Sinatra. It had a short run, and was nominated for a Tony Award. La Russo had two quasi-hits after that, both during the 1978–79 season, *Knock-out*, a ringside slugfest which ran 154 performances on Broadway, and *Momma's Little Angels*, a melodrama about family hatred after the death of the mother, which ran 108 performances Off-Broadway.

Michael Bennett saw Louis La Russo as a writerly reflection of himself, yet another street-smart American Italian kid making his way in the theater, John Breglio with an Olivetti. And he began talking to La Russo about Buffalo, about Sicily, the Mafia and the Magaddino crime family and, particularly, his own loving, if embattled, father-son relationship. The relationship had taken an odd turn with the *Chorus Line* success. Sal was now actively trying to compete with him in the theater, and Michael Bennett was amused. More than that, he wanted La Russo to turn the development into a play or, possibly, a movie. He even had the title in mind: *Our Father*.

Financially secure in his older son's success, Salvatore DiFiglia retired from the General Motors plant in Buffalo when he was only fifty-five. Both his sons were worried about their father's future. What was he going to do all day, play cards, the numbers, gamble? Frank DiFilia says he suggested to his father that he try an acting career.

DiFilia did so because his father was "a handsome guy who always looked younger than his years," so young that he and Bennett would frequently introduce him as their brother. "He was sitting between us at Joe Allen's, and we were asking him what he was going to do. He said, 'Maybe I'll buy some racehorses or something.' And I said, 'Dad, why don't you become an actor?' And I meant it. I always felt he had something in him, an artist, a poet—something! But he had never lived a life that would allow it. You could feel it in the man. He was incredibly gentle, sweet without being sweet. You always felt you could trust this man. He'd do anything for you. I always wanted to look like my dad. He had a big Italian nose but he was really handsome, he was really something!

"He went, 'An actor! That's a good idea!'

"Michael said, 'That's a *great* idea! I could help you out, get you going. You could play a policeman on a series. You have the look. You'd be perfect!'

"So Michael decides he's going to send Dad to acting school, then on to a career, and Dad enrolled at the American Academy of Dramatic Arts. At first Dad thought it was a joke. But there was enough— what?—vanity in him for us to convince him that there was something to it. We were doing it out of genuine concern that maybe there was something to it.

"We also thought, in a way, that he could prove himself. Maybe that was more in our minds than his; maybe he didn't feel he had to. In Buffalo he was highly respected by his peers, the street people, the bar people, the gamblers—none of whom were Mafia people; he wasn't part of that criminal element. It was a Damon Runyon world. You had certain guidelines and rules. Dad lived up to them and earned great respect. Everybody respected Sam. He'd take me around to the bars, and it was like all the men knew him. They were all great guys, but they didn't have a wide range of interest and I never knew what to talk to them about. Which is pretty much my story with Dad too. I loved him, respected him, realized he was a man of high standards, but you couldn't talk to him about much because he just wasn't interested. Same as Michael, just like Michael."

Salvatore DiFiglia took a six-week course at the American Academy of Dramatic Arts July 5–August 17, 1977. Classes ran Monday through Thursday, four hours a day of speech and movement, with a scene presentation at the end of the course. His teacher was Jorie Wyler, who remembers that DiFiglia's presentation scene was a short speech from *The Odd Couple*. Bennett wasn't present, and Donna McKechnie arrived too late to see her father-in-law's performance. George Cuttingham, president of the Academy, remembers Bennett telephoning during his father's attendance at the school and asking for classroom anecdotes, presumably for use in the proposed La Russo play. Jorie Wyler says that Bennett and La Russo visited her three years later, September 25, 1980, to talk about the possibility of doing *Our Father* as a musical. She remembers DiFiglia "as the sweetest of men, but out of his bailiwick and not seriously interested in acting or pursuing a career."

"We had more fun with *Our Father*," John Breglio says. "My recollection is that Michael always saw it as a movie, not a play, which is why I was cynical about anything happening with it. After Universal, I knew Michael would never do a movie. He was a man of the theater. He had every opportunity in the world to do a movie here, low budget, high budget, medium. There'd be calls all the time. 'Just tell us, Michael. We'll do it anywhere, Forty-fourth Street, Brooklyn, anywhere.' And he'd always wind up saying, 'I'm not going to do that.' "

Bennett's ready and "sweet" concern for his father gets a harsher interpretation from Sabine Cassel. During the months of their intimacy, Bennett constantly expressed his doubts about his heritage. "Michael was extremely fucked up about his mother and father," Cassell says. "What I know about them is through Michael. He love and hate her. The relationship with her is very difficult for him. And with him for his father too. I met them in Buffalo because we were supposed to get married. We stayed at the house. They came to pick us up at the airport with a white Cadillac. Hmmm!" she says, mocking the white Cadillac, whose Vegas-like ostentation had been consciously ridiculed by Bennett, first by his Rolls-Royce (white, then brown, but, either way, more sedate) and later by his two BMWs and a Porsche.

"His father was very nice, very much handsome, and I think Michael want to be like him, he liked what the father has.

"Michael wanted to prove a lot to his family. He was angry to prove he was the boss. He gave them money. He is the star! He had so much to prove to them he didn't have time for the rest, to show them he was okay, then to believe within himself that he was okay. But Michael he never liked himself. I told him one day, 'Listen, you don't love yourself, and you're wrong, because you're nice, very nice.' And he was.

"He could be extremely funny. Sometimes we were laughing until five o'clock in the morning! And talking! A lot of fun! And then he would . . . get crazy! And when he was doing that I'd go, 'Okay, okay . . .' "

Liz Smith offers another explanation about Bennett's family conflicts and his own complexities. "I think Michael had more prejudices against himself than anyone could ever have against him. His talent was dynamic, but I think essentially he didn't think he was so great. He had sort of an inferiority complex socially. He didn't get out of the theater. He just pretty much stayed in a world he could control. I always thought this thing of trying to measure up to his father's manliness—his father had a lot of women and all that—was just a role he decided to act out. He was driven more to men, I suppose, but it didn't make any difference. He still tried to make conquests of all the women he knew. I'd have married him in a minute if I'd been a little younger. I really loved that little guy!

"As far as Bernie Jacobs goes, I think Michael was just the excitement Bernie's life never had.

"At first Michael depended on Bernie, who is the greatest power behind the scenes, or in front of them, or anywhere else. He depended on Bernie to make things happen for him. Michael was smart. And then, maybe, he became genuinely fond of Bernie. But Bernie would faint if he knew how Michael talked about him behind his back. Nothing Bernie ever said about Michael could be worse. This is just the ways things are. These are powerful people who were using each other. The fact that they come to like and love each other isn't surprising. They just become like family, quarreling and fighting, loving and spiteful and making up and all that. Michael had that with everyone, with Hal and Steve, Tommy. He was a manly little fella—in that sense, I guess, his father's son."

When Michael Bennett heard about his father's death, he wasn't shocked; Sam had had a heart attack in his forties and, lately, a series of strokes. Bennett looked beyond the sadness of the death and saw inherent dramatic possibilities: a Sicilian tearjerker—only played out in Buffalo. There was the shared family grief and there was the lonely grief of the secret Other Woman, Mary Coniglio, and her out-of-wedlock child, little Sal, Bennett's half brother. He decided to stage a double funeral ceremony, one for his mother and the immediate family, one for Mary Coniglio and little Sal. He'd stage it as a low-keyed production number (minus light cues, of course). He'd have music, "Me and My Shadow" as a memorial melody. He and Frank would talk about their father.

And then, seeing himself in a larger role, he decided to attend the funeral dressed as a Mafia don and accompanied by his lover Gene Pruit. To his mother's bewilderment he appeared at the Lombardo Funeral Home, at 4614 Main Street, "like someone out of *The Godfather*," dressed in symbolic menace. He wore a costly chalk-stripe black Armani suit with shark-nose lapels, wide-collar white shirt, burgundy tie stippled with white dice, dark overcoat with shoulders padded heavily enough to bear the butt of a machine gun, broad-brim black fedora. The shoes on the dancing feet were as pointed and pliable as any of his deepest fantasies.

"Sam had a heart attack when he was forty-five, his first," Mrs. DiFiglia says. "He didn't look forty-five, he looked ten years younger. Then for fifteen years he was fine. Then at sixty there were a series

Not a single detail in any of his productions escaped Michael Bennett's attention. Here, he studies the precise fall of a costume in *Dreamgirls*. (© *1989 Martha Swope*)

Michael Bennett and Robert Avian during an early rehearsal of *Dreamgirls*. (© *1989 Martha Swope*)

As the lead singer of The Dreams in *Dreamgirls*, Sheryl Lee Ralph gets a lesson in attitude and deportment from Michael Bennett. (© *1989 Martha Swope*)

Sheryl Lee Ralph follows Michael Bennett's direction in this scene from *Dreamgirls*. Co-choreographer Michael Peters is behind Bennett. *(© 1989 Martha Swope)*

The Dreams Team: Jennifer Holliday, Sheryl Lee Ralph and Loretta Devine in a television sequence from *Dreamgirls*. *(© 1989 Martha Swope, Courtesy Billy Rose Theatre Collection, New York Public Library at Lincoln Center)*

Michael Bennett displays the first *Dreamgirls* logo to Robert Avian, Michael Peters (first row, left to right), Bernard Jacobs and general manager Marvin Krauss (second row). *(© 1989 Martha Swope)*

The romance between Jennifer Holliday and Michael Bennett was said to be all in Holliday's head, yet Bennett was her frequent escort. *(UPI/Bettmann Newsphotos)*

Michael Bennett discusses a scene from *Scandal* as Robert Avian looks on. *(Geoffrey Clifford/Wheeler Pictures)*

From a stepladder placed midway in the orchestra, Michael Bennett rehearses *Dreamgirls* during its Boston tryout at the Shubert Theatre. *(Cliff Lipson/Retna Ltd.)*

New Wave Director: a curly-haired Michael Bennett rehearses the ill-fated *Scandal* at 890 Broadway. *(Geoffrey Clifford/Wheeler Pictures)*

The tidy pink-and-white tin-canopied DiFiglia residence on East Delavan, Buffalo, New York. *(Richard W. Roeller/*The Buffalo News, *1987)*

Michael Bennett casts a languid eye at one of the erotic images from a dance sequence in *Scandal*, which set out to explore sexuality in the 1980s. *(Geoffrey Clifford/Wheeler Pictures)*

Robert Avian is overcome by it all while Michael Bennett beams acceptance of the awards and applause following *A Chorus Line*'s runaway success. *(Cliff Lipson/Retna Ltd.)*

40 James Lane, East Hampton. A $3.5 million estate on 10 oceanside acres that Michael Bennett bought from record producer David Geffen. *(Karen Gillham)*

Handsome, blue-eyed, blond males were Michael Bennett's "type." *(Cliff Lipson/Retna Ltd.)*

Although he sometimes considered himself ugly, the intensity in Michael Bennett's eyes and his driving intelligence were persuasively attractive. *(Courtesy of Mrs. Helen DiFiglia)*

Nominated for eight 1979 Tony Awards, *Ballroom* won only for its choreography, an award each to Robert Avian and Michael Bennett. *(Robin Platzer)*

Jennifer Holliday won a Tony Award for her performance in *Dreamgirls* and Michael Bennett won for his choreography with Michael Peters. *(Robin Platzer)*

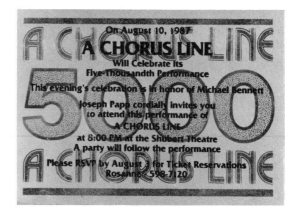

The August 10, 1987, announcement of a milestone. *(Karen Halverson, Courtesy of Merle Debusky & Associates)*

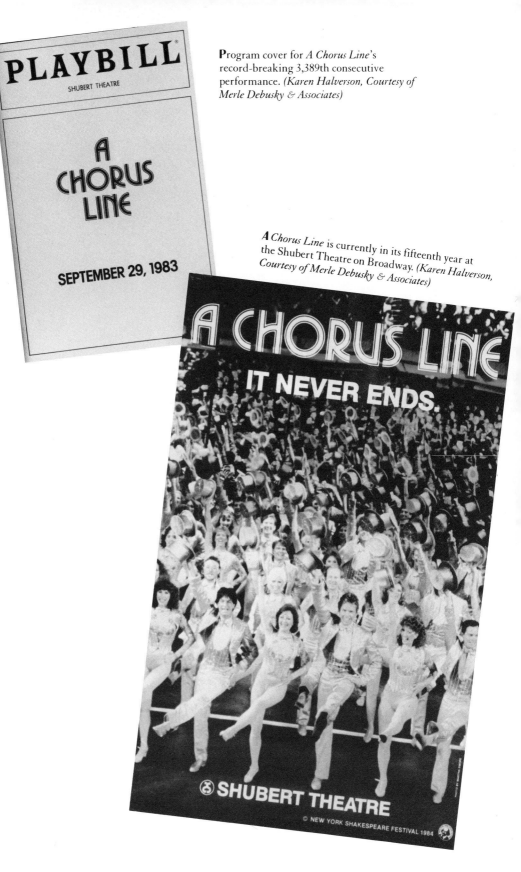

Program cover for *A Chorus Line*'s record-breaking 3,389th consecutive performance. *(Karen Halverson, Courtesy of Merle Debusky & Associates)*

A Chorus Line is currently in its fifteenth year at the Shubert Theatre on Broadway. *(Karen Halverson, Courtesy of Merle Debusky & Associates)*

A Chorus Line's exultant finale: the glittering top hat strut. *(© 1989 Martha Swope)*

A gold top hat and four historic Playbills. *(Karen Halverson, Courtesy of Merle Debusky & Associates)*

of strokes, and he wouldn't admit he was having them. Well, for one thing, look at what Sam did! He smoked three and a half packs of cigarettes a day, had high blood pressure, drank coffee all the time, didn't eat all day and would come home at eight and say, 'I don't know if I had anything to eat today.' And then the stress of gambling. He was losing very heavily the last few years. He'd gotten badly into debt, and probably didn't know how to get out. I wouldn't give him any more money but—oh, please!—Michael supported his father's habit the last few years, gave him enough money to gamble and get worse in debt!

"Luckily the banks were great to Sam. They'd loan him almost any amount of money because he paid back. When he died, well, he owed . . . I don't know the exact amount, thousands and thousands. Luckily I didn't have to pay it. I just got an attorney, who sent letters to all the banks saying I had nothing to do with it. I can remember a bookie telling me Sam lost ten thousand in one day. In one day! The bank loans probably came to a little over fifty thousand. I hadn't co-signed any of them, so I was home free. He'd just borrowed ten thousand a week before he died. It was bad enough I had to pay off his personal thousand-dollar loans, like a thousand he borrowed from his nurse and another thousand from a friend. I don't know how many bookies called me looking for money, and I said, 'Forget it, not one cent!'

"Worse thing was, Sam'd just bought me a car he didn't insure. He was ill, didn't know what he was doing. But here he dies and leaves me with this fourteen-thousand-dollar Le Sabre Buick I don't want. Funny part was, Michael had sent us a check for the car, only Sam used the money to gamble, then went and financed it. Which I didn't find out until I got to Sarasota. Sam was never down here. He was never interested in this place. I used to come down for a couple of months, then go back home, and he'd be happy to see me, he'd miss me. Then after I'd be home about a week, he'd be running off to his card games, so I'd come back here. It was crazy. I liked being here and there. I'd always go home for the holidays, Christmas and New Year's. I'd miss him.

"Sam never got excited about anything. If he did, he didn't show it. I'm more excitable. More like Michael. Or Michael's more like me. I like going places. Sam didn't like to travel, hated to go anywhere, rather stay at home, where I'm always looking for a place to go, things to do. Sam was very social at home, loved being around people. Everybody in Buffalo knew him, bar owners, policemen, the restaurants. He'd give anyone the shirt off his back. I used to tell him, 'How come you give money to everybody but me?' He'd just laugh. I really had to fight hard to get it.

"Well, Sam died and Michael came home dressed like the Mafia, and that Gene with him! He was so miserable to me that day, and the whole time he was in Buffalo. I wish he had never came!"

"Here's Michael in a nutshell," Frank DiFilia says. "He came to Dad's funeral dressed like a Mafia don. Who knows why? Success can really turn your head around. I think Michael really changed, something I didn't know for a long while. Michael didn't know how to relax with it. So he came to Dad's funeral and he had to put on a show instead of just being real—whatever that would have been. I'm sure he had gone out and bought this whole outfit. It was expensive and impeccable, like his shows. He insisted we both speak at the ceremony and, like, together. He had the organist play 'Me and My Shadow.' "

Mrs. DiFiglia: "We have a ceremony at the mausoleum after the funeral. Sam is a veteran, so they give me a flag and all that.

"Then Michael says to me, 'Mother, after breakfast we're coming back here. I've arranged to keep the funeral director, the priest, the limousines because we're picking up Sal and his mother and bringing them back for another ceremony.'

"I was in shock, 'Why, Michael, why?'

"He said, 'Because the kid has a right to be at his father's funeral.'

"I said, 'Wait a minute. What do you think's going to happen to him if he isn't?' 'Well, it's a traumatic experience and all that,' And I said, 'Michael, forget it! It doesn't matter.' He said, 'Mother, I've talked this over with my psychiatrist, and I'm doing it whether you like it or not.' "

Mrs. DiFiglia stares in disbelief above her words.

"Where I made my mistake, I should not have gone back with them. And I did. I had to be crazy! But at this point I *had* to see what she looked like, Mary Coniglio. I knew about the boy, little Sal, she had made sure of that! But I had to see her for myself! It didn't make it any worse. But, see, if I didn't, the thing was I'd still be imagining her as this gorgeous creature, and she wasn't. When I saw her—we picked her up, she got in the limousine with me. I didn't know whether she knew I'd be there or not. It wouldn't have made any difference to her. I was the one who resented her. She didn't mind me at all. I didn't do anything to her. In fact, I gave her part of my husband!"

Mrs. DiFiglia starts to whisper, as though she's talking through grief and wrath in the back seat of the black limousine.

"She was very friendly, telling me how sorry she was about Sam and all that. I'm thinking to myself: This woman is crazy. Her hair was cut real short, she looked like a man, very, very dark, dark hair, skin. I don't know who young Sal looks like. When I took Sam back and we patched things up, I took pity on the little kid, had him to the house, bought him clothes and things. We got to know each other. But now I'm looking at this woman, his mother, for the first time, and I don't know who Sal is like. I thought he was beautiful because he looked like his mother! Well, that wasn't so!

"I looked at Frank in the back seat, he looked at me and said, 'Mother, my God!' I said, 'Do you *believe* this, Frank?' See, it was we couldn't understand what Sam had been doing. At least if he had picked out someone gorgeous—but this woman was on welfare!

"When I walked in I didn't participate in the ceremony, the second one. I was in shock, I stood to one side. One of my nephews came over to me and said, 'Aunt Helen, Jacqueline Kennedy had nothing on you!' When the priest finished—Michael paid all extra for this—they got another flag, went through the whole ceremony, rolled it up and gave it to the boy. By this time the priest knew, the funeral director knew, everybody knew. How Michael had put it was, he said to the priest, 'My father has another son.'

"When it was over, the priest came to me and said, 'Helen, you're wonderful to allow this.' I said, 'Sometimes you have no control over what's going to happen . . .' "

Mary Coniglio tells about meeting Salvatore DiFiglia in 1972 in a Buffalo bar. He was fifty-two, she was thirty-one. She says Sam told her from the beginning about his wife and two sons, but adds that Michael Bennett "wasn't famous then, he got famous after Sam and me had been together a while." Their son, Salvatore Coniglio, was born August 12, 1974, at Millard Fillmore Hospital. Sam never promised marriage: "Mr. Lover Boy said he loved his wife and he loved me too. My Gawd, he had a lotta women, that's how he was." They kept their relationship from Helen DiFiglia. "Girlfriends knew. Sam's brothers knew. His sons knew. She didn't."

One night, in an argument with Sam, Mary Coniglio opted for truth.

"I was drunk and I just decided to call the wife, y'know, like clearin' the air. My son musta been about three, four. Sam and I were together four, five years before we broke up, and maybe my phone call helped. I was getting tired of it because of Helen. Broke up— and four years later he died.

"Helen's real nice, sweet, gentle. So was Sam. I loved Sam. But she usta leave him alone a lot. I mean, he liked to go out, drink, gamble, run around, and she just wanted to stay home, sometimes travel places. Two different personalities.

"His family knew about our son. His family, the DiFiglias, fantastic people! Fantastic! Accepted our kid right away, took him right in, all the uncles and cousins. Michael and Frank both said to me, 'He's not our half brother, he's our brother'—y'know, like that?

"When I met Helen at the cemetery, I couldn't understand why Sam cheated on her, but that's just the way Sam was. She comes to see Sal, takes him places. First time I met Michael, we were living in Cheektowaga. Sal was about eighteen months, and he said, 'He looks

just like Dad.' Sam was very proud of Michael. We were going together
about seven, eight months when he told me about him. He was just
a dancer on Broadway then, not well known. I mean, he got famous
when my son was about a year old. He sent money all the time, helped
Sam out and left money for his brother. Even when we weren't together
no more, Sam'd still come around once, twice a month with the money.
I was on welfare. Sam never had money of his own.

"A gambler, my Gawd! Always have five, ten thousand on him!
He was a bookmaker. I don't know about the Mafia, he didn't tell
me about it. But he did collect money time to time. I remember we
usta go places to pick it up. Once we went to Amherst to this guy he
was delivering to. But, personally like, Sam was always, always in
debt. Michael is the one sent money for our son, helped out—all the
time. He had little Sam visit him at his place. I've never been to New
York."

Bennett told Avian that the purpose behind the second funeral
ceremony was to give Salvatore Coniglio a sense of his true identity.
"Michael simply felt the kid had to grow up knowing what happened
to his father. He felt the kid should know what his last name really
was, who his father was. He didn't want that stuff phased out of his
life. The whole thing was so Italian. And he'd tell me over and over
about his father and the mistress, and the wife. He'd tell me these
things and I'd go, 'What? I'm changing the channel now.'

"Later Michael gets to know Sal, has him out to East Hampton.
The kid's a brat. Michael has two or three sessions with him on
different weekends until he can't handle it anymore. He's going, 'My
hands are full with this one. The kid questions everything—who are
you, what does this mean?' Then that was it with the kid! He left
him money in his will."

Elaine Krauss, whose married life and children Bennett supposedly adored, says, "Michael liked children, but only so far, although
he loved ours. His French girlfriend was married, and Michael said,
'I stole her away from her husband and I thought I'd marry her and
then I spent one vacation with her and her children at Disneyland.' "

Mrs. Krauss doubles up over the image.

"He said, 'Forget it! That's the end of that! I'm not going to bring up those two kids. What, are you kidding?' "

Frank DiFilia, without exonerating his father's infidelity, doesn't blame Mary Coniglio. Instead, repeating his self-stipulated role as a child caught between battling parents and a controlling brother, he tries to find some music in the latest disharmony.

"I think Mary Coniglio loved my father. A case could be made that it was more calculated, that she ended up pregnant because she thought there might be some profit in having this child because he would be related to Michael Bennett, but I wouldn't argue that case. I think she had the baby because she loved Dad, and her life didn't have that much. She has some good qualities. She's had a rough time.

"But the whole thing made it bad between Michael and Mom.

"When he heard Mom was upset about what Dad did, instead of laughing and trying to understand her, he got crazy with her.

"He said to me, 'That woman is so selfish all she can think about is her own feelings.' Michael had been so supersensitive as a child dealing with Mom when she was emotionally upset that he couldn't handle her in his adult life. He just didn't want to hear any of it. He put his foot down, closed the door. He wouldn't deal with anyone of us when we had problems, just like Dad."

Mrs. DiFiglia: "I will never understand why Michael came to the funeral like that. We weren't Mafia, our side of the family. Yah, sure, there'd been trouble in the past. Sam's brother Michael was killed by the Mafia. The family would never admit it but he was. He was killed in the 1930s before I met Sam. The family told everybody Michael parked his car at the top of a steep hill on a street called Albany that goes into the Niagara River, and fell asleep, and the car rolled into the water, and he drowned. When they found him, though, he was all beat up. The family claimed that was from the car rolling over in the river. But his wife told me it was the Mafia. The DiFiglias were all gamblers—all of them—from the mother and father down . . .

"What gets me is the way Michael started treating me—treating women!—after *Chorus Line*. He wasn't that way before. Oh, he changed. He could be very mean, then sorry after and try to make it up, but by then it was too late and he couldn't. He was such a wonderful man up to that point. I don't think it was the success, Michael had been successful all his life. I think someone was influencing him and I don't think it had anything to do with the *Chorus Line* success. He was fine for a long time with Donna. It started to happen after they got married. I'm not sure Gene had come along by that point, unless Michael knew him before. I've never put all that together, and Gene will never talk. Can you tell me Gene felt worse than I did at Michael's memorial service, yet I could attend it and he could not? Come on! I just can't believe that! I mean, *I had Michael!* He was my pride and joy. Oh, and the way they all treated me about the AIDS, and didn't tell me, and kept me away."

CHAPTER FIFTEEN

Thou Shalt Not Doctor

(1983)

At Eight Ninety Broadway on Saturday, April 9, 1983, show-business friends gave Michael Bennett "a rich, red, raucous party" to celebrate his fortieth birthday. The two hundred guests were asked to wear something red, Bennett's favorite color, and the big birthday gift was a red Porsche shipped in from California and adorned with a mammoth red satin bow. Everyone was given a red baseball cap at the door. The food was lavish, the liquor and wine unlimited and served by a staff of twelve from the kitchen next to Bennett's plush office. The office's usual rose-beige, potted-tree splendor became an all-night children's playland, a circusy Coney Island atmosphere punched up with red balloons, flowers, food booths, popcorn and candy machines stretching along a "boardwalk" that wound through the entire seventh floor, some of which was under renovation. Music from Bennett productions was provided by seven musicians from Richard Evans Music & Entertainment. All anyone had to do to turn the kids' corner into a combat zone was to sample the open (by request only) supply of "drugs of one's choice." Sober or stoned, the guests roamed through the vast inner workings of Bennett's workshop empire.

As successful as the party was, it had begun with pecking-order animosity between one or another of Bennett's friends. The rivalry was so severe among claimants of whose idea the party was in the first place that it resulted in backstage blacklisting, with—yet again —"some of the powerful people" making the (presumably) less powerful pay for their presumption. Michael Bennett was such "a dear friend" in the mind of nearly everyone he knew, closeness to him wasn't going to be shared. His friends—more aptly his co-workers— refused to carve him up as Solomon did with the biblical babe. Tommy Tune, one who could claim true friendship with Bennett, came to the party partly to fill the breach of having beaten him in the Tony Award competition between *Nine* and *Dreamgirls*, and partly to get his help on *My One and Only*. At that point *My One and Only* was a fiasco.

"It was going to be Michael's fortieth," Elaine Krauss says, "and Marvin said to me, 'Let's make him a surprise party.' We'd do it big, we'd turn Eight Ninety into a big boardwalk, Coney Island on lower Broadway, with red hats and red everything—"

Marvin Krauss beams. "Michael'd seen this red Porsche out in California! I was going to do the party myself. Had invitations printed up telling people something about wearing red. Then Matty Serino said he'd like to chip in. I said, 'Matty, you don't have to.' So I figured I'd better call Bob Avian, and it was Bobby, Matty and myself made the party. Oy!"

Mrs. Krauss: "At one point Betty Jacobs asked if she could help. I didn't think it was ruffled feelings. I'd have been more than happy to have them join in, it didn't make any difference. But from then on! They were—I mean! Marvin felt like—! Bernie once asked me, 'How could you let Matty do it and not me!?' I said, 'Why didn't you ask? How could I come to you and ask for money for a party? That's just against my nature. Matty happened to have helped Marvin on the invitation. Bobby is like Michael's brother.' I had just never thought about it. I certainly wasn't doing it to leave them out!"

Krauss: "I don't know if Bernie was worried about my friendship with Michael. If I had that answer maybe I could talk rational. I certainly didn't want to usurp any of his . . . persona. Bernie's a very influential man in the theater—and I mean you can't—and you aren't looking to . . . certainly you want to be his friend . . . but I don't know. The biggest problem was—for whatever reason—Bernie felt I was stepping on his shoes. That was not the case."

Mrs. Krauss: "Not only that, you couldn't with Michael anyway. Michael would be friends with whom he wanted. If he didn't choose you, you couldn't be close to him, in no way. It turned out to be an incredible party, a terrific special thing. And Bernie was very bitter about that."

Bennett, of course, knew nothing about the infighting behind the celebration. For him, it was a happy evening. And within the happiness, there suddenly seemed a fresh professional prospect in the troubled *My One and Only*.

Throughout his career he had maintained his reputation for doctoring shows out of town, and often the surgery was free of charge, done simply out of loyalty to the theater. "Call Michael!" had become a byword echoing from Baltimore to Washington/Philadelphia/New Haven/Boston. On *Seesaw* he had assumed total control of a seemingly terminal patient he helped recover and had been rewarded for his care. Much later—when, in fact, the first malignant splotch of Kaposi's sarcoma was festering beneath his skin—he briefly overcame his inevitable physical decline, and felt a surge of excitement, as he scheduled his AIDS treatment in Washington with the tryout of Marvin Hamlisch's stricken *Smile* in Baltimore. Aware of the negative gossip surrounding *My One and Only*, he offered Tune his help the night of his fortieth birthday, cornering Tommy Tune and his colleagues on the show, Thommie Walsh and Baayork Lee, when they arrived at the party. But Tune remembers Bennett's "offer" merely as professional interest.

"He took the three of us into the john, closed the door, and we had this little tête-à-tête," Tune says. "He asked what was going on, and I said, 'It's been killed but it's getting better.' Then he came to see it, and said, 'Okay, here's what's gotta happen . . .'

"No one asked him to come in on it. I was worried because it was so close to the end, ten days, maybe two weeks before the opening.

There was no more money, and we couldn't postpone anymore. It had gotten better. It was working. And suddenly Michael's there! We had a meeting the night before he was to start, Sam Cohn, Mike Nichols, Peter Stone, maybe Tony Walton. I thought it was too late, although, sure, I wanted everything he could give it."

Michael Bennett had ideas on how to improve—if not save— *My One and Only*. His presence doctoring the show was ironic. Peter Sellars, who had worked out the scheme of using the Gershwin *Funny Face* score against a new book by Timothy Mayer, had been fired during the chaotic Boston tryout, and one director after another had looked in on the shambles, including Mike Nichols, one of its producers (along with Paramount Films under the heading Paramount Theater Productions). By the time the tryout was being hauled to Broadway, Tune and Thommie Walsh were sharing credit for both direction and choreography. Tune, who was co-starring in the show with Twiggy, had denied directorial interference with Peter Sellars, yet Sellars, after he was fired, predicted the eventual lineup. Earlier, Sellars had sneered at the low-mindedness of most American musicals and skewered Michael Bennett as the King of Broadway.

There was even a much earlier irony.

In 1973, when Bennett took on the troubles of *Seesaw* in Detroit, he had called Tommy Tune, who was then living in Bennett's West Fifty-fifth Street apartment. Although Bennett was familiar with the process, he was often frustrated in clearing up somebody else's work and wanted help. Tune listened. Remembering similar frustrations Bennett had voiced about come-lately work on revivals of *By Jupiter* and *The Boys from Syracuse*, he gave him some advice. "Michael," Tommy Tune said, "thou shalt not doctor!" Tune then flew to Detroit and became part of *Seesaw*'s creative team and a member of the *Seesaw* cast.

Convinced he had the support of Tune and Nichols, Bennett felt he could doctor *My One and Only* into an evening of light entertainment. He moved fast, made changes and suggested more. The suggestions would require a quick $300,000. One April afternoon, at the St. James Theater, where the show was scheduled to open in less than a week, he was onstage with the chorus. Daniel Sherkow, a Paramount executive, walked up to him and told him he was fired. Where was friend Tommy Tune? As people shifted their gaze, Bennett lowered the visor of his red baseball cap and walked off the stage.

Tune: "It wasn't my position because I wasn't asking him to leave. Look—and I'm making no judgment on Michael's work—everyone—the whole production team—hated it. Everyone was appalled. They said they were going to have to let him go, and I said, 'You can't, you can't! You agreed to let him be here. Who's going to tell him?' Sam Cohn said he couldn't because it would break his heart. It came down to Sherkow, who was just this ineffectual *thing* who said no to everything, everybody.

"Michael called me immediately and said, 'Don't worry about me.' He asked me to write notes to the people he'd brought in, Michael Peters, Cleavant Derricks, Avian. I had a matinee that afternoon but I wrote them all thank-you letters before I left for the theater.

"I don't know if he got paid. I don't think he was around long enough for a contract to be drawn up. Sam was supposed to work that out. Michael expected one percent. I know he had bad feelings when the show became successful. He felt he should've been making some money off it. But not one piece of his work was used, not one. He wanted to throw away the book and make it a never-ending musical. It was a whole other concept, and there wasn't time for that. He was coming off *Dreamgirls* and still in that mode.

"There were a lot of drugs.

"Michael changed.

"There was a time when we all did drugs—like social drugs—but Michael got hooked. Drugs did nothing but make him paranoid. So I don't know what clarity we're talking about here. When he came to *My One and Only* he was a fella I hadn't been around a long time. He was very, very changed and, quite honestly, the work wasn't any good.

"We had dinner at the Algonquin one night. And he was quite . . . gone. Wine plus whatever! Gone! And he starts to sing low—like a hum—and slap the table. He sings, 'I see a never-ending musical.' Soft slap. 'I see a never-ending musical.' Harder slap. And then he repeats and accelerates until it gets louder and louder and he's beating the table—SLAP! SLAP!! SLAP!!! Dishes and silverware are rattling, and people are turning, and he's gone! He keeps up the melody. 'I see a never-ending musical, I see a never-ending musical.' Everyone in the dining room becomes quiet, everyone's looking. And Michael starts to laugh.

"That was passion, obsession and . . . and craziness."

Stricken, Tune wipes at tears.

"I've just come from an AIDS benefit in California. The last half of the second act was a tribute to Michael. The stage went to black and we heard the beginning of *Chorus Line*. The lights came up on this big picture of him sitting on a stairway, smoking and smiling, his little feet, his little calves, his little legs showing. Then, standing there, on the line in the logo, the original cast. And there they were: old and young, thick and thin, creased and smooth. They'd been through the wars. But there they were in the same old costumes, on the same old line with Michael up above them . . . I . . . I had no idea I had not released my feelings . . . So many have died from AIDS, you get numb to it . . . Yes, yes, there's grief—and then you just go to work.

"That was Michael up there on the stage. But he changed.

"It's not fair dropping back and saying, 'Well, he behaved like this.' What for? What's the point? He's gone and I miss him. Whatever troubles I had with him, I have only love, respect and admiration. Sometimes . . . the loss . . . is overwhelming."

John Breglio says flatly that Bennett wasn't paid for his work on *My One and Only*. "He spent at least three days talking to their writer. Then he worked with Tommy and Twiggy in his own rehearsal space at Eight Ninety, bringing in dancers and musicians and paying for it himself. He did it just because he was asked, out of friendship for Tommy, and this after a lot of ugly stuff on the street about the competition between *Dreamgirls* and *Nine*. Michael always rose above rivalry.

"Obviously when you bring in Michael Bennett, you spend

money, a lot of it. According to what he reported to me, there was an agreement with Sam Cohn he'd get one percent for working on the show. He told me not to worry about it, he trusted Sam. Then they fired him, and it had to be consensus. Sherkow walked on the stage and said, 'Please leave.' And Michael did."

A year or so later, after *My One and Only* had established itself as a hit, Bennett asked Breglio to collect his one percent. Breglio was told there had been no such agreement. Because Breglio had not been present during any of the negotiations, he had no comeback. He had only Bennett's word about the promise. "Michael was firm about what happened," Breglio says. "Since he wasn't about money, it's hard for me to believe that he dreamed up the one percent."

Avian: "The problem between Michael and Tommy wasn't that Tommy won for *Nine*. Of course Michael was upset, but he knew that's how the Tonys sometimes work. They weren't voting *for* something, they were voting *against* something, and it could have been against the fact that it was a Michael Bennett production or that it had been produced by the Shuberts or just that it was a black musical. That didn't cause any problems for Michael. He and Tommy were competitive, but everybody in the theater is. There's that classic line: 'You should do great and everybody else should fail.' That's just human nature.

"Michael and Tommy were friends from way back. *My One and Only* tore them apart where they didn't see each other anymore. When Michael was asked to leave, Tommy Tune didn't say anything in his defense. No one did."

Although they were in relatively close contact until 1983, Michael Bennett's relationship with Sabine Cassel was ending by 1981. For all his love and affection and plans for marriage, which his mother and the Jacobses hoped would happen, he was having second thoughts. If Donna McKechnie had been unable to fulfill the dual role he had intended for her (the glamorous and steadily sought-after Broadway star as well as the glamorous wife at home in the multilevel splendor of their Central Park South tower), neither could Sabine Cassel measure up to the role he had drawn for her (the charming Parisian coquette as steady helpmate in their East Sixty-fourth Street town house). If McKechnie wasn't bright enough for him, Cassel was perhaps too smart, too eager to manipulate *his* manipulations. By most descriptions she was "a party girl" who wanted people around all the time, and the more, the merrier.

As Bennett struggled through his accumulating fears, trying to find himself in their center while seeking another image for his father, another substitute for his family, the only thing holding him together was work, and the work process seemed to be ever slower and, finally, full of misgivings. At the point when he was dealing with the shadows of his own identity, Sabine Cassel was clearly trying to become his *semblable*. She even describes herself in his physical image, "small, short, dark like Michael," and balances his background—Buffalo, Jewish/Sicilian—with her own, which, she says, is "Nice, half Jewish, half Corsican."

Cassel: "We were looking very much alike, brother and sister, and I haven't any brother and sister, so that was fun. The way we were reacting, and talking, like brother and sister. And our pasts were much the same. My parents traveled a lot, then I went to Paris to stay with my great-aunt and met Jean-Pierre. I was twenty, and it was all very fast, and then I had my children.

"I love Michael, and think he love—loves me. I understand what happened with Donna, I understand why Michael married her. But the first thing he was in love with was his work. He was very comfortable working. When he was not working he was lost. Donna was like Michael onstage. When she was dancing, he was seeing himself, and they have, like, complicity to them, very strong. But when they were out of work, the magic was not there. And, *oui*, Michael was bored very fast. I don't think he was bored with me. He gave me all the excitement I didn't have with Jean-Pierre. But Michael was scared of what we had together because it was very strong. At one point we were very much in love. And it was passion. And passion never lasts! I didn't know passion before. One thing I have to thank Michael for is that I found passion through him.

"Even when we separate we were calling each other. After the town house was broken in, I went back to Central Park for a while. He went to San Francisco to see his boyfriend, but he kept calling me. When I was telling him things, like nobody keeps anyone, he was going, 'Oh, you are so wonderful, you understand,' and da-da-da-da, 'and I love you.' I couldn't be angry with him no matter what he did. He just couldn't be with anyone—man or woman—and probably that goes back to when he was a child, and he probably carried that loneliness with him until he died."

Sabine Cassel's forgiveness falters once.

"After it was over he took care of me for a while, then Marvin Schulman, his business manager, cut me back because Michael was buying the East Hampton house and there was not enough money for everything. He didn't leave me anything—it was not wonderful treatment—but that's all right. It would have been horrible if Jean-Pierre had done something like that because he is somebody who's really balanced! I can't be angry with somebody who was completely lost. Michael did not know what he was doing. He once said to me he wanted to be like Howard Hughes, and I said, 'Michael, he was crazy and that's crazy!'

"The only thing I cannot not forgive him is that he didn't call me when he knew he got AIDS. And I think that's not . . . correct. It's a long time since we were together, but there are things we don't know, like when did he get AIDS? That hurts me the most, then I think: Wow, but he was scared. He was like a child, no sense of responsibility. A lot of times when he couldn't face something, he was running away. I told him, 'Michael, running away is okay, but someday you have to come back.' Sometimes I was feeling like a mother."

Through the *One and Only* unpleasantness, *Dreamgirls* was still inhabiting Michael Bennett's head. The show was running smoothly at the Imperial. Given the finely tuned mechanism needed for Robin Wagner's cruising towers and Tharon Musser's patterned lights, the touring production was proving a financial headache and Bennett was trying to think of ways to simplify it. Simultaneously, he was developing a sexually explicit musical he intended to call *Scandal*. Treva Silverman and he were batting out a book, Jimmy Webb was writing songs, Wagner, Musser and Aldredge were investigating their insights. Splitting time between *Scandal* and *Dreamgirls*, and thinking about the upcoming milestone when *A Chorus Line* was going to surpass *Grease* as the longest-running musical, he spent $300,000 redesigning a simpler *Dreamgirls* for Los Angeles, principally by cutting seven minutes from the running time and devising a more cohesive opening for Act Two. The revisions were later incorporated into the New York production.

In Bennett's personal life Gene Pruit had now replaced all others, and Pruit's friend Robert Herr was now head man at Eight Ninety. In East Hampton visiting David Geffen, Bennett admired Geffen's house—with its neighboring pond stocked with geese and swans— and Geffen offered to sell it to him complete with its manicured ten-acre greensward fronting the Atlantic Ocean. For the boy from blue-collar Buffalo who, as a friend said, "never knew from trees," 40 James Lane was a dream he never dreamed. The dream would beguile him, then waver in agony.

CHAPTER SIXTEEN

Scandal

(1984)

By the end of 1983, eight months after Michael Bennett's fortieth birthday, the AIDS epidemic was being called the plague. Since most of its victims were homosexual men, it was also routinely called the gay plague, as though the qualifying label itself might somehow contain the virus in one specific segment of the population. The Centers for Disease Control (CDC) in Atlanta tabulated 3,000 Americans infected with the virus, and 1,283 of them were dead.* Forty-two percent of the cases belonged to New York, 12 percent to San Francisco, 8 to Los Angeles, 3 to Newark. The CDC now pegs the AIDS incubation period at eight years, with the low end of the scale at six months, the high at fifteen years.

To the majority of Americans (and the Reagan administration), 3,000 sick and dead people didn't mean much—and meant even less if the moribund could be scorned and forgotten as gay. But in the world of the arts, perhaps especially the theater, AIDS was the equivalent of a viral Holocaust, an almost systematic extermination of

---

*In March 1989, the CDC tabulated that 86,157 Americans had been infected with the AIDS virus since 1981, 49,390 of whom have died.

friends, colleagues and associates. The toll was devastating, and made more so by the ignobility of the scourge surrounding it. Christian fundamentalists, various religious leaders—and just plain homophobes —fulminated about unnatural sex practices, drugs, alternate lifestyles, then, descanting on hoarse breath, assailed the permissiveness of theater, movies, television and rock 'n' roll.

This was no time to be doing a musical charting a woman's erotomaniacal history, no time to be shifting upon heterosexual and homosexual mattresses. This was no time for *Scandal*. While *Scandal* could be—as it was—dismissed as a project, there was no way to dismiss—or even briefly mollify—the disease streaming through Michael Bennett's blood. If *Scandal* was to have been a celebration of sexual pleasure, the canceled celebration would come to signal Michael Bennett's death.

According to Avian, *Scandal** was scratched for two reasons: because of AIDS and because it wasn't good enough. "Here was a show about sex and sexuality, and everybody's starting to keel over; Michael was very worried about what was going on but not about himself." There were a couple of abortive attempts to escape the time-bomb tick of the 1980s by turning the sexual clock back to the 1950s or 1960s, but *Scandal* just wouldn't work as a scatterbrain frolic. The promise of painless promiscuity was proving deadly.

Scandal had come about when Ed Kleban, the *Chorus Line* lyricist, mentioned to Bennett and Avian a woman he knew named Treva Silverman, who had been story editor on *The Mary Tyler Moore Show*. Bennett was so taken by Kleban's enthusiasm that he contacted Silverman in Los Angeles, offering her a trip to New York. Silverman knew of Bennett only through *A Chorus Line*, which she had seen "nine million times," and from conversations with Kleban. Bennett, Avian and Silverman talked for months ("maybe it was as long as a year," says Avian) about possible ideas for a show.

Avian: "Every once in a while we'd ask about Treva's private life, which was built around her hidden sexuality. She told us she'd

---

*The show briefly had had two working titles, *Dreamgirl* and *The American Woman*.

go off to Europe periodically and become this other person . . . and the idea struck Michael. He wanted to do a show about the sexual history and fantasy of a woman. So we start writing this script about a wife who finds out her husband has been fucking around his entire life, the double standard, and all the while she's been Miss Goody Two-Shoes. We took all of Treva's experiences and applied them to the woman, and it was like *The Mary Tyler Moore Show Sucks and Fucks*."

As the dramatic narrative began taking shape, Bennett and Avian "developed outrageous sequences, like a ménage à trois with the woman under the covers trying to blow two guys, all done in a musical number! And a Botticelli orgy ballet where the angels on the ceiling came down on young French waiters!" The plot attempted to explore various sexual lifestyles. There was, for example, a big production number based on a Jimmy Webb song entitled "She's a Dyke," which took place in the Swiss Alps, Gstaad, on a resolve. One of the lyrics ran: "She's a dyke, you can tell by the way she stands / She's a dyke, uh-huh, you can tell by her glands." Swoosie Kurtz, playing the Silverman surrogate, would come down front during the scene and, referring to the lesbian, say to the audience, "She never discusses this person as him, only as the other person. Do you think she's gay?" Then she'd walk back into the scene, play it and say, "She's *definitely* gay." In addition, there was a big masturbation sequence and an erotic takeoff on the *American in Paris* ballet. "Originally we saw the whole thing as five ballets and a book, then we realized we needed songs," Avian says.

By this time Kleban was no longer involved on the project as a composer. Harold Wheeler had worked out a musical format so Bennett could demonstrate individual scenes. Meanwhile, Bennett and Avian had been considering other composers and lyricists, among them Peter Allen, Burt Bacharach, Ellen Fitzhugh, Marvin Hamlisch, Sheldon Harnick, Carolyn Leigh, Richard Maltby, Jr., Carole Bayer Sager, David Shire, and Stephen Sondheim. The composer they finally turned to was Jimmy Webb, an award-winning songwriter ("Up, Up and Away," "MacArthur Park," "By the Time I Get to Phoenix," "Wichita

Lineman"), who'd never done a musical. (Among Webb's awards is a 1968 triple Grammy—the only triple ever given—for music, lyrics and orchestration.) Bennett had been introduced to Webb through David Geffen. One weekend when Webb was visiting Jann Wenner at East Hampton, he was invited to James Lane for lunch with Bennett. As Webb tells it in the sway of his country accent: "I'd been in New York I reckon a coupla years trying to get started in the theater and zilch was happening. I had lunch with Michael at his house—walking in there with no future on Broadway, no connections, nothing happening for me—and I walked out with a show. The show was Michael's idea for a large musical about the Children's Crusade, and the script was by John Heilpern."

A short while later, during the last week of March 1984, Jimmy Webb found himself installed in an office at Eight Ninety Broadway. Bennett had said, "I want you very close to me because we're going to do lots of musicals, lots."

Webb began working on *The Children's Crusade*, with Bennett checking on him "every three or four hours every afternoon." These interruptions were always friendly and "wildly enthusiastic." One day Bennett brought Joe Papp to hear one of Webb's *Crusade* songs. "It went on like that for two months," Webb says, "because he had another musical ahead of ours, *Scandal*, and he was also working on something about his father."

Eventually Webb was drawn into *Scandal*, Bennett simply telling him that the script was ready to be punctuated with music. Webb read it and passed it back, saying it was funny but ran far too long. At that point *Scandal* "was really just a play with two fifteen-minute ballets." Webb suggested cutting, and the suggestion "caused some friction with Treva but, first, essentially we got along very well." Already trying out scenes with Swoosie Kurtz and Treat Williams, Bennett wanted the music immediately, if only the underscore, which Webb felt he could crank out in his sleep: "I wasn't worried. Then —just like a Mickey and Judy musical—he'd ask for a song, then ask for another, and it was that clichéd scene of the musician ripping pages off the piano, rushing them to the director and into the show."

His eagerness to produce outdistanced only by his astonishment at the vortex pulling him in, Jimmy Webb was exhilarated. He was going to write a Broadway show after all! He remembers finishing "a particularly herculean dance sequence" and rushing it to Bennett, who was waiting to rehearse it. Bennett took Webb's music, thanked him and turned his attention to the assembled dancers. Clearly dismissed but missing the dismissal, Webb lingered against a wall, waiting for the thrill of seeing the dancers moving to his music. "I stood awestruck for a few seconds. Then Michael turned around, saw me and said, 'Don't you have something you have to do?' He was so great—the most charming man who ever lived!"

The work went on for nine months.

Webb: "Michael was very seductive, and he definitely turned it on. He moved people around, could make them do anything he wanted them to do. He'd do funny, wonderful things. Like once he took a sneaker off and threw it at an actor, and everyone laughed. And he had the quickest analytical mind when it came to tearing music apart and putting it back together. The day he told me my talent was never in question, well, somehow that allowed me to drop all the barriers —the ego, the pretense, the clutter of the soul. It enabled myself to work with him with no restraint. Which is what I mean by seductive. He persuaded one to go along and—because he knew what he was doing—it was nice to go along with him."

"Michael was instant instant seduction," Treva Silverman says, gluing her words in place, then trying to unglue and rearrange them like photographs in an album. Are the assortment and memory better this way or that? She peers from a milky face, eyes nervous, emotions tremulous, and cautiously nibbles at truth as though it might contain poison. She was "in some sort of love with him," almost from the moment they met in his office at Eight Ninety Broadway, although there were times when she thought he was an "apparition."

"We started to work on *Scandal* June 18, 1980. We never slept together. Michael said, 'Let's put all our sexual intensity into the show.' The show itself was about sex, of course. Michael said, 'If we sleep together, and it's terrible, we're going to lose all the sexual intensity between us; if it's great, then we're going to want to keep doing it, and *then* what's going to happen is . . . that . . . you're . . . going . . . to . . . want . . . to . . . become . . . Mrs. Me. AND . . . I . . . DON'T . . . WANT . . . THERE . . . TO . . . BE . . . A . . . MRS. ME!!!'"

Remorse stimulates Treva Silverman's terror. Twitching, she begins the backstage story of *Scandal*, which Bennett finally shut down in anger and desperation. Near the end she weeps.

"We worked on it four and three-quarter years," she says.

Tears spill to her chin.

"Overnight he severed it. After our Thursday meeting he said, 'See you Monday, honey.' That was the last time I saw him. On Monday I heard from my lawyer. *Scandal* was over."

Bennett, she says, considered her "company." Further, he thought she was just as "smart" as he was. He also told her he was surrounded by people who were feverishly competing with him, gypsies as well as others who felt they were as competent and talented as he. Silverman says Bennett was always looking for "a soul mate" but the search was complicated by his "overriding need to control." He told her she was "the best writer he ever worked with," and outlined some future projects they'd do together, including a script about his father separate from the *Our Father* scenario, an idea Silverman would "supervise." It would involve two other writers, Silverman contributing "the man/ woman stuff," Louis La Russo the specific material on Salvatore DiFiglia, an unnamed third writer for the remainder.

Silverman talks about evenings of cocaine when the Mafia paranoia would be revealed. She was always amazed by his intellect. She recalls a night of hard give-and-take on *Scandal* when the phone rang "and it was Bernie—it was Bernie a lot on the phone." While she remained curled up with the script, Bennett took the call. Overhearing an extended conversation "about *Chorus Line* in Siberia or someplace," she worried that Bennett's concentration had been fractured and that he'd be unable to refocus on *Scandal*. But: "He hung up the phone and finished the sentence he had started when the phone rang."

Bennett was a "genius" to Treva Silverman. At first she thought his genius came from his own "cloud nine, from his own mysterious source of wonderment." Later she was surprised to learn he was capable of "deductive reasoning." He didn't just operate from "Genius Land," he used logic. To persons who say Michael Bennett was inarticulate, Silverman says, "He was among the most verbal I've known."

While approving Treva Silverman's work and, in his inimitable way, coddling its development ("You're the best, honey, the very best"), Bennett was having serious doubts about the show itself, doubts not yet fully empowered by the force of AIDS. He wanted a professional in the theater to read the script, someone not involved in the production. The person whose opinion he most wanted was Bernard Jacobs but—because of the attempt to sever his ties with the Shubert Organization and buy his own theater, the Mark Hellinger—he hadn't talked to Jacobs in over a year.

"Near the end of *Scandal*," Betty Jacobs says, "he asked Bernie and me to read it. They were still angry at each other. I was working at Eight Ninety. Their feud never had any effect on Michael's and my relationship. Lots of times I thought Bernie was wrong, lots of times I thought Michael was wrong. I'm a Libra and could see both sides.

"Bernie read it and agreed with Michael's hesitation. There was *sooo* much book! I never saw the choreography. I understand it was magnificent. I agreed there was too much book; it would have gone on like *Nicholas Nickleby*, forever. Some of it was graphic. But no more than anything else.

"Michael wanted to produce it himself, and he just wanted our opinion. That's when Bernie gave him the *Chess* album, and asked him if he wanted to do it. We were back friends again."

"*Scandal* was a long period of friction between Michael and Bernie," Bob Avian says. "By the time we dropped the show we were planning to switch from the Shuberts to the Nederlanders. Bernie had his own ego concerns. As head of the Shubert Organization, he figured Michael was one of his guys. You don't stray. Of course, this was all part of their ongoing relationship, in which they would fight and make up, fight and make up. They had a neurotic symbiosis. Michael knew it and fed his own neurosis right into it, and it all worked together. They were testing and challenging each other all the time, with love—I have to say—and great respect. But both trying to be in control and control the other. By the time we were thinking of buying the Hellinger, the road was getting pretty bumpy."

Jacobs: "Game playing, his relationship with everybody was always game playing."

Mrs. Jacobs: "Especially with Bernie."

Jacobs: "With me particularly. He regarded me always as a challenge.

"Betty and I are in Sicily, of all places, the telephone rings and it's Michael. 'How are ya? Where are you?' He doesn't know where I am. 'You know my family came from—' I forget where the devil he said. 'It's only about twenty-five miles from where you are. Why don't you go over to see the town. Maybe you can meet some people in my family.' Then he gets onto the real reason for the call. 'I just made a deal with Jimmy Nederlander to buy half interest in the Hellinger, and I want you to know it. I don't want you to hear it on the street.' "

Mrs. Jacobs laughs.

Jacobs: "I said, 'Michael there's nobody here on the streets of Taormina. So who's going to tell me, Michael, you made a deal with Jimmy Nederlander?'

"Obviously, he was just telling this to me because he had this conversation with Nederlander. I don't think he ever intended to go ahead with the deal, but he *wanted to stick it up my ass a little!*"

Only slightly startled by this burst of vulgarity, Mrs. Jacobs studies the floor. Reproach is not part of the Jacobses' relationship. Reprimand is used by common wives with lesser husbands. Attentive respect is the Jacobses' bond.

Jacobs is called away by a buzz from his secretary in an outer office.

Mrs. Jacobs: "I think Michael wanted to buy the Hellinger. I don't know if he ever would. Bernie was always watching over Michael as if he was his son. He was always worried if Michael was being taken for a ride because Michael was very naïve about some things, business things. He paid more for East Hampton than he should have. I don't remember why the Hellinger didn't happen."

Most people who observed the Jacobs/Bennett involvement saw it as a father/son connection. John Breglio suggests a competitiveness beyond that easy identification, a rivalry between businessmen complicated by commerce and art. "Here was Bernie as a real businessman/producer treating Michael as the artist/ director and Michael resisting being treated only as the artist/director and wanting to be treated equally as a businessman. Complex as that.

"Then, too, Michael needed in his life family members. Bernie was his father, I was like his brother, and we became family. He needed that badly. That's how he thought about people. *Dreamgirls* is so much about family. The song in it, 'Family,' is cynical in many ways but it has dual meanings. Two scenes after it's sung, the 'family' has kicked this woman out, which was a pattern in Michael's entertainment, people being thrown out and coming back in."

"Michael made the mistake all through his life of mixing business and friendship," his brother says. "Take Marvin Schulman, his friend across the hall at West Fifty-fifth who became his business manager. Marvin's now suing the estate.* I don't know if he's a bad person— yes he is, no he isn't. He's a human being whose peculiar aberration is money. Marvin will profit from any situation, and doesn't see anything wrong with that. I always kinda liked him, still do. But again,

---

*Marvin Schulman sued Michael Bennett in 1987 in New York Supreme Court after Bennett had severed his professional partnership with him, a partnership that had begun in 1963 when Schulman became Bennett's business manager. Schulman claimed that he and Bennett had an oral agreement, giving him 5 percent of Bennett's earnings. Initially denying this, Bennett finally admitted—in a deposition taken shortly before his death—that there had been such an agreement. On February 24, 1989, Schulman proved his argument, winning a $315,000 settlement from the Bennett estate, none of which has been paid. The money is to come from the sale of a building Bennett and Schulman owned at East Ninety-fourth Street. The settlement with the Bennett estate was reached by John Breglio.

he's in the middle of Michael mixing business and friendship, and that has a domino effect.

"For Michael business was personal, so his personal associates became his family, so his family couldn't be his family anymore because he had *another* family. Something's wrong at the root here. *They* are not your family. You may find people to trust but you can never trust them as you trust your family. Maybe there are people in your real family you can't trust, maybe. But Michael had it all flipped out."

Avian: "Marvin Schulman was our business manager, for five percent of Michael's total income from the sales of real estate and everything else. He feels he helped create Michael's stardom. Fuck him, he didn't. He was my business manager too. We questioned him on certain stuff and let him go. The suit is still in probate and it amounts to like five percent of the estate. Of course, he's willing to settle for $250,000!

"We'd known Marvin Schulman twenty-five years and, all of a sudden, we caught him on one real estate thing. He was supposed to take five percent on Michael's commission, the same on mine, and he was taking thirty percent! He thinks he's right. We didn't agree and said you're out. We just walked out. We never had a signed contract, but now he's talking verbal contract.

"Marvin's problem is: he watches his clients make a lot of money, and why shouldn't he make more? . . .

"Anyway, so we're buying the Mark Hellinger Theater! I'll never forget it! We had a night of celebration, Michael and I, at my apartment. He said, 'Let's get drunk and stoned *thinking* I might get the Hellinger Theater and own it, and we may have a show in it, and it may never happen, but let's celebrate tonight whether Bernie stops us or whatever!'

"So we have this rip-roaring drunken evening, the two of us screaming, going, 'Hey, baby, the Mark Hellinger belongs to us!' We have this real rush! We're dancing through the apartment screaming, 'Mickey DiFiglia owns a theater, Mickey DiFiglia owns a theater!' Laughing so hard we're crying. We can't believe it. We're so happy. It all seems so good."

Tracing the etched glass of his memory, Bob Avian catches his breath. The joy of the relived moment shatters.

The conquest of the Hellinger and the invasion of the Nederlander camp (where Bennett would have been the five-star general he was not under the Shuberts) never happened. Apparently, too many other wars were erupting simultaneously. *Scandal* was taking more and more time, and the bickering atmosphere behind it was steadily becoming as foul as the post-*Chorus Line* air.

The plan had been to repeat the *Chorus Line* process, with the workshop refinement finally to result in *Scandal* being staged at the small theater at Eight Ninety, a close enough facsimile of the Newman. Cast and technical people would work for minimum scale, then move uptown. *A Chorus Line* had, of course, long since proved the plan's feasibility and a number of Bennett's competing colleagues had followed it with their own shows. But by the time of *Scandal* Bennett had become a well-known figure. He and Avian were no longer Mickey and Judy putting on a show in the backyard and selling tickets out of a cardboard box. Although their come-on was the same, Mickey and Judy were big-time impresarios. They were successful and rich. Why should people work for them at scale? Work was work, whether in tryout or for real. The scandal behind *Scandal*, Avian says, was greed. The initial enthusiasm of the cast, chorus and creative personnel was quickly qualified by self-concern. "Everybody said, 'I'll work for nothing if I get twelve percent of the gross; I'll work for nothing if I get fifteen thousand a week; I'll work for nothing if I have a built-in retirement plan to last me the rest of my life . . .' "

In addition to this squawking, Treva Silverman was squabbling with the man from "Genius Land," as well as with Avian and Jimmy Webb. As though all this weren't enough, *A Chorus Line* was about to pass a milestone and the event needed Bennett's attention. On September 29, 1983, the show would pass the long-run record of 3,388 consecutive performances held by *Grease*, an accomplishment minimized only by the latter's utter lack of distinction. Divorcing himself from the hassles of *Scandal*, Bennett got caught up in the whirlwind celebration, turning *Chorus Line*'s 3,389th performance into a symbolic Broadway gala. It was not, however, a party absent of vipers.

There were hurt feelings within and without the Shubert for the celebration, "the *Grease*-breaker," as one disillusioned *Chorus Line* dancer dubbed it, but they were kept within the family. The family was extensive. Bennett's idea was to bring everyone together for a reunion and have the show performed by as many cast members from the original *Chorus Line* team as could be found, as well as by dancers from companies still performing it. Cassie, for example, would be danced by Donna McKechnie and her Broadway replacements, Ann Reinking, Vicki Frederick, Pamela Sousa, as well as by dancers from the road; Paul would be played by Sammy Williams, George Pesaturo, Rene Clemente; Zach would be acted by Robert LuPone, Joe Bennett, Eivind Harum. Some dancers, of course, had dropped out of show business. Some were unavailable. And some, like Robert LuPone, the original Zach, were still bandaging old wounds inflicted by Bennett and refused to participate.

The 3,389th performance set a record on its own. The silver-covered, black-lettered Playbill lists 290 performers but, with stragglers joining the production after Playbill had gone to press, the number reached 332. By the end of the performance, with all the me-and-my-shadow portraits crowding stage, wings and aisles, the Shubert re-sounded with an ovation that probably was heard in the nearby Booth, if not all the way to the Beaumont at Lincoln Center, where Joseph Papp first wanted *A Chorus Line* staged. When the huzzahs turned hoarse, the 1,472 invited guests gathered outside the lobby doors under a canopy strapped at the West Forty-fourth and Forty-fifth openings of Shubert Alley for a party that went on in the rain until five o'clock in the morning. At eight that night *A Chorus Line* would be giving its 3,390th consecutive performance.

Avian: "The way Michael pulled that together was amazing! In three days!"

"Michael called to find out how many costumes we had," Alyce Gilbert, the wardrobe mistress, says. "I said I'd have to count. He said, 'A hundred?' I said, 'Probably more like three hundred.' He said fine, and I started to count the stock. I'd been the dresser when *Chorus Line* closed at the Public Theater, and we'd made a lot of costumes since then, in the beginning for every new hire, usually a finale costume or two. We've only made about nine since the first bus-and-truck tour in 1982. We've mainly lived off stock since then.

"In the interim, of course, the look had changed. When *Chorus Line* first opened, dancers had a long, lean, narrow line, a lyric Thommie Walsh kind of thing. Now the look is much more muscular, athletic. Some of the clothes had been made for those earlier bodies. So when the dancers—*seven* Cassies, *seven* Zachs, *seven* Bobbys—started to show up, there were *a lot of alterations*! People were in tears because they didn't fit into their costumes anymore—and since they were five months pregnant it wasn't surprising!

"Somehow we managed to get something on all of them. We hauled stuff out of the basement, set it up on racks. We had tables with mirrors and outlets for hair dryers. Some of the people dressed on the stage next door at the Booth, and some had their old dressing rooms. At least forty boys dressed in the balcony. Most had arrived Monday or Tuesday, and the performance was Thursday. They only had a short time with us because the rehearsals were down at Eight Ninety. It was a giant class reunion. I knew practically all of them. Even the few hired on the road I had at least known by name because I had ordered shoes for all of them. *Chorus Line* has gone through more shoes!"

Coming down from the glitter of the *Chorus Line* gala and facing the uncertainty of *Scandal* was gruel after a banquet. The enmity behind the gala had been controlled. Bennett was not sure how long he could control Treva Silverman. Their relationship, Avian says, "got increasingly bumpy."

Silverman: "I was with Michael during *Dreamgirls* when he had hepatitis and he couldn't do coke, he couldn't do grass—he couldn't do anything—and he told me he was the clearest he had ever been.

To be around him when his mind made those leaps . . . to see it being created in front of my eyes . . .

"The first weeks of working together I couldn't believe what I was witnessing. I started imagining that, maybe somehow, he'd worked out all his responses before he came to a meeting, which, of course, was impossible. But everything he said . . . sprung out . . . so . . . evolved . . . I'd bring in some brand-new writing and he'd just take off from there instantly—no, actually not instantly. He'd start slowly, but then get to it *exactly*, saying, 'Suppose if . . . suppose if . . .'

"I kept being surprised at Michael's working method. He needed me to create something first and only then was he able to participate and develop it. I think that's where a lot of his ambivalence as a collaborator came in. He worked only with people he had enormous respect for, but then he started despising himself for needing them. Often he'd end up despising the other person for existing.

"After I would finish a scene, it would be a whole different thing. I initiated it, but I got it back triplefold. Like sex. Sex is like: you then him, him then you, you then him—until you don't know who's which, and all that. We sparked into each other creatively, emotionally, and what we were talking about all the time was sex. Sex as emotion, sex as metaphor, sex as sex. Everything in *Scandal* was about my relationships, my past, sexual anecdotes I'd heard about, my sexual what-ifs, Michael's what-ifs . . . It got so intense on every level."

Webb: "I think Michael made everyone feel they had something special with him. And maybe they did. But that's an awful lot of people! He was capable of romancing Treva, sure, and in her case I'd say he probably did. She lived in one of the nicest buildings in town—I should live so nice! He must have been supporting her. Treva wasn't writing anything other than *Scandal*. She was his willing disciple. And she *taped everything*! Must have a hundred—if not a thousand—hours of tape, every meeting, every session, every rehearsal. Michael seemed to know about the taping, which may be a reason he granted her some kind of insider status, if he did. A million times I must have asked Avian, 'What is this taping stuff?' and he'd roll his eyes at the ceiling.

"There are things Michael said on those tapes that are awe-inspiring in terms of what he really thought about this person or that person. I'm concerned because I'm on any number of them myself. Given what finally happened, it's likely Treva is gonna have to get her emotional investment back, is gonna have to get something out of *Scandal* through the tapes. I know Breglio's been negotiating with her. It may very well be to get those tapes in return for giving her the rights to *Scandal*. It's possible Michael's estate has some claim on it, and Breglio is saying, 'Gimme the tapes.' Michael did have a co-authorship deal with her when she started—before she started making waves."

Avian: "Treva had trouble with Jimmy Webb. She was tough on him. She didn't think he was the man for the job, where Michael and I adored him. I don't think she necessarily respected his work— maybe she did—but it really was the old story: she wanted to be Michael. She wanted to be in control and call the shots.

"At one point, in front of the two of us, she said, 'Michael, you told me I'd be in as much control as you, that I'd be a conceiver on the show and you'd give me that billing.'

"I looked at him and said, '*What* did you tell her?' Treva was sitting right there.

"He said, 'I don't remember saying that to her.'

"I said to Treva, 'You're telling me he said that! I don't buy it! If he did, I'm going to kill him right on the spot. I'm the co-producer on this show and I'll never let it happen, and you're full of shit!'

"Treva said, 'That's what he said.'

"I said, 'Sorry, it's over.' But we weren't over quite then. We survived that one. Michael might have skirted the issue because Treva really wanted ultimate control. He may have let her believe she had that kind of control. But he never would have used those words."

Then there came the day when Bennett received a disputed contract from a Silverman emissary.

"I was there when Treva's agent, or her lawyer, sent Michael this thick contract with a list of demands," Robin Wagner says. "One of the demands specified that her name be equal with Michael's. He went through the ceiling. I'd never seen him so angry. The contract was so thick he tried to tear it up and couldn't. He called in Bob Herr and had him rip it to shreds. And that was the end of *Scandal*."

Robert Herr doesn't remember shredding the contract. John Breglio says "a three-page document" came from Treva Silverman's lawyer, adding that the document's demands per se didn't end the work. At the time Breglio felt that he would have been able to smooth the difficulties with Silverman's lawyer. Again, the reason given for dropping *Scandal* is that it wasn't good enough. The contract—and its tone—merely poisoned an already sour pot. Between $750,000 and $1 million had been spent in four workshops, and the art hadn't developed. Beyond all that there was the specter of AIDS.

Had *Scandal* been produced, would Michael Bennett's standard four credits—for concept, production, direction and choreography— gone to five with co-authorship?

"Michael was arrogant in thinking he was a writer—tell me about it!" Jerome Kass says. "He was always feuding with writers. When we were working on *Roadshow* there was a piece in the *Times* about him and all his projects, all the things he was writing. He referred to *Roadshow* and never mentioned me! I was outraged and wrote an angry, angry letter to the *Times*, then never sent it.

"Michael wasn't a writer. He had a brilliant story mind, and he was an extraordinary director. One time he said to me, 'People can't believe I won the Pulitzer Prize for *Chorus Line*, but I did, I really did write it.' I know Kirkwood and Dante resented that deeply. Michael never knew what it was to put an empty piece of paper into a typewriter. He got enough credit. He was the show—but to take credit for the writing!"

Publicly as well as privately, Michael Bennett proclaimed *A Chorus Line* as basically his own. In a 1986 interview on National Public Radio he said, "It's the longest-running show in history. And it's mine! It's amazing. And it's the story of my life on top of it's amazing." Weaving memories of Buffalo and admitting the role of some of his friends in his career, he went on to say that *A Chorus Line* was "an idea I had in my head for a couple of years before I did it." Then:

"It's a lot about my life, not really so much about my life as the Zach character as people think. I'm much more Mike and Mark and other characters in the piece, and Don . . . We hired a cast, and we wrote for the cast. I had a beginning, middle and an end, and a point of view about what I was doing."

If this was characteristic self-aggrandizement, the genius buffing his ego, it included a surprisingly pretentious sweep. He attached part of *A Chorus Line*'s stimulus to the Watergate revelations. The country had lost its heroes and, supposedly, *A Chorus Line* established a new kind of heroism, the courageous little guy, specifically the littlest guy of all in the theater: the Broadway gypsy.

Having announced that his success was "hard to deal with, it's crowded at the top," Bennett found the crowds becoming claustrophobic by the end of *Scandal*. He wasn't feeling very well. Trying to escape some of the pressures, he was spending more and more time in East Hampton in thought, vividly imagining *The Children's Crusade* as a replacement for the circus, idly thinking about the Shuberts' insistence that he do *Chess*. Instead of tracking actors across a stage, he was watching swans cruising across Hook Pond; instead of digging into problems of dramatic structure and dialogue, he was wondering if his $50,000 sprinkling system would control the grubs pocking his lawn.

Eventually he agreed to do *Chess* and he flew to London, where he was seriously stricken. *"Chess,"* he said with a black smile, "is worse than AIDS."

CHAPTER SEVENTEEN

Checkmate and the Cover-up
1984–1985

Having danced all his life, he kept hearing the rattle of his aluminum, three-inch Capezio Teletone taps as he imagined them dangling a hairsbreadth from the heel and toe of so many pairs of forgotten shoes, hearing the rattle as he watched the wildlife at East Hampton. For the first time in his life the insistent sound of tapping was interrupted by wind whirling off the Atlantic Ocean, and he was happily distracted. He loved the quiet of East Hampton; its richly privileged pastoral charm became more and more a haven. Yet even as he came to appreciate the peace and beauty of James Lane he was never quite able to still the clatter of Times Square, the squeal and beat and rhythm that had orchestrated so much of his life.

Was it possible he was slowing down this early?

Was it possible he was losing interest in the theater?

Was it possible he was losing interest because *Chorus Line* was, as Matty's ads headlined it, the "One Singular Sensation"—and never to be duplicated or surpassed even by him?

Scandal was a mistake, but *The Children's Crusade* . . . !

Now there was an idea!

The logistics would be a mess, casts of 500 kids, audiences of 5,000, the Broadway musical in a democratic sweep no one had ever imagined before, a revolutionary idea, and it could play the world. Russia! China! In Beijing he'd be remembered for more than the Hustle! Mickey DiFiglia wouldn't need the credential of owning a theater. His name then would really be emblazoned. He would have flown the chorus line and, like Jerry Robbins, he'd exist in another orbit. If his mother had really been sharp, Barnum would have been a better name than Bennett.

No, Barnum wasn't right.

Barnum was crass.

The Children's Crusade was going to be art.

Another form of art.

Something completely different.

Something extraordinary.

And cyclically, in terms of his work, it would be a return to childhood, to the circus and the movies, to clowns and hoofing through the cellars and streets of Buffalo. It would be mammoth. What could be bigger? Sure—right there—the Atlantic Ocean maybe! As a metaphor, the Atlantic Ocean wasn't bad. He heard himself explaining to Bernie—Bobby and John and Jimmy already having been apprised—that *The Children's Crusade* was to be the equivalent of getting the Atlantic Ocean—whitecaps and all—into Madison Square Garden, into as many auditoriums, cow palaces, parking lots and hockey rinks as held two, three, four, five, six thousand people.

Right now, though, two swans were moving across the water with a beauty he might copy in a dance pattern but never really surpass. He was glad there was something out of reach. Maybe there was life after *Chorus Line* . . .

East Hampton was a haven. Bought for $3 million (which Bernard Jacobs says was far too much), it was later sold for $4.6 million. Avian says Bennett was proud of the place but that he wasn't "into it, it was a possession."

Avian: "The house had a lot to do with me. He was jealous of me—no, jealous isn't the right word . . . envious. He was envious I could have a country house, could come up here from the city and relax, do mundane things. He just couldn't do that. He'd go, 'What do you do in the country?' I'd tell him, 'Play in the garden, experiment with recipes.' He'd ask, 'Why?' 'I can't explain it to you, Michael. You should try it.' He'd go, 'Oh, I don't want to do that.'

"My house became my musical, and Michael couldn't understand that. I just escaped my way, and he wasn't able to transfer that to himself. In Connecticut I cook, read, garden, go antiquing. He'd try, then say, 'I tried and I don't know how to do that.' He wasn't into gardening but when he bought East Hampton he became interested. He had a gardener and he'd take me around and point out things. 'She put in something here, it's real pretty, it's red. And over there, I think it's blue and it's supposed to be all along here and next year we'll know.'

"East Hampton was a proud possession to him. If there was any paint peeling he'd go, 'Have that ceiling painted!' He was so immaculate it'd make him crazy if things weren't fixed, and with an estate like that there were always tons of things to do. The upkeep cost a fortune."

He began going to East Hampton on weekends. Then there would be long stretches when he'd spend all his time in New York. As he became sicker, a pattern of increasingly bad days relieved by days without symptoms, he gave up the Central Park South duplex tower, along with Eight Ninety Broadway, and moved to East Hampton. As the disease extracted its price, and he found himself fighting the odds in Tucson, he sold 40 James Lane.

If game playing had been one of the stimuli in the Bennett/Jacobs relationship, it reached its most competitive level in *Chess*, which, in September 1984, was a two-disc album described as a work in progress by its creators, Benny Andersson, Tim Rice and Björn Ulvaeus. Andersson and Ulvaeus were famous—in the 1970s with their wives—as the rock group Abba. A hit single had spun from the *Chess* album onto the world's disco floors, "One

Night in Bangkok," and another single, "I Know Him So Well," had made the charts. The Abba score was a shrewd amalgam of sources as diverse as Gilbert and Sullivan and Andrew Lloyd Webber. The Shuberts, Bernard Jacobs in particular, thought the music had the makings for a first-rate musical. Two things were needed: a book tying the eighteen songs together, and Michael Bennett with his team (Avian, Wagner, Musser, Aldredge).

Bennett listened to the album Jacobs had given him, and had some ideas.

The songs outlined a chess match between an American and a Russian, the match itself a metaphor for international relations, with a subplot involving an intriguing but politically dangerous romance between the American's second, a woman named Florence Vassy, and the Russian champion, who has a wife back in the Soviet Union named Svetlana. (At this stage the chess players were known merely as the American and the Russian; later they would be named Frederick Trumper and Anatoly Sergievsky; later still—for a brief run on Broadway—simply Freddie and Anatoly, with Florence picking up an inexplicable *e* in the surname Vassey.)

Bennett heard the music. The intrigue and melodrama in Rice's outline immediately suggested the Michael Curtiz movie *Casablanca*, where, similarly, in the end the noble hero gives up the woman because he loves her. Bennett thought he might be interested in doing *Chess* as *Casablanca*. Tim Rice, who was responsible for the original idea behind the musical, as well as its lyrics, flew to New York with Benny Andersson, then took a limousine to East Hampton for talks. *Casablanca* was slipped into the VCR. Everyone was impressed with the correspondence in Bennett's perception. Rice, who had written three shows with Andrew Lloyd Webber—*Joseph and the Amazing Technicolor Dreamcoat, Jesus Christ Superstar, Evita*—went off to write—and rewrite—a full script.

Avian: "Michael wanted the storytelling to have tension, and Rice kept coming back with dry, dry, dry material. He'd go off, work some more, and it was all very slow. And there was an odd thing in the center of it. Tim Rice seemed to be more about business than he was about the creative side of it. There were more business meetings! And always about how much would be made here, there; how much the hit singles, the album made. It was an odd way to write a musical. And everybody was a producer. The meetings went from East Hampton to London, and back again, and everything just always seemed to be in the process of . . . *developing*. Slowly."

By the time Bennett came to cast the show for workshop, Rice still had not come up with a script that met with Bennett's approval. Elaine Paige, Murray Head and Tommy Korberg were the singers on the album. Elaine Paige, a star of a certain magnitude in the West End, was Rice's girlfriend. Rice, in fact, had written *Chess* for her, and she was to be the name draw when *Chess* opened in London.

Avian: "Michael was still after *Casablanca*, but now he also saw the plot in ballet terms, with very little scenery, and played openly— only staged to death by Robin, with a tilting floor that did everything, with a whole battery of TV monitors. When Tim came to New York—in December, I guess—with the final draft, it just wasn't acceptable. Michael said it wasn't what we saw in our heads but we'd figure it out by the time we went to London.

"Then he said he was going to St. Bart's for three weeks, which he hadn't mentioned before. He had these . . . lesions. He went off and came back . . . very sick."

Mrs. Jacobs: "He called from St. Bart's and said he was coming back and wasn't doing *Chess*. He said he couldn't work it out, that he didn't like Elaine Paige, and—oh, I don't know—a lot of excuses. I couldn't understand it. Bernie didn't get angry and I said, 'How can he do that to you? It's the most unprofessional thing I've ever heard.'

"It was the only time I remember being angry with Michael. I used to make excuses for him—lots of times—when Bernie was annoyed. Then he invited us to dinner—just Bernie, me and Bobby. He said, 'I'm not going back to England because I have AIDS.'

"Just like that.

"We sat, the four of us, and . . . and cried."

Bernard Jacobs enters the room.

Jacobs: "He really told me first, Betty."

Mrs. Jacobs: "Well, I didn't know. That's why you didn't get angry with him—"

Jacobs: "He came up here to the office. We had a very unpleasant confrontation when he wasn't going back to London. He said he couldn't stand it, working with those people, the climate. We spent twenty minutes talking about it. Then he stood up and said, 'Come on,' and took me to the bathroom, opened his shirt and showed me lesions, purple scars. Kaposi syndrome. I had no idea!"

The AIDS stigma was granted glamour status on July 30, 1985, with the public announcement by the University of California at Los Angeles Medical Center that Rock Hudson was being "evaluated and treated for complications of Acquired Immune Deficiency Syndrome." Hounded by rumors, knowing he was probably doomed, Rock Hudson gave his doctors permission to go public about his illness. But this was not the brave act of a dying man as the subsequently developing myth had it.

Rock Hudson had spent his life hiding his homosexuality (even to the extent of marrying Phyllis Gates in 1955 to protect his career), and he tried to hide the fact that he had AIDS. Diagnosed in 1984, the exact moribund nature of Hudson's illness was known only to his doctors and four male friends. But by early 1985 the information had found its way into Army Archerd's column in *Variety*, the show-business weekly. If the scorn and humiliation resulting from the news in *Variety* came at first only from Hollywood, soon enough it was spread by less parochial newspapers. So, sixty-three days before his death, Rock Hudson confirmed for the world what had long been whispered.

And suddenly AIDS had shock value beyond the systematic recitation of the faceless numbers it had thus far claimed: 12,067 Americans had been diagnosed; 6,079 had succumbed. Now the disease had a recognizable, if distorted, physical symbol: Rock Hudson's once handsome, now serely withered profile. AIDS had happened to someone well known, a popular celebrity.

But the double revelation of a popular "heterosexual" Hollywood star finally being acknowledged both as gay and as a victim of his gayness created only a kind of sickly magnetism, like a fifteen-watt bulb eerily glowing inside a coffin. While Hudson's final, quasi-courageous moment may have sown some understanding, it didn't really change the weedy, ingrown repugnance most people felt about AIDS. No matter how you looked at it, or who got it, it was leprous and awful. It was also the New Scarlet A, and no longer restricted to a simple Puritan community. Aside from hemophiliacs and others "innocently" affected through tainted blood supplies, it offered immediate identification of almost everyone it touched as (1) homosexual, (2) bisexual, (3) sexually flagrant or (4) an intravenous drug user. Generally, it signaled promiscuity. As syphilis once had done, AIDS was a disease proclaiming a person's psychosexual history and revealing tangled secrets, desires, taboos, fetishes and furious erotic practices.

If Rock Hudson's closeted life came to mean far less than his last breaths of weak bravery, Michael Bennett—who had never really been closeted—decided to control as many moments of his own life as he could until it finally lapsed. He had his lawyers, John Breglio and Robert Montgomery, send letters to London getting him out of the *Chess* contract without stating the reason. Bernard Jacobs stepped in and offered to negotiate a substitute deal to palliate Rice, Andersson and Ulvaeus, and to prevent Bennett from being sued. Everyone was sworn to secrecy. Realizing they would need a strong story line, someone came up with the idea of a heart attack: Michael Bennett had serious arrhythmia, would probably require surgery and would surely recover.

Mrs. Jacobs: "Tim Rice was very angry at Michael. He thought he wasn't doing *Chess* because of Elaine. And Michael had had some trouble with her when he first went to London."

Jacobs: "Tim didn't think Michael had a heart attack. But when Michael did get sick, Tim thought it was AIDS. When he came to our suite in London—if you remember, Betty—he said, 'Maybe I shouldn't touch you.' Tim can be very snide."

Meanwhile newspapers carried the story about Michael Bennett's heart condition and the imminence of open-heart surgery.

Jacobs: "I created the story? Well . . . I know Michael said he didn't want anyone to know. When he opened his shirt he said, 'How can I work with dancers? They're going to see these lesions, know what I have and run away from me."

Mrs. Jacobs: "He did say that to go back to those drafty rehearsal halls in London would kill him, that his doctors had told him. He did go to Washington to have his chest opened, cancer in the lungs. When people asked me, I said, 'I know he's had open-heart surgery, I've seen the scars.' He never told anybody about AIDS."

Jacobs: "We were the only ones who knew, and Bobby, and Michael Peters."

Liz Smith: "Someone said to me—maybe Bob Herr—that Michael took perverse delight in the AIDS cover-up because it would eventually make Bernie into a liar."

When Bennett pulled out of *Chess*, Trevor Nunn took over. And what was eventually produced in London was a two-minded musical, some of it with the post-*Dreamgirls* look of Bennett's work, more of it a numbing replay of lost causes. Robin Wagner's scenic design—a horizontal version of his blueprint for *Dreamgirls* with tilting platform replacing shifting towers—was put to bad use the moment the show began. The first image was a vast black-and-white floor, a massive chessboard, the space around it limitless in shadows, limitless in the suggestion of a world where black and white merge (in terms of narrative, more aptly the merging of chauvinistic red, white and blue and plain commissar red). The immediate focus suggested a spare filmic style, only to be instantly blurred by a choreographic onslaught devised by Molly Molloy, dancers brought on in the chiseled attitudes of chess pieces, all got up in shades of ivory. Suddenly, in the midst of what seemed promising, *Chess* became the Solid Gold Dancers being very still and concentrating on "art."

Chess never recovered from the basic inconsistency of attaching Trevor Nunn to Bennett's incomplete plans. While it ran in the West End for two and a half years, it was greeted with critical dismay when it opened in May 1986.* It was greeted with more dismay when—in yet another version, uniting Nunn with playwright Richard Nelson —it opened in 1988 on Broadway (at a cost of $6 million) and canceled itself out after sixty-eight performances.

Like a father whose son abruptly turns away from a costly toy he has given him, Bernard Jacobs continues to believe that Michael Bennett could have manipulated *Chess* into a masterpiece. Others are not so sure. It wasn't "a Bennett kind of show." Its political ramifications took it to places he had never been; more damaging, perhaps, to places in which he had no interest. His attention span was short, concentrated, very specific. He understood heartache, the need for hope. He didn't understand—or didn't wish to understand—more sweeping issues, although, by the very nature of the undertaking, *The Children's Crusade* might have changed that.

What Bennett saw in *The Children's Crusade* is clear enough. In the year 1212 a ragtag group of children tried to accomplish a pilgrimage that had politically corrupted their elders, a march—for Christ's glory—that would make up for their parents' spiritual betrayal during the Fourth Crusade. As the truly innocent must, the children failed. It's likely that Michael Bennett saw himself mirrored in Stephen of Cloyes, the visionary French peasant boy who led the march. Yet whatever hope Bennett may have seen in the idealism of Stephen and his young followers finally would have had to be darkened by the grim record of what actually happened. The Children's Crusade ended

---

*Chess closed in London on April 29, 1989.

with some of its adolescent wanderers drowned in a shipwreck, others dead from deprivation and disease, still others sold into slavery in Egypt. Had Michael Bennett lived and the musical he had envisioned been developed, the perhaps too easy optimism of *A Chorus Line*, *Ballroom* and *Dreamgirls* would have found a harsh sweep in historical reality.

CHAPTER EIGHTEEN

Roadrunners, the Prayerful Saguaro and the Last Party

(1985 . . .)

"**W**hen *The New York Times* put it in the paper that Michael had the AIDS, I wasn't home," Helen DiFiglia says quietly but with outrage, "and everybody was calling me. Frank was trying to get me before I saw it. When I got in—must have been about ten—there were all these different messages, my nieces in North Carolina and Buffalo. They wanted to get me before I saw it. And there was a message from Michael. He'd called, wanted to get me before I saw it, but I didn't know where he was. He had told me before he was in Hawaii, and all the time he was in Tucson. He didn't ever leave a number, all that time.

"Frank finally got me and told me why Michael was trying to get me, and I just had to wait until Michael called back. Michael called and said, 'Mother, did you hear about—' and I said, 'Yes.' "

The light dims in Mrs. DiFiglia's eyes, dies, then rises to a harsh flare.

"He said, '*It's not true.*' "

She waits, as though the prolonged moment would, indeed, prove it not true.

"He never admitted it to me. I said, 'Okay, you're sick.' He could hardly talk. His lungs had been affected, he had trouble breathing. He said, 'I have lymphoma.' Which he did. But he wasn't talking about the AIDS. I said, 'When can I come see you?' 'I don't know but I'll call you back in a couple of days.' I said, 'Don't wait too long, Michael, because I'm coming whether you like it or not.'

"They called a few days later. Vicky Allen, his nurse, and Bob Herr had talked him into it. Vicky kept saying, 'You've got to tell your mother.' But Michael didn't want me to see him that way because . . . he had always been so strong with me. And now . . . he was the weakest.

Earlier, explaining her son's understanding of things he couldn't "possibly have known," his mother had referred to an incident when he was a little boy. Complaining of stomach cramps, he had searched out the cause in a medical book, then diagnosed his own appendicitis.

"He was a little bit of hypochondriac, and every time he'd look in this medical book I had he'd say, 'Oh my God, I've got this, I've got that!' I'd say, 'Forget it, Michael, you don't have it.' Then this appendicitis came up all of a sudden, and I didn't pay much attention. It wasn't as if it'd been going on for a long time—I mean, it was sudden. He said, 'I know I have appendicitis,' and I said, 'Wait and see—then we'll take you to a doctor.' I went to work and said, 'Now, you call me if you don't feel well.'

"Well, he did call about twelve. 'Mom, I'm sick.' I said, 'Okay, I'll get your father and have him take you right to the doctor.' He said, 'And I'm telling you I got appendicitis.' I said, 'Okay.'

"I never even got to the hospital before . . . they had him there to operate so fast! That's how bad it was! And he knew! How did he know this stuff? He didn't know anything about medicine. I sure didn't. He was creepy at times, would know stuff he couldn't possibly have known. I think he was born with all this knowledge or something . . ."

There is a pattern to AIDS, five psychological stages first identified by Elisabeth Kübler-Ross in patients facing imminent death. For AIDS victims—most of whom are young—the five stages, heightened as they are by the sexual stigma of the disease, are like a purification rite decreed by a pitiless god, or a ritual defined in hell. First there's denial, then depression, then anger, then bargaining and then, for some, acceptance. When Michael Bennett learned he had the virus he was as susceptible to these five stages as anyone else, and, in fact, passed through them many times, sometimes jokingly: "Today, by the way, I'm in denial; tomorrow maybe there'll be anger." The persons who watched those wrenching transformations were steadily amazed at his will. A number of AIDS patients give up. He battled. Convinced "by who he was and his money," he was certain he was going to beat it, Kenneth Lipper says. "He would fly anywhere, try anything, but he did say he wasn't going to die suffering." John Breglio says, "He had hoped to keep it a secret in Tucson, and thought the press would respect his privacy. He had no objection to everyone knowing he had AIDS after he died. God knows, that should have been his decision. It all goes back to what he felt happened on the heart attack story."

Diagnosed in New York, Bennett was one of the first patients on the experimental drug AZT. AZT interrupts the cycle of the virus and, although pulsing with side effects, extends the patient's life. Whatever benefits it provides, and to most of those suffering, even a single day shy of death is a blessing, AZT is an oxymoron. Cruelly it offers hope but the hope is curtailed. AIDS is death. To scientists searching for a cure, AZT is a temporary poultice offering time. If a patient's life can be stretched three or four years after the incubation of the virus, which ranges from eight to fifteen years, there is the possibility some new discovery could extend it further. The contradictory force in Matthew Arnold's lines: "Still nursing the unconquerable hope, / Still clutching the inviolable shade," is what drives medical research, perhaps especially AIDS research, where time is crucial. Hope is based on tomorrow.

AIDS research has been complicated—some would say compromised—by far more than a deadline. The image of white-smocked scientists holding vials to fluorescent light as they work selflessly into the night—their concentration intensified by a soundlessly ticking clock—is real enough, but it shares time with at least two other considerations, one political, one economic.

The AIDS struggle has been burdened by rivalry: first between scientists (Dr. Robert Gallo, a retrovirologist at the National Cancer Institute in Bethesda, and Drs. Luc Montagnier and Jean-Claude Chermann of the Pasteur Institute in Paris, where the virus was originally isolated); second between countries (specifically the United States and France). Scientists anxious to establish a breakthrough—to curb suffering, to foster health—are well aware of the rewards such an achievement could mean: glittering honor and cold hard cash, more directly the Nobel Prize, a sizable lump settlement and attendant royalties amounting to a lifetime annuity. The research often seems to have been distorted by ego, with Dr. Gallo, for example, championing himself as the one who discovered the cause of AIDS and belittling Dr. Montagnier and Dr. Chermann in the process. Beyond that is the perplexity of the disease itself, with hypotheses attaching it to a particular green monkey in Zaire and the suggestion that the power of the virus may have been dormant "in some simian population for thousands of years before being transferred to humans."*

Wherever it started, however long its history, AIDS is now recognized as a scourge, although to some—tempering the evidence—not a pandemic. It has been linked in the public mind with homosexual or bisexual promiscuity and/or with drugs shot through needles. In other words, the general perception is that it happens to people who are willful (and asking for it) and to others who are simply ignorant. As mysterious as some of the facts behind AIDS are, the route of infection is through the bloodstream. Virulent microbes attack and defeat the body's immune system, in some cases creating a rare disease known as pneumocystis carinii pneumonia (PCP), in others a rare skin cancer known as Kaposi's sarcoma (KS), in still others both PCP and KS, in some invasion by parasitic infections (cryptococcus, toxoplasmosis).

Avian: "Michael was on the AZT program when it was an un-

---

*Randy Shilts, *And the Band Played On* (New York: St. Martin's Press, 1987), p. 459.

finding out it prolonged life by about six months, and at the end of the six months it could cause terrible reactions, anemia, and the opportunistic infections could return doublefold. But it was a great 'up' period for Michael. AZT is made from the sperm of herrings. *How did they ever find that out?* So, tomorrow, maybe from a snail they'll find something . . ."

In his desperation to live ("and shine again on the next Tony Awards," as he said to Lipper), Bennett went from hospital to hospital, medical center to medical center. One of the first trips was to the University of Minnesota, where Dr. Fritz Bach was conducting sibling blood tests in relation to the AIDS virus. According to Avian, Frank DiFilia—without knowing his brother had AIDS—was persuaded to make a blood donation in New York. The brothers' blood didn't match, and eventually the test proved unworkable. In Minneapolis, Bennett and Avian were first given the details of the terrifying prognosis.

Bennett said to the doctor, "How much time does a person have once diagnosed?"

The doctor—his words coldly factual—answered, "Approximately eighty-five weeks from the point of diagnosis to death."

Bennett and Avian looked at each other, the space between them thrumming with fear. *Eighty-five weeks! How long is eighty-five weeks?* In unison they said, "Eighty-five weeks." Said right out like that, it seemed a long time, almost a reprieve. Usually quick with figures, Bennett couldn't calculate the time and, for a moment, neither could Avian. The clock was ticking mercilessly. The day Bennett's life span was given to him cut-and-dried and inexorable was January 2, 1986. There was to be no reprieve. In effect, he would be cheated forty-nine days and die within seventy-eight weeks.

After adjusting to the shock of the Minnesota verdict, there were further consultations in New York, including several with his psychiatrist, Dr. Emmanuel Feurer. Michael Bennett then enrolled in an outpatient AIDS program at the National Institutes of Health (NIH) in Washington. His participation in the program meant grueling biweekly trips on the shuttle from La Guardia to National Airport, with, increasingly, the jet's pressurization causing him shortness of breath, vomiting and often paralyzing anxiety. At NIH he met a young nurse, Victoria Allen, who at first had no idea who he was (during his illness he had dropped Bennett and reverted to Michael DiFiglia) and who, had she known, could not have cared less. Victoria Allen is as far away from Broadway as an emergency ward is from center stage.

Trained to maintain professional distance from patients, both for her own emotional protection and for theirs, Victoria Allen found her discipline waning as she became personally involved with her once-every-other-week patient Michael DiFiglia. She admired his "give-it-all attitude," but was startled when she realized the skill he used in manipulating her. Bennett, having witnessed firsthand the rivalry among AIDS scientists and doctors, many of whom seemed as much interested in copping a Nobel Prize as in conquering the disease, saw Victoria Allen for precisely what she was: a clearly focused, totally dedicated nurse who had had dreams of becoming a doctor. Besides that, she was pretty. She resembled both Donna and Sabine. She had a boyfriend in Washington and, soon enough, Bennett was conversationally directing her love life. Then he hired her away from NIH as his private nurse.

Victoria Allen, Gene Pruit and Bob Herr lived with him in Tucson for eight months until he died. At Bennett's insistence, Bob Avian's job was to keep things going in New York. Near the end, explaining his dismay at the behavior of some of his old friends, Michael Bennett said to Lipper, one of the few allowed to visit him in Tucson, "Ironic, isn't it, that the people I want with me as I die aren't my old friends or even the people I worked with."

"When I was at NIH," Victoria Allen says, "the AIDS patients would come in and be divided up among the nurses. I didn't know who he was the first time he came. The second time he told me. I said, 'Oh, that's nice.' I'd seen a lot of Broadway shows, but I mean I had no appreciation of him that way. He was just somebody doing nothing because he was sick, and I was taking care of him.

"At NIH the way it's set up it's not like a regular hospital. In a lot of them a patient can't just come in for treatment, then go out, because the doctors aren't around all the time. There's a nine-to-five Monday-to-Friday schedule at NIH. The doctors are around, and most patients get a pass for the evening and go out to dinner. And activities are provided: bus tours through Washington to see the monuments, the Smithsonian, Mount Vernon. It takes some of the grimness away, it's paid for by the hospital. Michael's financial situation was different from a lot of the other patients, and he insisted on paying his own tickets. He wouldn't just take advantage of what was being offered."

"Hooked by his charm," Allen admits that he got special treatment.

"You're supposed to be impartial, but the more I knew him, the more he became my favorite patient. He'd come skipping in, ready for anything, he was going to beat it! He'd fly down to Washington and back the same day. I got to know he was coming at a certain time, and I'd have it all set up to draw a blood test, have the doctors lined up to see him. Everything was ready so we could do it as fast as possible, and he could be back on the shuttle to New York. At the time I didn't realize he was manipulating me! I was doing it because I wanted to, I guess . . .

"I was planning on leaving NIH, and I went to New York one weekend and talked to him about it. Then I changed my mind. He wanted to try out some new experimental drugs, and he was flying around a lot. I knew some doctors in Tucson, I'd been planning to come here after NIH. He flew to Tucson, got sick on the way out and entered the hospital. I came to visit and he asked me to be his nurse. At first we lived in a rented house on Longfellow Lane, then he bought the house on Camino Miraval."

The house at 2150 Camino Miraval sits on a slight rise of parched soil here and there thrust with scrub and squat trees, a small stucco fortress facing the strange omnipresent haze of the Catalina Mountains. The Catalinas seem to wall in part of the sprawl of the city, earth mounded up against a world beyond, the sun hanging like a glinting gong stamped on the back "Made in Arizona." The rise and fall of the Tucson basin, where houses, motels, churches, colleges, hospitals, banks, supermarkets and gas stations sit helter-skelter, suggests a paradoxically miniature landscape inside a vast steaming whorl, the desert made habitable but still hot, still dry as bone. Quails, roadrunners, coyotes, jackrabbits scurry on and off the tarmac, scraping through the sand and underbrush to scavenge what they can from back stoops of kitchen doors and open decks. Random two-pronged, thirty-feet-tall saguaro cacti stand like prayerful sentinels, flowering arms raised to the limitless sky.

Michael Bennett thought Tucson was ugly when he first arrived, then he came to find its aridity and remoteness peaceful. He moved out of the rented house on Longfellow Lane because he wanted more room, wanted something closer—in spirit if not style—to East Hampton, and because he thought the move would prove to the unseen religious forces behind his life that he was going to be around for a long time. He was still in control. He bought Camino Miraval for $500,000 the day it went on the market. Designed by Joseph Thomas Joesler, a locally admired 1930s specialist in Southwest architecture, the low-lying adobe had a room next to his for Victoria Allen, separate quarters for Pruit and Herr, a top deck, a wood porch, a swimming pool, privacy, a view of the Catalinas from the front and downtown Tucson from the back. The house was seven minutes from the hospital at the Arizona Medical Center. The boy from Buffalo who made it to the lush, thalassic lawns of East Hampton was now St. Anthony lost and withering in the dry beauty of the desert.

Reliving discussions and arguments with writers that had sometimes become outright shouting matches, the good ones with Neil Simon, John Guare and John Heilpern, the bad ones with Michael Stewart, Jerome Kass, Tom Eyen, Peter Stone, Treva Silverman, he sat out on the patio and thought about writing his life story. If anything, he'd collaborate with the quails and roadrunners who came close enough to fly off with his thoughts, if not his words. It wouldn't be easy (although Neil had said all you do is do it), but it would be about him and Buffalo, and English had always been his best subject; he had never skipped those classes.

How many times had he come up with writing ideas, themes, metaphors, characters, situations? How many lines of dialogue had he fed into Jerry's, Tom's, Treva's scripts? He'd try; he could do it now alone. Where to begin? Images of Helen, Sam; time steps in the basement with Frank; then the shows, God, all the shows; looking back, looking back, his grandmother's ninetieth when he gave the big party toasting her as someone as admirable as Katharine Hepburn; the joy of all the *Chorus Line* parties; the misery at Windows on the World at the *Ballroom* party; the ups, the downs, the hits, the flops; echoes from songs: "I'm still here . . ." "What I did for love . . ." "I am changing . . ."

Maybe he couldn't do it the usual way, words accumulating into paragraphs, paragraphs into chapters . . .

What about a new form . . .

What about autobiography as play . . .

Two titles tilted in his head. He remembered telling Bobby that if he ever got around to writing about his life he'd call it *Please Don't Dance in Shanghai*. He could see Bobby in front of him countering with a second title, could even hear the sarcasm in Bobby's voice: "No, darling, no. I've a much better idea. From Buffalo. Remember you always telling me how poor you were, with Helen buying you sneakers instead of shoes, and you trudging off to dance class through a blizzard in your sneakers? Remember you told me that same sad old story about not having money for the bus and hiking in your sneakers? Must have told me a hundred times. So how about *Sneakers in the Snow*? Perfect!"

    Bennett lived those last months as
normally as he could with his Vizsla, Kila* and a new dog, Bosco,
"a handsome pug" Herr and Pruit bought, which he thought looked
like Ben Vereen. He fixed up Camino Miraval, ordering furniture
and materials from New York; shopped for house plants; bought new
white sneakers when a slightly less new pair developed a smudge or
a scar; and, close to his forty-fourth birthday, April 3, 1987, replaced
his slightly less new black BMW with a new blue BMW. Although
the black car had tinted windows and air conditioning, he felt it was
both funereal and a firebox. He talked up a new BMW to Pruit, Herr
and Allen, all of whom were to help him convince John Breglio, who
was managing his money, that it wasn't a needless extravagance. Allen
says that he acted like a little boy afraid to ask for something he
wanted. "It was fun when he'd spend his money on himself so openly
because, in a funny way, he was a haggler, bargain-conscious. He'd
love to buy these Mexican baskets that are everywhere. He'd ask how
much, then say, 'That's too much,' and not buy one! You'd think:
Michael, you have enough, buy it! He was so funny. Here's a man
who could have anything he wanted."

  The day of the new BMW the three conspirators went with him
to the Grand Prix dealership at 4635 East Twenty-second Street. Leading the way, Bennett walked in, saw two BMWs, one blue, one bronze,
and chose the blue, which was on display in the showroom. Sitting
behind the wheel, he studied the dashboard, said, "Okay, this is it."
While Herr went off to write a check for the sale, Allen and Pruit
got in the back seat. When Herr joined them, Bennett drove the car
off the cool showroom floor and onto the baking tarmac, marveling
at the much lower sun glare blue afforded over black.

  On the way home to Camino Miravel, he decided to celebrate
and pulled into a Dairy Queen. Inside, the car was streaming cool
air-conditioned air; outside, it was hell. "He made us all get out to

*Originally the Vizsla's name was Killer, which the doorman at 40 Central Park South pronounced
Kila.

have our ice cream," Vicky Allen says, "so we wouldn't spill any of it on his new blue car!"

"There were times in Tucson he forgot he had AIDS," Bob Herr says. "He found out he had it somewhere near the last months of 1985. He didn't tell me, but I felt the mood change at Eight Ninety, and I just knew before he told me. And he didn't really tell me. He sensed I knew, and just said, 'Okay,' and dropped it. A while after that we started making the trips. At NIH he was constantly reminded he had it because he was on their experimental program. The nature is that you have agreed to their program so they can see what's happening. We flew to Washington every other week, so he was constantly aware of it. But in Tucson he was on the program, then off."

The medical attention in Tucson was thorough, so thorough that even the most remote possible cause of the AIDS virus was tracked and analyzed. For example, in 1981, five years before Michael Bennett had enrolled at NIH, the Centers for Disease Control in Atlanta had investigated an infection associated with cats, toxoplasmosis, for any latent connection with AIDS. Once in bodily tissue, toxoplasmosis has the power to cripple the central nervous system. This disease is found in man and other mammals, and in birds as well. It's the paramount cause of death among cats. Like pneumocystis carinii pneumonia, it's an opportunistic infection, a vicious parasite that attaches itself to an already depleted immune system, then works through a long incubation period. It—or something like it—had begun to appear in the new disease. Eventually the CDC's partial list of ailments attached to AIDS was to include, as Randy Shilts has reported, "fungal infections of birds, sheep, cat, and deer, as well as cancers that appeared all over the body, on the tongue, in the rectum, or most horrifically, in the brain."

In Tucson, Bennett was tested for toxoplasmosis by Dr. David Yocum. The results were negative. Checking all the symptomatic clues, doctors found no relationship between his illness and his love of cats. Later, as AIDS researchers struggled to find possible links in the disease they wondered if Michael Bennett's steady drug abuse had played a role in his death. Did his cocaine inhalation, in partnership with Quaaludes, further weaken his system, leaving him even more vulnerable to the ravages of acquired immune deficiency?

Herr: "In Tucson he'd feel great, then not so hot. At times it was very painful, not from the drugs but from the various things he had, all the problems that happened to him in the time he was fighting it. He had a lung biopsy at NIH, then in Tucson chemotherapy nausea different from the standard chemo sickness, digestive problems, Kaposi sarcoma, which was how he was diagnosed. It was hard to watch. He gained weight at NIH. He was about 150 to 160 pounds—had a little potbelly, and we had to shop for clothes all the time, which he loved.

"Then . . . well, he just wasted . . .

"He didn't want to see people, just a few."

In fact, the list was short: Bob Avian, Robin Wagner, Michael Peters, John Breglio, Kenneth Lipper. He might even have preferred not to see his mother and brother, and he instructed Herr and Allen to keep others away. Vicky Allen is quite clear about former best friends who had wounded him in one way or another and whom he had no desire to see. She feels a lot of people used him for who he was and didn't really care about him, saying darkly, "Certain things I learned about people who were supposedly Michael's friends; in a way it was sad, so many were superficial." She sensed that "a woman friend's" phone calls were motivated by gossip: "She wanted to know [about AIDS], not because she cared about Michael, but because she wanted to be the first person in New York that knew more than other people." If these and similar calls made Allen "want to scream," the visit from Marvin Hamlisch drove her "crazy."

Allen: "Michael felt Marvin Hamlisch betrayed him. I know Marvin Hamlisch told people in New York Michael had AIDS. Michael had told him because he was going to help get certain drugs; Marvin knew a lot of doctors. Then he told people when Michael had asked him not to. I'd always thought they were friends, but when Marvin came here I saw he was a very selfish person. All he cared about was Michael making him money, making him famous. The first time he came through, he was supposed to stop back in a month. We never saw him again."

"When I visited Michael in Arizona," Marvin Hamlisch says, "it was after AZT had come out. There was no other drug. I had already spoken to Mathilde Krim [oncologist who organized the AIDS Medical Foundation] about other possible drugs. When I visited him I knew he was dying. Yet I was trying to say, 'Every day you're alive research is going on and I'm out there, Michael, I'm out there!' That was the level of Michael and me.

"I loved the man, and the love we had over the years couldn't be killed by lawyers who'd tell me his demands and I'd go, 'That little friggin' bastard!' The love was based on: he knew I was good and he was a genius. When you worked with Michael you put yourself in his camp, as opposed, say, to the Hal Prince camp. I knew forever I probably would never work for Hal Prince unless this happened [Bennett's death]. It's scary if you want to work on shows, but that's the name of the game."

Herr: "Michael said various things about his mother and Frank coming to see him. He didn't want them to go through the anguish of his dying, which we always approached as *maybe* dying. For a while I thought the *maybe* was right. He did so well on AZT. He also didn't want Helen and Frank here because of what he'd have to go through dealing with them. He wasn't close to them. He created that kind of family closeness elsewhere. But Gene and Vicky and Feurer and I kept saying, 'Maybe your mom should come.' We didn't want to say maybe this would be your last chance; on the other hand, maybe it was."

"Bob Herr picked me up at the airport," Mrs. DiFiglia says. "He said Michael was in the hospital and we were going there. He wouldn't tell me anything more than he was sick. I walked in and I could tell right away it was the quarantine floor. People were wearing gloves. You had to sign in and out, and oh, I kinda knew. But since Michael didn't want to admit it, I said to myself, I can't tell him he's lying and I know he's got the AIDS; I just have to let it go because if I get upset with him he's going to get upset with me. We just couldn't have agreed.

"He was like a skeleton, gasping, on oxygen, like a skeleton, nothing left of him. And I knew! Oh, I knew! He was dying, and I didn't know what from, only I know it, I know it! So I tried to be as calm as I could be. I talked to him and he tried to talk to me and he couldn't, he was gasping. 'Michael, don't talk. Do you want something?' He said no. I just sat there.

"I called Frank when I got back to the hotel. 'Frank, I want you here immediately if you want to see him alive.' Michael didn't want Frank there. I said, 'I want Frank here and he's coming!' "

Withered and wracked as he was, Bennett was determined his brother was not going to see him at a further disadvantage, lying down—waiting for death—in a hospital bed or at home. The day Frank DiFilia was to come, Gene Pruit brought Bennett home from the Medical Center in the BMW, then, at his direction, dressed him in slacks, a sweater and his usual immaculate sneakers. Pruit helped him into a wheelchair, kissed him and wheeled him outside to wait.

Mrs. DiFiglia: "He sat and waited, oh, a long time. The plane was delayed. He was getting tired, so tired, and I could see him fighting to sit up. I said, 'Michael, you can go to bed. Frank won't care.' He said no. And he was . . . sitting up when Frank came. They talked a few minutes, and then Michael said, 'I'd like to go to bed now.'

"Oh, Frank was shocked. But I'd prepared him somewhat—more so than they had the decency to prepare me!"

Mrs. DiFiglia trembles. She twists the wedding ring on her finger.

"Frank . . . was very angry that Michael had permitted this to happen and not let us know, particularly him. Why couldn't he tell his brother? Maybe because he knows Frank and I are close and Frank would've told me? But why couldn't he have said, 'Frank, you're my brother and I want you to know but please don't tell Mother . . . ?' I mean, why did he do things like that? I don't know, I don't know."

A spasm invades her, slowly retreats. She stands by the slider to the balcony touching the Star of David, staring for a long moment at the Gulf of Mexico.

"I hadn't seen him for about a year and half," Frank DiFilia says, "and it was maybe longer with Mother. When the article appeared about the heart attack, I had such faith in him I believed it, and I said to Mom he was in Arizona being treated for heart disease. Then he called and told me he had lymphoma. He let me know it was pretty bad, but he was still saying cancer. Couple days later he called again, said 'I can't tell you how serious it is but you gotta understand I want to see you again.' I didn't want to say I want to see you again before you die, but . . . well, I was going away to work on *Cats* for a couple of weeks. He said to come after that. My mother flew to Arizona, called and said he's in really bad shape. I was angry. He had lied to me for a year. He had called every once in a while saying he was in Hawaii, saying he was swimming, writing his autobiography, moving around. He called me on his birthday and I remember singing 'Happy Birthday,' just a bit of it, and he said, 'Sing the rest of it, sing it all,' and I did.

"Over the past couple of years he started pulling away once he knew he had AIDS. Prior to that my dealings with him were of such little consequence, or satisfaction, I let it go, and didn't ever plan on seeing him. I stopped trying to make it an active communicative relationship. I wanted him to change, to finally wake up. 'If you're going to have a relationship with anyone, do it with me, Michael, because I'm your brother. You have nothing to hold back, to fear, to hide. Wake up! Relax! Open up! Be human!' It was like Mom trying to wake up Dad. Neither of them were able to achieve what Mom or I wanted."

For a short time Bennett was spared the chorus of spite circling his death in New York, but he heard it loudly during his final weeks at Camino Miraval. Ingratitude, Shakespeare's "marble-hearted fiend," found its way from Times Square to Tucson. And it came from an unexpected source, not from friends used and perhaps abused, or from disgruntled co-workers, but, rather, from a handful of associates in theater and dance he had genuinely tried to help: his tenants at Eight Ninety Broadway.

From the day he bought the building he had seen it as a replica of the New York Shakespeare Festival several blocks away, a replica that one day might be as important as the Festival itself and, possibly, even overtake it. Although Joe Papp was a hardworking visionary, he wasn't what Michael Bennett was: a hardworking visionary who also happened to be an artist. Bennett had come to think that he was outdistancing Jerome Robbins on Broadway, and he saw no reason why the same competitive spirit wouldn't leave Joe Papp faltering at some midpoint hurdle. Eight Ninety would become an important cultural address, its small downstairs theater an Off-Broadway landmark. The place already had an associative reputation based on the *Chorus Line* workshops.

He had found the building through Cora Cahan, the wife of Bernard Gersten. Cora Cahan was the administrator of the Eliot Feld Ballet. The Feld Ballet was represented by Paul, Weiss, Rifkind, Wharton & Garrison, where John Breglio worked. In the tight, ambitious circle that is show business itself, Feld had known Gersten through the New York Shakespeare Festival, from which—in a furious argument with Joe Papp—Gersten later fled to replace Breglio as one of the producers of *Ballroom*. Bennett heard there was rental space available at Eight Ninety, which then housed the Feld Ballet, an arts group and some light-manufacturing companies, and he planned on leasing a floor. Told the building was for sale, he bought it. It turned out that he also bought a houseful of tenants crying poormouth.

Eventually he displaced the manufacturers and created office and workshop space for his allies. Committed as he was to the dream of turning Eight Ninety into an arts complex, he was forced to absorb the monthly shortfalls of some of his tenants. Signed to a long-term lease in the mid-1970s, the Feld Ballet was paying approximately $1.50 a square foot, not an unreasonable sum in those days. As the 1980s approached (with the area surrounding Eight Ninety now discovered and in process of reclamation), square footage was renting for between $7.00 and $8.00, and sometimes as high as $9.00. According to Breglio, Bennett approached Cora Cahan with a rent increase and was told any increase would "drive the ballet into the streets." He met opposition on every floor. People were taking the *Chorus Line* King for granted. The attitude seems to have been: He eats cake, let him support us.

And Bennett began pouring money into the building.

"All you have to do is sit down and figure out what it cost to run Eight Ninety," Breglio says. "The maintenance, the insurance, the capital improvements, the taxes, the whatever. All you have to do is add up what was being paid out and you could see it had to lose money. It was a ten-year losing proposition, and no sensible real estate man would have kept it going on that basis. For example, the Feld Ballet had a lease, and for a while there was no legal way Michael could raise the rent. Then, when he could legally do it, they said there was no way they could pay. So he carried them."

Bennett simply had to get rid of the building. He didn't have much time left. He wanted to simplify his last few months, to have his estate in order and his assets as liquid as possible. Eight Ninety Broadway was put up for sale, for these reasons alone. "He didn't do it to throw out any of the arts group people," Breglio says. Although he sold the business for what seemed an enormous profit, the take was illusory. "The income was never there," Breglio says. "He lost over a million a year on it for close to ten years. And the steady income was no longer there. He wasn't generating any new projects; *Dreamgirls* had closed; *Chorus Line* was only running in New York, and on limited profits, and the road company hadn't earned that much. He was dying in Arizona."

Yet with the announcement alone of an impending $15 million price tag, the tenants he had supported for nearly ten years shrieked greed. Michael Bennett saw himself publicly portrayed as the Donald

Trump of lower Broadway. The first complaint was that the selling price automatically disqualified the poor struggling arts groups, the suggestion being that the price itself was proof of Bennett's avarice and revenge. All he was interested in was a fortune from a third-party developer. It was as though he had never thought about Eight Ninety as a possible creative center for the arts. He was pictured as a nimble Simon Legree dancing through his countinghouse. Overnight, and in the sickly light of death, he—not his colleagues—became the ingrate.

Breglio: "He could barely speak. He wasn't able. The *Times* followed the story. At the same time we were being told that certain people would go to the press saying they weren't being given an opportunity to buy the building. The point is: Michael never didn't want to sell it to them. They simply had to come up with the money, which they finally did through a white knight. To everyone's delight the money was suddenly there and Michael was able to sell Eight Ninety to a consortium of American Ballet Theatre and Eliot Feld. It couldn't have made him happier. He wanted the place for dancers and performers. But the awful thing was, he saw himself perceived as this terrible antagonist, the exact opposite of what he was. It was very painful!"

Avian says the tenants were in arrears all the time, some not even paying enough for their heat. "Every time Michael would ask for an increase, they'd say, 'We can't, we'll go under.' 'We can't' was constant, constant. Then Cora Cahan and Eliot Feld, who'd been crying the blues, all of a sudden came up with $14 million to buy the building. They hurt him so bad at the end, the things they said in the papers. I mean, he was dying. He had enough to deal with in Tucson without that!

"I saw Michael for the last time in the spring. I was doing *Follies* in London, and he really didn't push me into it but he kept saying, 'This is your last chance, do it, do it; it's the perfect bridge for you; keep working; you've got to keep working.' The last time I went out there, and I didn't see him at his worst, he was down to 100, 105 pounds. Not a hair on his body because of all the chemotherapy, and looking like a hundred-year-old man, all shriveled up, with a wild look in his eyes. It was so terrible. So awful. And he stared in my eyes and . . . and . . . it was like, 'Don't look at me that way, I know how sick I am.' It was . . . devastating."

On Sunday, June 28, 1987, four days and a few hours before he died, Michael Bennett had a party unlike any other he had ever staged. There were no colleagues or anonymous well-wishers at this one, no passersby or autograph seekers craning after stars or celebrities. But he planned it with the same meticulous care he had given to the Shubert Alley bash when *A Chorus Line* had broken the long-run record. This party was for the doctors and staff of the Arizona Medical Center Hospital who were shepherding him on his certain way to death.

If, in fact, he had been "living a script" all his life, he was going to spotlight one last moment before the stage went to black. He was weak and depleted but probably didn't know how close death really was. Whatever grim final thoughts he had were frequently interrupted by fantasy. It wasn't the act of contritition that eased his guilt and temporarily dispelled his fear. It was a sentimental image he had of himself striding down the aisle at the 1988 Tony Awards, surprising everyone as cheers suddenly encircled him. The whole house was smiling and crying as he walked onstage in his tails. Waiting for the adulation to taper off, he bowed and bowed again. Then, standing at the edge of the stage as the final hush fell over the audience, just as he was about to speak, someone hollered out from the balcony, "Fuck! He did it again!" He had repeated this fantasy over and over to Kenneth Lipper. It ended with a *Newsweek* cover story headlined "Bennett Back on Broadway," his smile stretching to the margins and scoring the odds.

The party was for about fifty people from the hospital staff, according to Herr, "every doctor, intern, nurse, technician, sweeper he came in contact with." It was catered by a Tucson restaurant known as Katherine & Company, Katherine herself in charge of the menu and service. The food was a particular problem. Bennett was concerned about people coming to the house of an AIDS patient and being worried about "possible contamination."

Herr: "We hand-wrote the invitations, and he wanted a line saying 'Catered by Katherine & Company.' I thought that was tacky, like bragging, but he said that's not what he meant. He wanted the guests to know we weren't handling the food so they'd be comfortable. He had been worried about that at East Hampton too, and was adamant that we use plastic glasses to put people at ease."

During the week leading up to the party, he was in and out of the hospital for treatment. He was getting progressively weaker, but in the scale of his physical deterioration the changes were imperceptible. His amusements now were few. When he found Camino Miraval oppressive, Vicky Allen would drive him to La Paloma, a nearby resort, where he would sit in the lounge and sip a single piña colada without alcohol, which had been forbidden. He was getting ready for his party little by little. Vicky Allen brought him home from the hospital the day of the party, and took him back when it was over.

Allen: "Everyone came. He was Michael DiFiglia, but most of the people knew who he was, and it didn't make any difference one way or the other. They had no more appreciation of Broadway than I did. Everyone just liked him. Katherine & Company did these big ice chunks with all the food laid out. There was an open bar, people outside, people swimming. There must have been fifty people, maybe more. He wasn't as spunky as he had been. We didn't know he was that close to dying. He was quiet, sat on the sofa, different people would come to talk to him. He didn't really go outside, it was hot. Then he went to bed, and a few people went in there to talk to him.

"It ended like a farewell party, and we didn't quite realize . . ."

"**M**ichael changed at the end, really changed," Kenneth Lipper says, "and it started at East Hampton. He never went to parties at East Hampton—oh, he'd come to our house. It was like: the only thing that had attracted him was the turbulence of the theater, then somehow there was the sea and the land! He couldn't believe he was on this beautiful piece of land, the idea he came from the city, had an inner-city kind of personality, all that. More than being sick, the land changed him. He'd sit for hours watching the trees, the wind, the ocean.

"I don't know about religion but he had strong belief in fate. Which is religion, in a sense. He wanted to live life to the fullest, and he did. His vision was bigger than the environment permitted. Even to the day he died he said, 'I can't complain, because in forty-four years I did what people couldn't do in ninety-six years!'"

Mrs. DiFiglia: "The torment and the drive! Nothing was ever enough! It had to be bigger, then bigger the next time, and one person isn't capable of handling all this. And that's why I think it was time for him to leave this earth. What more could he do? How could he top that? And he would have kept on trying until he killed himself anyway. He really did, in a way!"

Herr: "I never saw any signs of religion. He joked about coming back and haunting us all, the implication being that he would come back and watch what was going on. And, you know something, I believe it!"

Echoing Horace's "I shall not wholly die," Herr says, "Sometimes I really think Michael is with us. The dead do live in the living."

Allen: "We were paid to be with him. I mean, my job was helping him to die. But that wasn't Gene's or Bob's job, and it was tough on them; I could see the strain.

"He went through several crises but, through all of them, he wasn't ready to die. I could tell from day to day whether it was going to be a good day or it wasn't. I guess I knew he was going to die the day he died. I think he had decided the time was right. He knew there was nothing going to cure him, and he had fought so hard, through so much pain. He had no problem dying when he did. It was, like, 'Okay, I'm ready.' He died so peaceful. I had never been with a patient who died, so I was scared, thinking: I've got to be here when Michael dies and I'm really frightened. The weird thing was, I wasn't."

Victoria Allen hesitates.

"I had a couch . . . right outside . . . a little sofa. He was still breathing when I went out to lie down. I dozed off for a minute, woke up, went in and he wasn't breathing. And the strangest thing is, I think he knew I was afraid and he waited until I fell asleep until . . . I don't know, it really was . . . weird.

"I got Gene and Bob, and the three of us felt: There's just a body there, the soul is gone, the soul—like this energy—is . . . just gone . . .

"The day he died I saw the films they played of him on TV, and I didn't know that person. That's him, the voice, the eyes, but it wasn't him. It was a whole different person, and I thought: Gosh, he's smart. He kept everyone away and everyone who knew him is going to remember him as that person and not the sickly dying one. If people see you sick, that's the way they remember you, not the way you were before when you were healthy. And he really wasn't that person on the television screen, at least not to me. I asked Dr. Feurer about it. He said the Michael I got to know was the real Michael."

CHAPTER NINETEEN

Advice to the Players

(. . .1987)

Had the 1987 memorial service at the Shubert Theater not been postponed from July 27 to September 29, its memories might have been untarnished. In the interim, on August 10, *A Chorus Line* passed its 5,000th consecutive performance, and the shock and embarrassment caused at the after-theater party hosted by the New York Shakespeare Festival at the Palladium on East Fourteenth Street scorched the eulogies that were delivered seven weeks later. While the bickering behind *A Chorus Line* was common enough backstage, it still amounted to a family squabble kept in the kitchen. Although there were rumors about a book in process which would detail the hurt, humiliation, financial deprivation and lack of promised stardom among the original *Chorus Line* cast members, that too was family stew simmering on a back burner. James Kirkwood turned the flame to high with an egomaniacal and mean-spirited display publicly rivaling anything Michael Bennett had ever done privately. What happened that night released some of the long-held hostility behind *A Chrous Line*, the show Michael Bennett proclaimed he "had done for love."

At the conclusion of the 5,000th performance, Joseph Papp appeared on the Shubert stage to make a short spe⌄ ut Michael Bennett. The evening was dedicated to Bennett, whose remains—turned to ash soon after his death—were now in the possession of Gene Pruit and Robert Herr. (After his death, Pruit and Herr moved directly from Tucson to Hollywood.) Papp spoke only about Michael Bennett, no one else. He was thinking, he says, "solely about Michael, not his collaborators—this was my testimony to Michael."

Amid applause and some tears, a cake on a trolley was rolled onstage. The 5,000th performance was history, the 5,001st waiting in the wings. Papp and some 750 guests moved on to the party at the Palladium.

Without a trace of remorse, Kirkwood tells what he did, and without any attempt to explain himself, even denying the out some people have given him. He said he wasn't drunk ("I had one drink at Sardi's at seven, with a shrimp cocktail") and wasn't "on anything." His date for the evening was Sydney Biddle Barrows, the media-labeled Mayflower Madam.

"I got to the party," Kirkwood says, "and went right up to Bob MacDonald, who was standing with somebody else from the New York Shakespeare Festival, and said, 'I really find that reprehensible.'

" 'What?' they said.

" 'You know *what*. That none of our names was mentioned, any of our contributions, any of that, and I find it embarrassing and Jesus Christ awful.'

" 'Here,' they said, 'we got you a good table.'

"I was with Sydney and six or eight people, and we sat down. I asked the waiter for vodka. He said there was only champagne. I said, 'I'm going home. I can't drink champagne.' Which I can't, because I have gout. 'I want vodka or I'm going home.' So they sent out and got vodka. But I wasn't drunk. I had one drink at Sardi's at seven, with a shrimp cocktail.

"Then Joe came in with his wife and LuEsther Mertz, and they sat right there, and I looked over and thought: I can't believe this! People were coming up to Joe. I was waiting to eat until the vodka came. I turned to Sydney and said, 'Jesus! I'm not going to have a good time at this party unless I go over and tell him how I feel.'

"And I got up and went over.

"He was sitting down. There were about eight or ten people at his table. I wasn't drunk but I was angry. I didn't swear. I said, 'Joe, I don't understand your behavior tonight.' He said, 'What behavior?' 'I don't understand you getting up there and not mentioning Marvin, Ed, Nick or me, especially after Michael's death. I find that totally reprehensible, demeaning, embarrassing—and I really would like an explanation.'

"He started to get up.

"Just as he stood up, he shouted, 'GO FUCK YOURSELF!'

"And I hit him, hit him in the chest, knocked him down on the floor. Somebody picked him up, and then we were right out on the floor sparring around. He shouted, 'YOU MOTHERFUCKER PRICK!' I said, 'YOU COCKSUCKER!' You know the kind of stuff you start to say, but I didn't go any lower and call him shithead. We cuffed each other, we didn't really hurt each other. Then thirty, forty people rush over breaking us apart, grabbing everybody, and that was that.

"I went back and sat down. Someone came over, his daughter-in-law, I think—does he have one?—and she said, 'That was unfair to Joe, you know he's not good with names.' I said, 'Jesus Christ, lady, it's been thirteen years! And if you're not good with names, have a little card with names on it. There'd only have to be about seven!'

"I stayed at the party until about three. I had a good time then. Joe left early."

"There's not much to say," Joe Papp says. "It was in the papers. His ego, that's all, and then there's his reputation with drink and coke—who wants to get into all that. This was to have been an evening *for* and *to* and *about* Michael, and his contribution to the theater."

Kirkwood: "The next day I called a florist. 'I want black flowers, and if you don't have them, I want the worst, the most awful floral arrangement you can make, money's no object.' 'Okay, Mr. Kirkwood.' Then I added a note: 'Dear Joe, Last night you told me to go fuck myself. I'm afraid I can't offer you the same advice. You're such a megalomaniacal prick you'd probably enjoy it far too much. Signed, James Kirkwood. P.S. In the event you don't remember the name, I'm one of the co-authors of *Chorus Line*."

"It was so humiliating! I know why Jimmy did it, and it's so ironic to me," Nicholas Dante says. "I cannot tell you how often Jimmy and I have been pushed aside because of Michael and the Shuberts and Joe Papp taking all the credit for the show—as if we didn't exist. It sticks in your craw. However, after thirteen years, you should be used to it. Papp gave his speech, and he spoke badly, by the way, and he called Tharon 'the lighting lady'! Her name is *Tharon Musser*! And she's a genius! And how dare you!

"He didn't even mention us, which didn't bother me—there's been thirteen years of this! But it infuriated Jimmy. Which makes me laugh because he got too much credit anyway! He went up to Joe and said you don't even know your authors' names after all these years, how could you do that, he was sick of it, and Joe said, 'Fuck you,' and Jimmy hit him. It makes me laugh that that should have made Jimmy so angry, because, really, he's gotten too much credit. And much too much money!

"Recently it occurred to me that Bernie Jacobs has *never* spoken to me in thirteen years! The man's a jerk. I don't think Michael ever told any of them what I did, what my role really was. And I think they all think I'm this little fag dancer who got some money and who should shut up. I *can* talk about it now because I've been through therapy, I can talk about it now and it's okay. And I can talk about Jimmy now—and it will shock the shit out of me—but I have nothing against him personally."

Kirkwood: "Papp's a megalomaniac, ask anyone in the theater! He's also a prick. The papers had him saying he wished he'd killed me, and that I wanted to break his neck. I haven't seen him since. I really didn't use abusive language until he started, not at his table."

Having stated its sting, the bee briefly buzzes a flower.

"Christ only knows, you have to admire the man. Look at all the employment he's done in the theater. But the ego is tremendous.

"So now—in big BIG letters—it's going to be: JOE PAPP'S 'CHORUS LINE.' It'll probably happen."

"I just think Jimmy takes too much cocaine," Liz Smith says. "I just think he's a person who's very envious, has a mediocre talent. I've been his friend for years and have just gotten totally fed up with him. Joe Papp is a jerk and horrible, but he was wonderful at Michael's memorial service. What Jimmy did is unforgivable, but then it must be terrible to have the Pulitzer Prize and know that you only have it because of something someone else did. I mean, all this stuff about *Chorus Line* being a group effort! I think *Chorus Line* is Michael, really Michael, with some very good music from Marvin."

As publicly distressing as the Kirkwood/Papp ringside rancor was, there was a quieter—but no less distressing—reaction to the public dispersal of Michael Bennett's goods and fortune. Filed five days before what was to have been the memorial service, his last will and testament so shocked his immediate family that its *Gianni Schicchi* aftereffect could only escalate in the interim of the memorial service postponement. Although it focused on ego and not money, the bitterness displayed by Kirkwood and Papp at the Palladium was the equivalent of family resentment gone public, hidden feelings suddenly headlined.

The will—Document P-15809—signed by Michael Bennett in a strong hand July 17, 1986, in New York, with a first codicil dated December 28, 1986, a second May 30, 1987—was filed in Tucson July 22, 1987. The signature below the first codicil has a flourish similar to that in the will; the second is a juddering scratch. The will runs to twenty-four pages, the codicils together to six, with an additional two-page document of testators.

The disbursement of Michael Bennett's $25 million estate includes $600,000 in trust (with John Breglio as trustee) and the deed to the condominium at 2110 Ben Franklin Drive in Sarasota to his mother; a $400,000 legacy in equal shares to Gene Pruit and Robert Herr, plus

$300,000 in trust to Gene Pruit; a grant of $100,000 to Frank DiFiglia (DiFilia), reduced in the first codicil to $50,000; $50,000 in trust to his half brother Salvatore Coniglio, terminating when Coniglio reaches twenty-one; $25,000 to his cousin Joanne DiGiulio; and gifts to various friends, including, in the first codicil, $10,000 to Victoria Allen plus $90,000 specifically to further her studies at medical school. The first codicil also channels 15 percent of Bennett's residuary estate to AIDS research.

The major inheritor of the *Chorus Line* copyrights are Robert Avian and John Breglio, with a special trust involving the possible "commercial value" of the original tapes (with interest to be paid to any of the persons originally interviewed, the interest passing to Frank DiFiglia if those individuals die or cannot be found). In the will the balance of the residuary estate was first shared at 42.5 percent each between Frank DiFiglia and Robert Avian. The first codicil reduces DiFiglia to 20 percent and raises Avian to 50, with other changes, and the additional substitution of Pruit's name for that of Robert Fox for a 5 percent share.

Michael Bennett's Pulitzer Prize, his "solid gold Tony for *A Chorus Line*," and all other Tonys and awards, were willed to Avian, along with certain rights surrounding the revival or development of the Bennett musicals. "A solid silver top hat" inscribed by *A Chorus Line*'s original cast was left to Bernard and Betty Jacobs. The red Porsche went to DiFiglia, the blue BMW and Kila to Pruit, a grand piano to Michael Peters, a gold watch to Dr. Emmanuel Feurer, the contents at 40 James Lane to Pruit and Herr, the contents at 40 Central Park South to DiFiglia; and a Paul Jasmin "painting of Kennedy in a box with a flag on his chest" to Scott Pierson (Pearson).

"I never—never!—asked Michael for money," Mrs. DiFiglia says angrily. "I was on his payroll at one time, so was his father—that's how he supported his father's habit. But this will! He didn't take care of me as well as he took care of Gene Pruit. After he met that Gene, Michael wasn't smart about a son and a mother relationship. Until then it was the greatest. He only left little Sal $50,000. His half brother, and that's all he left him! And when Sal's twenty-one—$10,000 and that's it! Who's going to pay for his education? Frank and I are thinking of that.

"Why didn't he take care of me better? Why is my money all tied up with Breglio?

"He did a lot for Bob Avian, who didn't need the money—50 percent of the estate to Bob Avian and only 25 percent to Frank! Breglio's not going to give me beans! John's a nice man but he just doesn't have my interest at heart. Frank and I want to buy a home together, so we can see more of each other. We've looked at places on Long Island, Glen Cove, where I have friends. How much longer am I going to live anyway? Pruit gets his money right away, mine's tied up. Was Michael trying to protect me? Did he think someone was going to marry me for my money? I'm not that stupid. Oh, I'm just so sick of it all.

"Bob Avian has his own Tonys, why does he need Michael's? I would have liked one.

"You see, Michael is still controlling all our lives. I mean, in death it makes no difference. He is still telling us what to do, when to do it and how to do it . . ."

There were people who felt—John Breglio in fact said so—that Michael Bennett was sorely needed to tell everyone what to do at his own memorial service.

Bob Avian postponed the tribute because the grief was new, raw and unappeasable, a daily unconquerable battle that hadn't yet retreated to a neutral zone. Michael Bennett may have been able to whack a production together in three days to celebrate *A Chorus Line*'s 3,389th performance, but Avian was emotionally unable to honor Bennett's death so soon after it happened. As his "control freak" friend had told him to do, Avian by now was fully involved in the London revival of *Follies*. Not completely convinced he wanted to continue in show business, Avian was going through the motions ("Michael made me want to try"). When his *Follies* schedule permitted, he arranged the memorial service, which was by invitation only.

At three in the afternoon of September 29, the same date *A Chorus Line* had broken the record four years early, the Shubert Theater momentarily became a shrine. The people gathering there—relatives, close friends, self-styled "best friends," colleagues, critics, business acquaintances, briefly reformed enemies and possibly the plain curious—were all, in one way or another, affected by Michael Bennett, some personally, some just by his work. There were speeches, some genuinely moving, some mawkish, some honest, some not. Stephen Sondheim played and sang and wept; so did Jimmy Webb. Frank DiFilia read a note from his mother, who wished not to speak. Bernard Jacobs spoke about late-night phone calls; Marvin Krauss flattered himself and his family in memories of the deceased's career; Liz Smith told about being the onstage hostess of a charity benefit directed by Bennett during which he convinced her that she could dance like Betty Grable; Donna McKechnie talked about similar inspiration. And John Breglio wondered how Bennett would have staged the memorial itself, suggesting that maybe his friends and colleagues had gotten it all wrong.

Midway through, a cracked and grainy home movie showed a tiny Mickey DiFiglia, in tap shoes, bow tie and tuxedo, spinning so feverishly across a dance floor that he seemed about to shatter inside the centrifugal force. At the end there was the top-hat-and-cane finale from *A Chorus Line*. Dissolving the image of dancers and the audience, the mirrored screen turned to reveal a blowup of Michael Bennett leaning into the camera, a whimsically smiling Merlin, arms in a wide embrace encompassing the Shubert and everyone in the theater.

EPILOGUE

An Offstage Voice

Leaning out from the picture, above the chorus line, he saw them all.

But the space shifted, slid away. He seemed to be inside a rotating tower, the tower sliding, crossing, recrossing a taped line, the line diminishing, thinning out to ribbon, winding, coming back again thick enough for a shroud. It led from dimly seen snowy street to glaring crossway, then to the spilling ocean before curling back on itself at the base of dark mountains.

Where was he, sea or desert?

Where was God, anchored or with the wind?

If he could see Him, he'd shout, "Move downstage, darling."

The light could be better.

And then the light changed, opened. There was no more time. He saw them all. Each had an identity fading in an instant. Infinitesimal images. Grains of sand on a pearl. Only four could be perceived before disappearing in the life lines of his hand.

There was Sam: betting where the waves would break and—when proved right, then wrong—mimicking the exaggerated grimaces of Greek comedy, then tragedy.

There was Helen: strapped in a ball gown, waltzing waltzing waltzing soundlessly across sand, and behind her Frank stumbling a two-step, reaching for her hand. And then the three of them, Sam, Helen and Frank, staring at him.

Sea became desert.

He saw himself filling it with life, whispering as he moved from person to person, group to group. Then he heard applause, a sound like the wind, with figures wavering behind it in gold costumes, top hats, canes: Bobby, Robin, John . . . Donna, Sabine, Tommy, Jimmy . . . Bernie, Treva—all lining up, expectant, waiting.

And from over the ridge of the highest hill, he heard himself count: "Five . . . six . . . seven . . . eight . . ."

BIBLIOGRAPHY

Altman, Richard, with Merv Kaufman. *The Making of a Musical, "Fiddler on the Roof."* New York: Crown, 1971.

Atkinson, Brooks. *Broadway.* New York: Macmillan, 1974.

Bordman, Gerald. *American Musical Theater.* New York: Oxford, 1978.

Botsworth, Patricia. "The Fight to Save 'Seesaw.'" *New York Times*, Sunday, April 8, 1973.

Engel, Lehman. *The Making of a Musical.* New York: Macmillan, 1977.

———. *The Critics.* New York: Macmillan, 1976.

Ewen, David. *American Musical Theater.* New York: Holt, Rinehart and Winston, 1970.

Goldman, William. *The Season: A Candid Look at Broadway.* New York: Harcourt, Brace, 1969.

Gottfried, Martin. *Broadway Musicals.* New York: Abrams, 1979.

———. *Opening Nights: Theater Criticism of the Sixties.* New York: Putnam, 1969.

Green, Stanley, *Broadway Musicals: Show by Show.* Milwaukee: Leonard, 1987.

Guernsey, Otis L., Jr. *Curtain Times: The New York Theater, 1965–1987.* New York: Applause, 1987.

———. *The Best Plays of the Year. The Burns Mantle Theater Yearbook.* New York: Dodd, Mead, 1973, 1974, 1975, 1976, 1977, 1978, 1979, 1980, 1981, 1982, 1983, 1984, 1985, 1986, 1987.

———. *Broadway Song & Story.* New York: Dodd, Mead, 1985.

Hudson, Rock, and Sara Davidson. *Rock Hudson: His Story.* New York: Morrow, 1986.

Kasha, Al, and Joel Hirschhorn. *Notes on Broadway: Conversations with the Great Songwriters.* Chicago: 1985.

Kerr, Walter. *Journey to the Center of the Theater.* New York: Knopf, 1979.

———. *God on the Gymnasium Floor and Other Theatrical Adventures.* New York: Simon and Schuster, 1971.

Kübler-Ross, Elisabeth. *AIDS: The Ultimate Challenge.* New York: Macmillan, 1987.

Mordden, Ethan. *Broadway Babies: The People Who Made the American Musical.* New York: Oxford University Press, 1983.

Prince, Hal. *Contradictions: Twenty-six Years in the Theatre.* New York: Dodd, Mead, 1974.

Rich, Frank. *The Theater of Boris Aronson.* New York: Knopf, 1987.

Shilts, Randy. *And the Band Played On.* New York: St. Martin's Press, 1987.

Sifakis, Carl. *The Mafia Encyclopedia.* New York: Facts on File, 1987.

Simon, John. *Uneasy Stages: A Chronicle of the New York Theater, 1963–1973.* New York: Random House, 1975.

———. *Singularities: Essays on the Theater, 1964–1974.* New York: Random House, 1975.

Zadan, Craig. *Sondheim & Co.* New York: Harper & Row, 1974.

INDEX

BOOK MARK

The text of this book
was set in the typeface Granjon
and the display was set in Britannic
by Crane Typesetting Service, Inc.
West Barnstable, Massachusetts.

It was printed on 55 lb Glatfelter, an acid-free paper,
and bound by Berryville Graphics,
Berryville, Virginia.

DESIGNED BY CLAIRE M. NAYLON